WHO'S THERE?

WHO'S THERE?

The life and career of
WILLIAM HARTNELL

Written by his granddaughter
JESSICA CARNEY

fantom
publishing

First published in 1996 by Virgin Books, an imprint of Ebury Publishing

This revised and updated edition published in 2013 by Fantom Films
fantomfilms.co.uk

A catalogue record for this book is available from the British Library.

Hardback edition ISBN: 978-1-78196-107-0

Typeset by Phil Reynolds Media Services, Leamington Spa
Printed and bound by CPI Group (UK) Ltd, Croydon, CR0 4YY

Jacket design by Stuart Manning

Contents

Acknowledgements

WHEN MY BIOGRAPHY OF my grandfather was originally published, in 1996, *Doctor Who* was no longer being made and many I'm sure believed the programme would never be brought back to our screens; but largely because of the hugely loyal fans, in 2005 the programme was recreated for the twenty-first century by the BBC. With the programme about to celebrate its fiftieth anniversary, I am thrilled that seventeen years after the original publication of the book there is another edition being brought out, with minor amendments. So my thanks to Fantom Publishing, and also to Cathy Kilgariff for her recommendations.

But I would not be writing this now without the assistance of those who helped the first time round: so I should like to thank again Anne Morbey and Leslie O'Hara (who has sadly since died) for making sure that what I had written made sense; then I'd like to thank other friends for giving me their opinions and being supportive – Cheryl Robson, Eleri Sampson, Helen Walker; and Ciaran Baker for encouraging me to start the project and Alan Felton for being a fount of knowledge. Thanks also to Alan Mason and Eric Dobby for their professional advice, and to all those at Virgin Publishing who brought the first edition to life. I am very grateful to the many people – too numerous to mention – who took the time to answer my letters asking for anecdotes or stories, and especially those who agreed to meet me and talk about my grandfather – particularly Peter Purves, Carole Ann Ford, William Russell and Maureen O'Brien, Verity Lambert and Lord Attenborough, as well as others. A special mention should go to those in the catalogue room at the BFI who were always helpful, and to Stephen James Walker who enabled me to view so many of my grandfather's films which I had not seen before. Many, many thanks to Terry Carroll and of course to my family – my mother above all – who allowed me to rifle through their memories, and lived with me turning out every cupboard and drawer for any last scrap of information. And of course to my grandparents, without whom…

Preface

IN 1963 I WAS asked to produce a new children's drama series for the BBC. Unlike any other programme of its kind, it emanated from the Drama Department and not, as was the norm, the Children's Department. The series was called *Doctor Who* and it was, ambitiously, planned to run for fifty-two weeks of the year.

Choosing the actor to play the title role of the Doctor was obviously the most important and crucial piece of casting. The Doctor was a mysterious and complex character. He had a child-like quality, was unpredictable, sometimes crotchety, very knowledgeable about some things and completely ignorant about others. He could be frightening but was also stalwart and kind. Above all, he was an outsider who did things in his own individual way.

I had known William Hartnell's work from his appearances in many classic British films including *Odd Man Out* and *Brighton Rock*; but I felt that two of his performances – that of the irascible Sergeant Major in the television series *The Army Game* and his moving performance as 'Johnson' in *This Sporting Life* – revealed his range as an actor and proved that he had all the attributes required to play Doctor Who.

Waris Hussein, the director, and I approached him with some trepidation as, in those days, to ask an actor to commit himself to a series for a year was fairly unusual, and Bill was never short of work. Before he came to meet us, I know he had some reservations about this commitment but these were soon dispelled. He immediately understood the character of the Doctor and went on to play him and win the hearts of many millions of viewers – children and adults. He was a wonderful actor and, for me, the perfect Doctor Who.

Verity Lambert

Introduction

FIRST OF ALL, I think I should explain myself. Those of you who are avid *Doctor Who* fans may well have seen a picture of me as a baby – looking podgy and uncertain – being held aloft by my grandfather in one of the books published to celebrate thirty years of *Doctor Who*, or you may have noticed a comment made by my grandfather about me in the *Doctor Who Handbook*. In both of these my name is correctly given as *Judith* Carney. The reason I am now called Jessica is that a long time ago I had to change my name for Equity when I became a professional actor, as there was another actor with a similar name; for various reasons I kept my surname and changed my first name, and I have kept the name Jessica all my professional life as, although no longer an actress, I am still in the industry. So I am not an impostor (but it does get a little confusing at times). William Hartnell was my grandfather's real name, though he was known as Bill, Billy, Will (by his mother), and William; to my brother and me, however, he was always 'Sampa'. For simplicity I have referred to him throughout as either my grandfather, or Bill.

There are many reasons why I originally decided to write this book. Firstly, as a family (my mother was Bill's only child) we were always receiving letters asking questions about him. Several fans had said they wanted to write biographies of him, and in a couple of *Doctor Who* books very intelligently researched chapters had been written about his life. But these of course were largely compiled from press cuttings and interviews he gave, and I knew that such sources can give a false impression of what a person is really like. I was also aware that he had told a few white lies about his origins. Secondly, while I knew that *Doctor Who* is the main reason he still has a fan following many years after his death, he only played the Doctor for three years, and there was so much more to his life than that. My generation and younger think of him as the eccentric Time Lord, but anyone older remembers him perhaps for *The Army Game*, or for his film performances. Nevertheless, various movies in which he appeared during the 1940s and fifties are regularly shown on television: it is still possible to catch his work in films such as *Brighton Rock* or *Carry On Sergeant*, as well as lesser known ones, without too much trouble.

The third reason for the project was purely personal. I never knew my grandfather well, and by all accounts he was not easy to get close to. Although *Doctor Who* made a big impression on me as a child, by the time I was in my early teens he had begun to suffer from arteriosclerosis, which made a more adult relationship with him difficult. He had never talked to me at length and so researching his life and his career was fascinating. He didn't keep a diary, apart from his teenage journal, though my grandmother Heather did for more than twenty years, and she often wrote down the bare facts of what Bill was doing. My grandparents also kept countless programmes and reviews of shows in which they appeared, and for a while Bill employed a professional cuttings agency. I wrote to a selection of people who had worked with him, and received many helpful letters back. I met with old acquaintances and spoke to some on the phone: all helped me to piece together his life.

As I hope I have implied, this is not a *Doctor Who* book. So much has been published about the programme, by writers who know far more about the series than I do. Indeed, the wonderful *Doctor Who – The Handbook: The First Doctor*, by Howe, Stammers and Walker, told me everything I needed to know about what went on behind the scenes and I was able to compare the production diary section with my grandmother's notes. I did not want to duplicate any of the work carried out by others, or include stories that have been quoted elsewhere. I have tried to give a more personal view of the show, and if there are any anecdotes that have appeared in other publications, it is because they were told to me personally by those concerned.

My grandfather had a reputation for being irritable and perfectionist, but as with many performers, his 'image' and reputation were often at odds with the description I had from those who got on well with him. I wanted in this book to explain some of the insecurities which often accounted for his behaviour, and show how witty and charming many people found him. One of the directors I consulted dismissed my queries about his irascibility by saying that many performers who are really talented are difficult to work with, largely because they care so much about their performances. And he did care. He took acting very seriously, and I received unanimous praise for his ability from those within the profession.

I very much wanted the success my grandfather found on *Doctor Who* to be seen in the context of his career as a whole. There are huge contrasts in his life. He started out training with a classical company, then played many leads in farce and musical comedies, and ended up as the archetypal British character actor. I hope this biography will show how varied his career was, and demonstrate how the different strands came together at the end of his life to enable him to create a totally convincing character which inspired one of the biggest fan followings in British television. He helped to create a character which has entered the national psyche and has perhaps become as iconic as Robin Hood or Sherlock Holmes did in other ages. I trust I will not shatter too many illusions, nor incur accusations of being too biased.

Chapter One

MY GRANDFATHER WAS A TIME LORD

'KNOCK KNOCK.'

　'Who's there?'

　'Doctor.'

　'Doctor who?'

　'Doctor *Who*, silly…'

When I was seven, this was the favourite game in the playground at my junior school. The other children never tired of trying it out on me. Much giggling and nudging always followed: after all, Doctor Who was my grandfather. Everyone knew who Doctor Who was – the programme was first shown in November 1963 and very rapidly it seemed to catch the imagination of every child in the country. Or perhaps I was just biased. I really didn't mind the 'Knock, knock' joke, even though no one was supposed to know that William Hartnell was my mother's father. My brother and I were under strict instructions not to talk about him as my mother didn't want us to appear to be showing off or to be teased about the connection. I don't think I ever volunteered information about him, but after a while our 'secret' became impossible to hide. Particularly when he opened the village fête, held in the local hospital grounds, at which our family were guests of honour. It was Saturday 22nd May 1965.

He arrived at the fête, wearing his Doctor Who costume, in an open-topped vintage car. It wasn't quite the TARDIS (after all, you could never guarantee where the TARDIS was going to land), but it was spectacular enough for Pembury, the village in Kent where my parents lived. He wore his black astrakhan hat over the flowing white wig, which many people thought was his own hair: it made him look so much older than his real age of fifty-six. A black cape and suit in a rather loud check completed the outfit which so epitomised his character: quirky, stylish and eccentric. As his friend Bob Pither brought the car to a halt, he smiled and waved at all the children. I felt proud and excited as the crowds cheered my own grandfather.

Looking back at childhood, just as tradition has it, the days always seemed sunny. According to my grandmother's diary, the day of the fête really *was* sunny. A photographer tailed my grandfather as he did the round of the stalls, admiring the home-made cakes, taking aim at the coconuts on the coconut shy and generally helping to raise money for whichever hospital fund was to benefit. He handed out *Doctor Who* photographs and signed endless autograph books. Then he watched as my brother Paul and I were taken for a ride on the miniature railway. We joined other excited children and clambered on top of the carriages which were no more than fifteen inches high. Wearing my favourite summer dress, short white socks and polished Clark's sandals, I shrieked with laughter as the engine trundled slowly along the tracks, which had been specially laid around the lawns. But the best moment of the whole day was when someone from my own school sidled up to me and wanted *my* autograph! But then not everyone had a grandfather who was a Time Lord.

I now know that my grandfather had always been good at making personal appearances: he spent a lot of time throughout his life judging competitions, giving out prizes and signing autographs. He was always appreciative of his fans, but the adoration he received from children as a result of *Doctor Who* was something quite different. He felt it was very special. My grandmother, Heather, dealt with the fan mail and meticulously replied to everyone who wrote. Sometimes she showed me the letters. They included countless hand-drawn pictures of Doctor Who himself, the Daleks and the TARDIS; some people even sent photos of themselves and their families.

The Pembury Fête took place about a year and a half after the programme began. I was six when it started, so I must have some memories of my grandfather from before then, but they are difficult to separate from the others. It didn't seem particularly odd to see him on television with funny hair, wearing a strange costume. It was just his job.

Almost all my family worked in TV, theatre or films, and I was brought up on theatrical anecdotes. Although my mother never went on stage, my father, Terry Carney, was an actor before becoming a theatrical agent. Both he and my mother had been born in the proverbial trunk, as all four grandparents had been actors. I never met my father's parents: they both died before I was born. My paternal grandfather, George Carney, was a music hall star who moved over to play character parts in films at a slightly earlier date than my mother's father. Both grandfathers actually appeared together in the same films on more than one occasion, long before my parents met – *Brighton Rock* is probably the best known of these. So while most of my earliest recollections of William Hartnell are bound up with his famous creation, all my knowledge of George Carney is gleaned from the roles he played in old British movies. Especially as my father had himself few memories of him: his parents split up while he was still very young. His mother had also been in music hall as one half of the singing and dancing duo Vesta and Minnie Pine – but enough of my complicated family heritage! Suffice to say that we still had several old trunks, left over from touring days, in our loft. Rummaging among the clothes and costumes in these kept me quiet for hours. Dressing up was my favourite pastime: I was always acting out some story or other. I never thought I would be anything other than an actress (though I am very glad that I am no longer acting).

Watching *Doctor Who* was a Saturday afternoon ritual, in a way that those born into the digital age could never now appreciate. The end of the preceding programme, *Grandstand*, with its distinctive music and final shots looking through the end of four camera lenses, is indelibly etched on my memory. Following this sports round-up, anyone who grew up in the sixties will remember the amazing electronic sounds and opening titles of *Doctor Who* because they were so utterly innovative, and they have been justly celebrated since. Then, they really did seem other-worldly. Even though I knew it was my grandfather in the role, I still got wrapped up in the stories and the suspense of the cliff-hanger endings. I didn't have to hide behind the sofa, like some of my contemporaries, as I knew that no harm would really come to him, but the monsters still fascinated and frightened my brother and me. The lack of sophistication of the creatures and the effects has of course been commented on and laughed at many times when compared with the twenty-first-century version, but it was only to be expected given the money available for making the show and the constraints of shooting in those days. Our excitement at that time was very real however. There had never been a television programme like it. In the eyes of children who were not accustomed to huge-budget American science-fiction films, and who had never seen anything as remotely inventive as *Doctor Who* on television, the programme was captivating. Space travel was now a possibility and time travel therefore a logical development. Even those who were never fans attested to the universality of the effect that *Doctor Who* had on children then. Some of this was due to the uniqueness of the concept, but also the timing of the slot meant that the programme was created to interest a wide age group. It was aimed particularly at eleven- to fourteen-year-olds, but placed between a sports and a pop programme it captured a real family audience, with children as young as myself and my brother (six and nearly five) as well as parents. I also like to think that some of the success of the series was to do with the performance my grandfather gave, creating such an enigmatic character. Some weekends we would watch the programme with our grandparents, which added an extra dimension to the enjoyment, but my grandfather never gave the story away. I believe it gave him a thrill to view it with us, delighting in our reactions. Evidently he was impressed by my early attention to detail – though I'm sure it had more to do with my predilection for the costumes – as he commented in an interview for *Reveille*:

> My granddaughter Judith [my real as opposed to my stage name], who is seven, will probably be a producer one day. With Doctor Who in the middle of some terrible global disaster she'll ask me what I've done with that pretty tall hat I was wearing in the previous scene.

My brother and I couldn't bear to miss an episode, and with no such things as videos, DVDs, or catch-up, perhaps more than for most fans, our Saturdays revolved around the show.

*

One of the highlights of my childhood was a visit to the Riverside Studios where *Doctor Who* was made. Today the building houses an arts centre with theatre and cinema, but then it was a fully functioning television studio used by the BBC. It was Friday 19th February 1965, and I was seven and a half. My grandmother travelled up to London with me by train; we met my father for lunch and then she took me to the studios in Hammersmith. After meeting various members of the cast, including Maureen O'Brien, William Russell and Jacqueline Hill, I sat with my grandfather in the make-up room and watched him get ready. I was fascinated by the wig. Close to, the net round the hairline was clearly visible, although it wasn't discernible on screen. There were all sorts of wonderful potions and lotions and sticks of greasepaint in front of the mirror. To keep me entertained, a friendly make-up girl showed me how the effect of a bruise was created, and she put one on my arm. I was terribly proud of this bluish fake bump and went round showing it to everybody, pretending I'd hurt myself; they were all suitably impressed and made concerned remarks. Then I was shown into the studios.

The episode being made was called 'Invasion', part five of 'The Web Planet', a story set in a world inhabited by huge moth-like creatures, the Menoptra, and giant ants, the Zarbi. Friday was recording day, following the rehearsals which took place Monday to Thursday each week. I've since read that the special effects for 'The Web Planet' were the most ambitious they had tried to date. Each episode had a budget of approximately £2,750, and very little editing could take place after filming. Because of these financial and technical limitations, location shots were rarely used and everything had to be achieved on the cramped sets. Even to one so young (when usually everyone and everything seems so huge), the studios seemed very small, so I can appreciate how difficult this must have been. When I was briefly given a glimpse into another room, I remember being slightly disappointed at the sight of a scaled-down TARDIS on a heap of sand in the corner – it looked tiny, decidedly unmagical and didn't suggest to me the surface of a mysterious planet at all. But of course I had no idea about what it would look like through a camera lens. The costumes, however, were far more fascinating to me. The actors looked funny dressed up as moths with their yellow and black stripy bodies, but the ant costumes were quite intimidating. I recall touching the hard fibreglass heads, and then having one put over my shoulders – but it was much too heavy for me.

Suddenly, the camera rehearsal began and everyone started to concentrate on their own jobs. For a short while I was left to my own devices. I was so excited: it felt as if I had *carte blanche* and could wander anywhere, although I'm sure someone was watching over me very carefully. All around me there were cameras and lights and cables and other things to trip over. Then someone came up to me and asked me to move as somehow I was in shot. What a thrill! I stepped aside reluctantly, as I was longing to join in too. There were times when I must have been in the way, but everyone was very tolerant, friendly and kind, and my grandfather gave me as much attention as he could. On the way home later that afternoon, my grandmother took me for tea at Lyons Corner House, near Charing Cross: a special treat to end a special day.

My brother Paul also visited the studios, a few months later on Friday 21st May. This was during the shooting of an episode featuring Frankenstein's House of Horrors, part of the Dalek serial called 'The Chase'. It must have been great fun for him, but he was barely six at the time and quite shy, and he can't remember much about it. Like me, however, he was thrilled by the make-up room: he watched as an actor was made up to look like Frankenstein's monster. He was too young to appreciate the mechanical gadgetry of lights and cameras, and the scenery didn't seem as exciting in the studio as it looked on screen, but the idea of dressing up and putting on strange make-up appeals to most children. I'm happy to report that it didn't have a lasting effect, and he was sensible enough to work on the other side of the camera, in production. However, I was always slightly jealous of the fact that he got the chance to sit inside a Dalek body.

As with millions of other young children, the Daleks became an obsession. I perfected the voice of a Dalek and would run around the playground intoning, 'I am a Dalek, I will exterminate...' On Christmas Day 1964, Paul and I were the lucky recipients of the first Dalek play-suits. They were very sturdy: the rigid body section was held up by straps which went over the shoulders and from this hung a blue plastic 'skirt' with a silver-grey stud pattern, held in shape by an oval metal hoop at the bottom. The head consisted of a plastic dome with an eyestalk, and a cage of wire, which hid the face very well but allowed you to see out. The mesh was surrounded by slats of hard pressed card, kept in place by metal rods which then slotted into the body section. The two arms could be manoeuvred independently from inside, one with the familiar suction pad at the end, the other simulating the 'extermination rod', with a bulb which flashed on and off when the battery was activated.

JESSICA CARNEY

Although my brother and I didn't realise it, we nearly didn't get our presents. The Dalek dressing-up costumes were produced by Scorpion Automotives, but the factory where they were made burnt down just before Christmas. Perhaps our two were the first ever completed, as they were rushed to my parents' house on Christmas Eve night, after much panic. They were too big to wrap, but this didn't detract from our excitement as they were hidden in the garage until the last moment. My brother, a few inches shorter than me, was nearly swamped by his, as they were quite heavy and not the easiest of things to walk in. While he was completely hidden by his suit, you could just see my feet at the bottom. My mother watched the two of us trundling off down the street to show our friends, one Dalek slightly taller than the other. We rang the doorbell at the house where Paul's friend Melvyn Bragg (not the famous TV presenter, I should point out!) lived, and were greeted by screams. No one had seen a Dalek in Greenleas, Pembury, before. Soon we felt like Pied Pipers, as several children followed us along the street where we lived, down on to the lower road of the estate. This was where my Dalek impression ('I will exterminate...') came in useful. Everyone wanted to have a go in them, and it's surprising that they survived at all (they are very battered now) as we played with them so often. If you didn't get the balance of the straps right, you were liable to topple over. This seemed to happen to my brother fairly frequently and it looked so funny as his head always fell off. Eventually, like most kids, we grew tired of dressing up in the suits, and they spent years in the loft at my parents' house. Then in the early 1990s they were dusted down and the one in better condition was taken to the BBC studios where the *Doctor Who* documentary (shown in November 1993) was being made for the thirtieth anniversary. It was worn by Josh, the six-year-old who was used as a link in the programme. He had seen all the videos and probably knew more about the series than I did. I was thrilled to find that the magic of *Doctor Who* lived on and that a whole new generation was excited by it and it was delightful to see a small boy, about the same size as my brother had been, wearing the costume again. Since then of course *Doctor Who* has been brought back to our screens by Russell T. Davies, Julie Gardner, Steven Moffat, Mark Gatiss and others. The merchandising has become very sophisticated and I'm sure one of the reasons that helped keep alive the enthusiasm of the fans during its hiatus is because they had, from the very early days, something tangible to collect. I was asked again in early 2013 if one of our original Dalek suits was in good enough condition to use in the re-creation of the early years of *Doctor Who* in *An Adventure in Space and Time*. Sadly they were too far gone.

Once *Doctor Who* merchandising had taken off, my brother and I were given some of the other products at Christmas time. It was fun having annuals and puzzles starring your grandfather, and we often laughed at some of the cartoon versions of him, which weren't very good likenesses. We also had the 6½-inch-high battery-powered Dalek toys. They charged over the floor on little wheels but didn't seem to have much sense of direction and tended to bump into walls and bits of furniture; the arms and eyestalks snapped off very easily when this happened. My grandfather was given several of these model Daleks as souvenirs. There were four silver-grey ones and a black one, the most menacing of all. When my brother and I went to stay, we were always exhorted to be careful when we played with them because of their self-destructive tendencies. They were more for decoration, and sat on the window ledge in the hallway, as if keeping watch on all who entered their cottage.

*

During my childhood I often stayed with Bill (as my grandfather was known to his friends) and Heather at their home near Mayfield, Sussex. I adored spending time there, even though I felt I had to be on my best behaviour. Their world seemed enchanted. Perhaps all children think their grandparents' houses are special, but theirs felt and smelt and looked so different from my parents' home (which was modern and white and very 'sixties'). It was probably the first time I had come into contact with antiques and curios. Their weatherboarded cottage was set back a little from a country lane and was surrounded by trees and meadows. The nearest house was several fields away, fields which were golden with wheat in the summer, and splashed with red poppies. The back garden was separated from beautiful dense woodland by an old fence and rickety gate: this was the entrance into my 'magic woods'. The garden was green, grassy and undulating, with a rocky stream running through it. Flowerbeds were laid around the house and along the pathways, which sloped up to a garage at the top end. My grandfather was proud of his garden, and even though it was my grandmother who did most of the gardening, he enjoyed pottering about in it. There was an old well in the middle, and from this same source the water was piped into the house. It had been tested and found to be pure, but I was fascinated by the fact that, because of its high iron content, the water had a reddish-brown tinge. I was always a little dubious about getting into a bath full of orangey-coloured water.

Old Mill Cottage must have been built in about 1600 and was actually two semi-detached cottages, though Bill and Heather only lived in one side, and never did up the second half. I still don't understand why, as the part they lived in was quite small. It was like the TARDIS in reverse: it seemed larger on the outside than on the inside. Their front door opened into a hall with a narrow staircase leading up to the bedrooms: one reasonable-sized room in which I always stayed with my grandmother, and a much smaller one which was my grandfather's. There was also a tiny box room. Downstairs, the living room had an inglenook with a red-brick grate which always seemed to have a roaring fire burning in it. The kitchen, cluttered with odd cupboards, was old-fashioned, and you had to walk through it to reach the bathroom, which had been added later. The low ceilings and small windows, so characteristic of seventeenth-century houses, meant it always seemed dark inside. I can only describe the atmosphere in there as 'brown'. But with the dark brown beams and old furniture it was a warm, cosy, brownness, added to by the dim lights, the wood smoke and the nicotine – everything was tinged with it as both my grandparents smoked heavily. Years later when they moved out, everything had to be washed down to remove the patina of tar. It was fashionable to smoke then of course, as no one knew the real dangers, and I used to watch as my grandparents took the Du Maurier cigarettes from their glamorous red boxes, tapping them before they lit up (though Bill also smoked Players). At the time, it seemed a curious habit, but not one I was tempted by. I don't remember finding the smell unpleasant, which as an ardent non-smoker shocks me somewhat, but then at that age I had nothing to compare it with. Anyway, their cottage had its own unique homely smell; it felt very safe and comfortable and had an aura of incredible stillness. Perhaps I've made it sound dingy, but it wasn't because there were pretty chintz curtains at the window, a golden yellow fabric on the three-piece suite and in the spring and summer my grandmother filled the rooms with vases of bright flowers – bluebells or primroses, and many wild flowers which grew like weeds everywhere in the fields and ditches then.

The nooks and crannies were filled with simple ornaments – mugs, ashtrays, bits of Rye pottery, spills for lighting the fire, little baskets brimming with old buttons – and they all seemed to have stood in exactly the same place for an eternity. In the corner of the living room sat a death mask of the poet Keats. It was fascinating but slightly frightening, with its closed eyes and pallid, smooth, expressionless face. My grandfather also owned a plaster cast of a hand, eerie and disembodied, which was mounted by the fireplace. I used to look at these things with a kind of reverence. My brother felt the same kind of awe; perhaps, because we weren't surrounded by our toys, we had time to be contemplative. Presiding over everything in the living room, the stillness and oldness and brownness, was the clock. The large brass-edged glass carriage clock sat high up on the mantelpiece above the inglenook. I was mesmerised by its ticking, waiting eagerly for it to strike. It had a mind of its own and instead of one, it actually struck thirteen. By that clock I knew the house was magical. A spell was cast on me in that place: I felt as if time stood still and that to shout or be childish in that room would violate the calmness. I must at some time have been told that my grandfather didn't like noisy children. I don't ever remember incurring his wrath. Perhaps I was afraid to. Perhaps my mother's fear of angering him had been instilled into me subliminally, so that the very walls of the sitting room where I usually encountered him inhibited me from noisy pursuits. He seemed to me, as a child, always slightly aloof, slightly mysterious. I was never quite certain whether he would be grumpy or friendly. Although I wasn't overtly aware of it because I had no other grandfather to compare him with, there was a slight lack of warmth between him and my mother which it took years for me to understand. But my grandmother always made up for this with her enthusiasm and energy, and her unfailing good humour.

My mother says that having grandchildren gave my grandfather a new insight, and he became more aware of a child's point of view. I don't, however, remember him often actively playing with me. He did occasionally join in board games and once or twice played cricket with us. I don't think he was terribly good on a one-to-one basis with children at this stage of his life, though he was thrilled with all the fan mail he got from them for *Doctor Who*. He was proud of his grandchildren, but could only cope when we were quiet and well behaved. That's why I usually stayed with my grandparents on my own: my brother was younger and somewhat noisier. But as a young child it is impossible to understand how work affects adults, and that sometimes they need peace and quiet. If my grandfather was there when I visited Mayfield, it meant he wasn't working: and, as I now understand, many actors feel insecure if they don't know when their next job is coming along. During the period of *Doctor Who*, apart from occasional weeks off, he was only at home at the weekends, and presumably was then quite tired, and even perhaps had lines to learn. But there *were* times when Bill played the joker: he would tell funny stories to make me laugh and I remember his recurring tease that strawberries grew on trees. He used to say it quite seriously and I never knew whether or not to believe him, which probably amused him no end. This dry sense of humour seems to have confused even adults, as in my research I have heard people say he would relate a story with such a serious expression that no one knew whether or not he was joking.

I was good at occupying myself – I had to be as Heather couldn't spend all her time amusing me. I was never bored because the house was like a museum where, with care and permission, one could handle the exhibits. Every basket I peered into and every tin I opened revealed fresh treasures: old pens, or a fascinating array of buttons and buckles which provided me with hours of play, sorting them, finding matching sets and then jumbling them up again when I tired of that particular amusement. Then I'd frighten myself by reading Babar the Elephant stories. My grandparents had wonderful old copies of the books, printed in 1940 with 'joined-up' writing instead of normal typeface, and the original illustrations. I can still recall the fear I felt at the page depicting the elephants whose behinds had been painted to frighten off the enemy, and how upset I was when the old king died after eating poisoned mushrooms. These books came down off the shelf without fail every time I stayed. In the same way, I always asked for the little brown drum to be unhooked from its nail in the beam. The hide, painted with weird Chinese dragons in green and red, was beautifully taut and it made a delicious twangy sound when hit with the wooden sticks. There was something both scary and sacred about it. It belonged to my grandfather; he had brought it back from the Chinese quarter in one of the cities in Canada where he had worked in the late twenties. I only ever banged the drum gently, and I'm sure it was only allowed down from its hook when Bill was out of earshot.

One day, at the age of seven, I decided to 'do up' the other half of the cottage. It was completely empty, unconverted and very dusty but I was undaunted. I spent a day and a half sweeping, cleaning and making it into my imaginary home. Then I carried in some chairs and a little table and invited my grandparents to tea. They duly joined in the game and drank tea from toy cups and saucers. I always called my grandparents Ya Ya and Sampa, rather than 'Grandma' and 'Grandpa'. Presumably, when I was very little, my first attempts at saying the words had sounded like these strangulated versions, and they stuck. They both refused to be called anything else, even when my brother and I were in our teens, which was a little embarrassing. I suspect they didn't like the idea of 'grandma' and 'grandpa' because it made them feel old. One of Bill's favourite words was 'barmy' – he was always using it – and he loved it when I called him 'barmy Sampa' when he played the fool – so he wasn't always serious when I was around.

*

Bill and Heather had two pets: a black cat called Crumpet and a Staffordshire bull terrier called Stumpy. They both liked dogs and had always owned terriers: the first one, a feisty little wire-haired terrier, had been called Dickie, and he was followed by an Irish terrier called Jolly Dog, who often used to go on tour with my grandmother. They adored Stumpy, who had been bought for them by my parents some years before. He was brindle and had a good pedigree, but had a broken tail – hence the name. Though Staffies are now considered rather tough aggressive dogs, he had a wonderful personality and I was never afraid of him. Stumpy died in October 1965: Bill and Heather were devastated and both cried their eyes out. They bought another brindle Staffordshire bull terrier and called her Honeybunch, but she was never quite the same. Whenever I stayed, taking the dog out was a daily excuse for a walk. 'Sampa' sometimes joined us when we went for a wander across the fields. Bill was rather taciturn on some of these trips. He and my grandmother rarely walked together. I now know that they weren't particularly happy at this time, and perhaps I picked up the bad vibrations, though I was too small to understand.

The countryside around the cottage was very beautiful and I used to pick bunches of cowslips and scabious which grew in abundance on the South Downs. In springtime, the 'magic wood' behind the cottage was carpeted with bluebells. I tried not to tread on any of them during our walks, and I was always looking out for the rarer white variants. I felt guilty picking handfuls of flowers but persuaded myself that there were so many it didn't matter.

Not far from the rickety gate, two majestic silver birch trees stood out among all the alders and beeches; their wonderful papery bark gleamed in the sunbeams which broke through the canopy of shimmering leaves. To my brother and me, they were guardians of the forest, and if we had been very good children, we would find a small gift at their roots at the end of our stay. As with Father Christmas, there must have been a point when we realised where the presents came from but carried on with the fantasy so as not to disappoint the adults. We always hugged the trees to thank them, and sometimes wrote little thank-you notes. We imagined that we could hear the trees talking to us when the branches scraped together in the breeze, high above our heads. To any outsider, it would have looked funny to see two small children hugging and talking to trees, but it was a very good way to get us to behave!

A love of nature was something which Bill and Heather shared. Heather used to go badger watching, as there were badger setts in the woods. Once she took me; to catch a glimpse of these nocturnal creatures we had to lie on tarpaulins from early dusk until it was dark, not moving, not speaking, just watching. My patience was rewarded by the wonderful sight of a badger and her babies coming out to play. I felt honoured – and somewhat pleased with myself for not being scared of the darkness. Heather was also involved in various conservation societies, doing surveys on the number of orchids or rare plants or grasses in the area. I helped her with these at various times, and remember proudly showing my grandfather the different types of grasses I had collected and mounted on paper with their proper names. He was very impressed. Bill could wax lyrical himself about the countryside, and I found several photographs annotated with poetical lines about natural beauty. Neither of them went to church but both saw God in nature, so if they had any beliefs they were perhaps more to do with the majesty of the wilderness than any orthodox teachings.

Bill's love of the countryside stemmed from his childhood, and most of his hobbies were country pursuits – gardening, fishing and horses. Although I never saw him ride, I knew about his love of horses – and his love of gambling on them – even when I was small. He had passed his interest onto my mother, who worked at various stables before she was married and was keenly interested in horse racing. She occasionally placed a bet and so whenever any of my family watched racing on the television they used to get (I thought) unnecessarily excited. Sometimes it even ended in tears. They would sit on the edges of their chairs, shrieking, or jump up and down shouting encouragement to their chosen horse. Although I could see there was a thrill to it, I could never fully understand the emotional effect it had. Not that my mother ever put more than a few pounds on the tote, unlike her father. He went to the races frequently, followed form and bet heavily.

He took me to the races once, when I was very little. It was a family outing but I spent a lot of time with Bill that day. He made me feel very grown up as he pressed a ten-shilling note in my hand. I had never possessed so much money. He told me I could bet on whichever horse I liked. We stood and watched the majestic creatures as they paraded round the paddock before the start of the race. They snorted and skitted as their jockeys tried to keep them calm in front of the crowds. There were brown ones, chestnuts and some that were almost black. Their riders had strangely patterned shirts and caps. The only way I could think of deciding which horse to put money on was to choose the one I thought was the prettiest. My favourite were what I called 'white' horses, which had the added advantage of being very visible on the field. So I was taken over to the tote to place my crumpled ten-bob note on a silver-grey filly. We watched as they galloped round the circuit, and I peered through binoculars when they were almost out of sight. Must have been beginner's luck, because my brilliant animal came in in the first three. I took my ticket back to the man in the little kiosk. The brown note which I handed over earlier had miraculously been turned into a green one. I had doubled my money. I felt so proud. Ever cautious, I was quite satisfied with my winnings, and didn't risk losing it. I went home at the end of the day with that self-same pound note and put it in my savings box. Even at that age I had been imbued with the idea that putting lots of money on the horses in the way that my grandfather did was not sensible, and so luckily I didn't inherit his desire to gamble.

I did, however, inherit the love of horses. When I was little they were definitely my favourite animal. I liked drawing them, stroking them, feeling their soft muzzles and warm breath. Like many young girls around the age of ten, I longed for a pony. In time my grandparents gave me riding lessons for my birthday. Bill rashly promised to buy me a horse. My parents had by this time moved to the country and we had a small patch of orchard beside the old farmhouse in which we lived and which my father was restoring. Perhaps, being realistic, there wasn't enough land, or perhaps as my grandfather was by then no longer doing *Doctor Who* he was not as financially secure and couldn't afford to help with the upkeep. But, for whatever reason, owning one of these beautiful animals remained a dream. I was disappointed, but in a few years I had other interests and a fascination with horses became merely a phase I had passed through.

*

There were occasions when Bill really enjoyed his role as grandfather. When I was very little, in 1960, he took the whole family out to lunch on Christmas Day. We ate at the White Hart Hotel in Lewes, near Brighton. My brother was still in a high chair, but I sat at the table like a grown-up. It was exciting to be taken to such a smart place. Some of the other guests groaned when they saw two small children sitting down to eat but Bill was proud of us as we were very well behaved. The other revellers had no need to worry.

There were a few other times when he took the whole family out: another favourite place of his to eat was the Rose and Crown, a wooden-beamed seventeenth-century hotel and restaurant in Brenchley, a pretty little Kentish village. It was run by Mollie and Jack, friends of my grandparents. Bill would sit at the head of the table and revel in having his family around him, enjoying playing the host – I even remember him indulgently allowing me to have a place set for my favourite doll at the table.

On Saturday 7th January 1967 my father took us all to Southend to see a pantomime. I had been to a couple of pantomimes before, but this one was very special as it starred my grandfather. The touring production of *Puss in Boots* had visited several other big towns for a week at a time, including Ipswich and Cheltenham. He was the star attraction, and although the character he played was called Buskin the Cobbler, most people still considered him Doctor Who, as his last episode playing the character had been transmitted at the end of October 1966. I'm sure for many of the children in the audience that character of Buskin merged completely with that of the Doctor… especially as Doctor Who had often dressed up in strange clothes in the historical stories. Besides, there was a 'Win a Dalek' competition in the foyer, and on the programme there was a picture of him wearing his black astrakhan hat. This conscious character confusion would have arisen because of copyright issues over the BBC character, so presumably the management tried not to incur the wrath of the Corporation, whilst also attracting audiences who wanted to see Doctor Who. At one point in the show Bill stood at the edge of the stage and threw sweets out into the audience – children ran up the aisles to the front of the auditorium, eagerly jumping to grab them. I joined the throng and managed to catch my grandfather's eye. He smiled at me and aimed a couple of sweets in my direction. I caught them and grinned back. It made me feel as if I was sharing some wonderful secret that nobody else knew about.

As I got older and more involved in school and with various friends, I saw less of my grandparents. But how much does a child really know about his or her grandparents? I was closer to my grandmother as she lived with us after Bill's death and she had always been a mentor to me. These childhood memories of my grandfather are the happiest I have and they are how I should like to remember him, considering what was to follow. My brother and I were, I suspect, protected from seeing him as he became more difficult to cope with. Growing up, I found out about aspects of his character I'd been unaware of as a child. But these early recollections will always be strongest because every time I see an episode of *Doctor Who* on television or DVD they all come flooding back. You see, Doctor Who *was* my grandfather. He incorporated so many of his own characteristics into the character that this grumpy, amusing, moody Time Lord, who had a huge following of loyal fans, was the person I called 'Sampa'.

Chapter Two

HIS EARLY LIFE: FACT OR FANTASY?

> William Hartnell was born on a very down-to-earth farm in the village of
> Seaton in Devon on 8th January 1908. He was the only child of a dairy
> farmer whose family could trace their ancestry back for over three
> hundred years.

THIS IS THE ACCEPTED version of my grandfather's origins, given in
various interviews and reproduced here from Peter Haining's *Doctor Who:
A Celebration*. But there is an earlier 'official' version of his background,
given in the William Hartnell fan club bulletin, published in 1947:

> 'Billy' Hartnell… was brought up on a Devon farm, and developed a great
> love of horses… Son of a professional soldier turned stockbroker, Billy was
> educated in military tradition for the most part at Imperial College
> Windsor.

This is not dissimilar to the first, but did his father really have three
changes of career, from soldier to stockbroker to dairy farmer?

When interviewed on *Desert Island Discs* in 1965, Bill said he was born
in the little village of Seaton in Devon. While his mother's family did
indeed come from an old Devon farming family, a glance at my
grandfather's birth certificate will show that he was in fact born in
London, in the unromantic district of South Pancras. His mother, Lucy
Hartnell, was then living at 24 Regent Square, which was a few streets
south of King's Cross and St Pancras Station, between Gray's Inn Road
and Judd Street. Today it is a rather uninspiring area, and sadly three sides
of the square now consist of modern sixties- or seventies-style blocks of

flats. The house where he was born is one of those which has been demolished. The one remaining side shows how the square must have looked at the beginning of the century – a terrace of Regency houses with their characteristically elegant arched windows on the ground and first floors, and small wrought-iron balconies at first-floor level. This sounds grand, but it was very run down and considered a slum area in the early 1900s. Presumably Lucy was living in furnished rooms at the time.

Why didn't Bill tell the truth about his place of birth? Perhaps he wished he had been born in Devon – he was certainly fond of his aunt who lived there and enjoyed staying with her in the country as a boy. But it is the birth certificate which holds the clue. Either side of the entry stating his mother's job – her occupation is given as 'Commercial Clerk' – the space under 'Father's name' and 'Occupation of father' is ominously blank, and there we see the real reason for the stories he made up about his background.

Illegitimacy in Edwardian times carried a huge stigma. The worst aspect for Bill was that he never even knew the identity of his father. His mother apparently told no one, and the insecurity of not knowing where he came from stayed with him all his life. As an adult he tried to trace his origins but could find out no more than I can. Family history has it that his mother and her sister, Bessie, were both 'in service', and it is possible Lucy was seduced by someone at the 'big house'. This could have been the lord of the manor, his son, or the butler. It could have been a visitor or another servant; we shall never know. Or perhaps Lucy just helped out somewhere with housekeeping. For some reason Bill thought his father could have been French – though his fair looks certainly don't suggest Gallic origins. My grandmother always thought he looked rather like the French actor Jean Gabin, whose colouring was similar – as, of course, not all French men are tall, dark and handsome.

Lucy was nearly twenty-four at the time of her son's birth. She wasn't a particular beauty and she never married, but always called herself 'Mrs Hartnell'. Her family came from the West Country and she must have gone to London to have her baby to escape the censure of the close-knit farming community. In the early 1900s there were several farms owned by Hartnells in the Devon and Somerset area; and, as with many farming communities, a lot of the families were related to each other. Lucy's parents were Jane and James Hartnell, and they were probably cousins as

Jane herself was a Hartnell even before marriage. They lived at Curland, a small parish just south of Taunton, at the time of Lucy's birth in January 1884, and had one other daughter, Bessie, who was born in 1879. Bill was very fond of his Aunt Bessie. Late in life she married a widowed farmer, Tom Andrew, who lived in Bideford. They had no children of their own, but Bill stayed close to her throughout his life. I met her – when I was very young – as she lived to the ripe old age of 86.

*

My grandfather never talked about his past to family or friends. Everyone I have interviewed for the book says that he never mentioned his childhood or where he came from. Those who got quite close to him still felt they didn't know him intimately. My mother had only a vague idea about his background; she knew that her father hadn't been happy as a child so she never probed. I would know little more than the above if it were not for an exercise book carefully preserved among his effects; even my mother never saw it until years after his death. In this book, at the age of fifteen, he set out to write the history of his life as a cautionary tale. It's called 'The Life of a London Urchin' and in it he describes his upbringing, where he lived, and all the scrapes he used to get into. It's written in a slightly florid 'Dear reader' style: there are exhortations to be honest as we are told that although he was a 'devil and an artful bounder' he has now been offered the opportunity to go straight. Taking a very moral stance, he hopes people will understand how hard it was for a child in his circumstances. He gives himself the name 'William Fenn' but all the facts mentioned fit in with his own childhood, and inside the back cover he has scribbled in a slightly older hand, 'The story of my life – WH'.

Much of the story is very poignant, and, even allowing for a certain amount of self-dramatisation, it is clear he was made very unhappy by his illegitimacy. In the fifty-two pages of the journal, my grandfather records his thoughts and vividly describes various incidents in almost stream-of-consciousness fashion. The writing is rather spidery, his punctuation rudimentary and there are some spelling mistakes, but nevertheless it has a great vitality. He starts by telling the reader:

> I am writing this in the year 1923 the month of May 12th. I have now got a good start in life and my master suggested that I should write the story of my early life, things before I came across this lucky job.

It would seem that my grandfather stayed with his mother when he was very young and was then 'fostered' by a family called Harris, while his mother went to Brussels to work in service as a nanny. Mrs Harris was small, dark, elderly and 'kind as an angel', and he called her 'granny':

> She was very good to me, would make me anything like shirts, pants, night-shirts anything that she could, she was good, I shall never forget her all my life… I don't suppose she is my granny but just an old woman to look after me and nurse me up…

It seems strange that his mother should go all the way to Belgium to look after children, but there is a passage in the first 'chapter' of his journal which suggests that this was true. He writes about how much the Belgians suffered during the war:

> Look at the poor Belgians how they had to rough it not just once or twice but for two or three years, turned out of their homes, homes burnt down, thousands killed more than whatever we will know, how I know all this, is because I used to study the papers, read the news every evening…

As he was only six at the start of the First World War, and ten by the end, it would suggest that he had a personal motive for such an early interest in reading about the fate of the Belgians. If his mother was out there it would have given him the impetus to follow the news closely. The other possible explanation for her time on the continent is that Lucy and her sister Bessie went out to Belgium as nurses, because the one picture we have of them together when young shows them in nurses' uniforms. Perhaps Lucy went out initially as a nurse and then stayed on as a nanny.

My grandfather does admit in the first few pages that it is difficult to remember the facts about his early life accurately and he has relied on what other people have told him. Whatever the exact movements of Lucy Hartnell, as an unmarried mother from a family which was not well off she would have found it very hard to earn her keep and bring up her son. Bill was certainly living with the Harrises in Camden, a couple of miles north of his birthplace, by the age of six, as this was when he started school. He attended St Michael's in Arlington Road: founded in 1850, it still exists but moved to 88 Camden Street in 1955. The school was only a couple of streets away from where they lived, at 9 James Street. This road changed its name in 1938 to Jamestown Road* and it runs alongside the canal at Camden Lock. The houses in that section of the road have since been pulled down, but they certainly weren't very smart – Mr Harris was a boot mender and he had a small shop in the parlour looking out on to the street. Bill used to help him sometimes. John Harris's little business is recorded in the Kelly's street directories of the period, and these also told me that the family moved from 9 James Street to number 7 in 1915, a fact which is borne out by the rate records.

The Harrises had a grown up son called Harry who went to work but still lived at home. Uncle 'Harry' was obviously fun as he would hide nuts, sweets or apples in his pockets for Bill to find when he came home. Most Sundays he would take my grandfather up to Hampstead Heath to watch football. On several occasions they got separated and Bill recalls crying his eyes out because he didn't know the way home. Sometimes he ended up at the police station until Harry collected him.

One day, Bill found his way up to Hampstead Heath on his own and while playing around he fell in the pond. Someone must have fished him out and taken him to the police station again, and when he finally arrived home, his 'grandfather' gave him a thrashing. Remaining in wet clothes for so long gave him a cold which then developed into whooping cough, and he had to stay in bed for a while. Once he felt a bit better, Bill was bored with staying in his bedroom, so he slipped out when no one else was at home and met up with some local kids. They started to play 'Knocking Down Ginger' – knocking on doors and then running away. He stayed out until around 9.30 p.m. that night and by the time he got home his 'grandfather' had heard about his escapades. He was given the belt and sent to bed without supper.

Bill complains that Mr Harris was very strict with him, but it certainly sounds as if he was a very disobedient child. Two days after the above incident he was told he could go out, but was under strict instructions not to go up to Hampstead. As it was Sunday he put on his best suit, but as soon as he'd met up with friends, they went up to Hampstead to play by

---

* There were originally a large number of roads with 'royal' names, such as James, Charles, Victoria, etc. This caused confusion, so many street names were changed at the beginning of the century.

the pond, despite the warning. This time Bill slipped on the bank and got his velvet suit covered in mud. He went home crying knowing he was going to get the belt again. He was punished and sent to bed without tea once more. When his 'granny' came in he heard her saying, 'I don't know what has come over him, he is very disobedient lately.' When she came up to his room, he 'swanked' that he was asleep, then:

When she had gone down I got off the bed and went to the door again and I heard her say, you have frightened him, he has gone to sleep poor boy. I thought poor old granny you are good to take my part. I did not really deserve it but the more my grandfather hit me the more I would do it. Well later I heard them go out so I crept downstairs and made some tea, and I went out [to] the bakers and pinched some cakes for my tea then I ran home and eat them after upsetting the tea pot on the tablecloth. When I had finished it I hid the tablecloth and got a bag and put a lot of jam jars inside and bottles and took them to a rag shop and got five pence on them then I met my mate and we bunked in the pictures nobody saw us before we went in my mate say 'let's knock off some apples and suckers' so we stood in a crowd by a fruit stall and pinched a lot of apples then went in a sweet shop and I ask for an empty box well while she had gone my mate pinched handfuls of toffee and a shiny shilling behind the counter when she came back she said here you are sonny, I said tar.

Bill seems to have concertinaed several escapades into one in the above passage, but his journal is full of such stories. He was only young, about eight or nine, but he seems already to have been adept at shoplifting. His 'grandmother' would send him out to buy food and he would manage to steal what was required and pocket the coins she had given him to pay for it. He spent a lot of time with one particular mate and they had various ruses for earning themselves a bit of money; on one occasion they went to Euston Station and carried bags and called taxis. They ended up with several shillings' worth of tips between them which they spent on tea and cake, sweets and, after bunking into the cinema, fish and chips on the way home. 'Bunking' into a cinema was a favourite pastime; he adored the movies of Pearl White, heroine of *The Perils of Pauline* and other serials, and this was also when his love of comedians such as Charlie Chaplin began (Chaplin's first short in which he wore his tramp costume was made in 1913). Although he doesn't mention Chaplin by name in the journal, Bill always admired him and frequently did impressions of him at home.

Years later when Bill appeared on *Desert Island Discs* he called him 'the greatest genius of all time'.

Bill and his friend also used to 'bunk' on to the tube and he recounts one incident when they nearly got caught for not having a ticket. Somehow they talked their way out of it. They were always just avoiding trouble by the skin of their teeth. They had to be on the lookout for the police when they were trying to cadge a few tips, whether carrying luggage at one of the stations or attempting to get taxis for theatregoers in the Strand. His mate – whom he never names – seems to be the older of the two and was responsible for initiating him into all sorts of bad habits. Bill must have been very young when he started smoking and the journal contains a wonderful description that would be enough to put most people off:

> we went to the dogend round that's picking up fag ends and smoking them, and when we had finished it made me ill so when I went home my grandfather said I looked ill so he said you had better go to bed so I went up groggy.

Growing up during the First World War when most young men, including young male teachers, were away fighting, he felt the lack of a father figure keenly. It is hardly surprising that Bill behaved like the London urchin he used for the title of his journal, considering the kind of company he was keeping. At one point he goes into great detail about a bookmaker he ran errands for. This bookie forged banknotes which he used to pay out to punters. One Derby day, after making a killing, he disappeared. The police traced him to Southampton and boarded a boat on which he was evidently heading for the Continent. The bookie jumped overboard and drowned, but his accomplice got away with the money. This happened in about 1918 and Bill writes:

> I remember it all because I was very paly [sic] with him and used to give me money to go places for him. He was a decent chap and it was very silly of him to go crooked. It was money that tempted him, but you see it didn't pay he got trapped.

*

The first chapter of the journal contains several passages of such moralising, and by the age of fifteen he had clearly developed a marked philosophical streak:

> I was wondering the other night that why some boys are sent into the world with no troubles and a happy home and plenty of food and money everything they want and others hardly have a thing no food or clothes and no affection or friends while the others live on the fat of the land everything they want they get, while we get nothing, have to look for it and told to get out of the house that's your parents for you. I have wondered to that why all the good and kind get taken from you, die in agony some of them, yet the wicked and rogues live and gain a happy life. There must be some reason for it, the world does go round funny.

As he ponders the unfairness of life, he offers one answer which sounds as if it came straight from his Sunday School teaching: that the good are ready to die while the wicked are given a chance to repent. However, by his own admission he spent more time chucking apple cores around and mucking about than listening to the Sunday School teacher.

For someone with no more than a basic education and foster parents who were certainly not well educated, though perhaps keen on pontificating on the state of the nation after the war, his journal shows a great deal of awareness and compassion for the underprivileged. He knew what it was like to be broke through no fault of one's own – he says that his people weren't bad, nor were they drunkards, just unlucky. He manages to be objective about poverty and does not just consider his own difficulties. For example, he was very concerned about the number of tramps and beggars he saw:

> Look at the unemployment they mostly consist of Englishmen in most cases its no fault of there [sic] own, they have done there bit and there ought to be work for them all, they have given up good homes and wives to fight for king and country to come back to nothing, no work, no money and limbs off most of them then when they go for work, nobody will look at them… what's the good of medals without a home and money medals don't keep you.

Considering his views then, it's surprising that he didn't grow up to be politically active; he wasn't, but he did marry someone who was very left wing when she was young. Later in life, though, he was always willing to help someone going through a bad patch, and was quite often a soft touch for a hard luck story. He never used his own difficult childhood to get sympathy; he simply internalised it. I believe it was this which was largely responsible for the 'chip' many people said they felt he had when he was older.

*

Bill makes one mention of seeing his mother during this period, so whether she was working abroad and just making a swift visit or whether there were many visits is unclear. The passage is very matter of fact and unemotional – he obviously doesn't feel particularly close to her – and everything in the journal suggests that he had few memories of his early time spent with his mother before being sent to live with the Harrises. He says simply that when he returned home one day his mother was there. She gave him a present – a little toy motor car, some plums and 2s 6d – then he said goodbye and went out to play. He remarks that the next time he went to the cinema he was good and paid for himself, instead of 'bunking' in.

Bill appears to have been closer to his aunt and he used to spend some of his school holidays with her in Devon. I can find no record of a farm in Seaton being owned by Hartnells, so perhaps saying he grew up there was wishful thinking on the part of my grandfather, as it was a pretty little seaside town on the south coast. But there was a farm owned by the family not far away where his Aunt Bessie worked in the dairy. When he was about ten or eleven he spent the summer there before going to live with his mother. He used to help his aunt, though he was often more of a hindrance, as he was always dipping his fingers in the cream or being generally mischievous. Sometimes he would go on the milk round with his great-uncle in the cart, from five in the morning until lunchtime at half past twelve. It was on the farm that his lifelong love of horses began. Riding round the fields with his friend was his favourite pastime; occasionally they would even ride round in the small trap which they hitched up to one of the ponies.

He also loved climbing trees in the orchard and pinching apples. Another amusement was to put a bowl of water on a table outside in the yard beside some flowers, then knock wasps off the blossoms with sticks and watch them drown. All these pranks sound like normal boyish high spirits, though somehow he always managed to tear his trousers on a branch or do something to provoke a telling off when he got in. He did, however, get into more serious trouble when he and his friend got so drunk on cider that they passed out. They sneaked round the back of the house with mugs and drank the cider his uncle had made straight from the barrels:

> till we could not move, then we got so dazy that we fell off to sleep next morning when I woke I looked round and found myself in blankets. I properly got the breezes up because I knew when my uncle went round to look and see if everything was alright he must have found us asleep.

Unfortunately for Bill and his partner in crime, they had left the bung out of the barrel and all the cider had drained away, swamping the place. His aunt warned him to steer clear of his uncle for as long as possible. Her advice was heeded because Bill says bluntly, he was 'a grumpy old pig'. Auntie Bessie was always very protective of her nephew especially when he was teased by the local kids who used to shout 'bastard' at him. When Bill and his uncle finally met up at tea-time he was warned never to go near the barrels again, otherwise he would be sent home. The lure of the cider was too great nevertheless, and a few days later the youngsters were caught drinking again. This time his uncle kept his word and sent for Lucy, who was back in England for good.

*

My grandfather went back to London to live with his mother in Holborn. She was now no longer looking after children, or perhaps injured soldiers, but was trying to earn a living by taking in lodgers. He started at St John's School just off Red Lion Square, where he got on well to begin with but was soon frequently getting the cane on his hand and backside. Though corporal punishment was so much more prevalent then, he claims that he was blamed for everything, and was always fighting the other boys – no doubt they teased him for being illegitimate there as well. After a while he made friends with some of the ringleaders, and subsequently went with them on shoplifting expeditions to Gamages, a large department store in the Holborn district. They used to steal things like torches, mouth organs and paintboxes. Soon they were recognised there and so moved on to

Selfridges, where they took knives and forks, leather bags, sweets and books. Somehow they always managed to escape being caught.

After a while it became more difficult for Lucy to get lodgers, probably owing to the depression after the First World War. She became short of money and owed rent, and started taking her worries out on her son. He says he got bullied for the least misdemeanour and people were always telling tales on him. Once he shinned up a lamp post for a bit of a laugh, but his mother came out of the house and shamed him by thrashing him in the street in front of everybody. He began to dread going home. His mother would hit him with a broom and throw anything she could lay her hands on at him. A lot of children feel hard done by and that their parents are too strict, but the situation does seem to have been genuinely very bad – he was hungry a lot of the time and got very skinny, as well as being short of clothes.

Then his mother found herself a boyfriend and things looked up for a while. A tall good-looking police constable from Beak Street police station, he used to stay some weekends and occasionally during the week. Lucy was obviously very insecure about the whole situation because:

> my mother used to treat him very badly always rowing with him... when it was time for him to go back to the station she would not let him go, used to lock the door, and smack his face and smash his nice hats and burn his gloves all sorts of vile things. One day he came in and caught her thrashing me for something and he stopped her, at least he got in front of me and pushed her away so she threw a glass tumbler at him and cut his face, he was a gentle man he did not move, did not lay a finger on her, and never did the whole time he came to us.

But Bill adored him and even called him Dad. For a short while he became the father figure Bill lacked and he used to go and look for him when he was on the beat. When the policeman advised him to be a good honest boy, he says he took the advice and genuinely tried to behave better. But Lucy seems to have been jealous of their closeness:

> No one seemed to love me only my policeman father. It almost broke my heart to think mother was so cruel to me. I shall never forget that man I called dad he was not really my father I found that out later on. I haven't a father because I am illegitimate. That's why my mother hated me so much I suppose.

Sadly the relationship didn't last as the policeman was transferred to Woolwich Arsenal police station. This upset Bill a great deal as he didn't see him for a long time. Without his influence Lucy started bullying her son again, and Bill went back to his old ways.

The journal ends at this point, which is very frustrating as we are tantalisingly told that in the next chapter he will tell more about 'getting into worse holes than ever'. What could these have been? The book was not written in one go and had been continued on several different occasions: he tells us the last section was started in December 1925 after a long break. In the first quote from Bill's journal it mentioned his 'master'. It is this mysterious figure who encouraged him to write down the story of his life, but he never gets to the point of explaining how they met. It is this person who is responsible for giving him a chance in life, a 'chance to run straight and play the game in other words be a "sport"'. Going back to his moralising, Bill sees himself as a 'rogue' who has been given the opportunity to repent. His earnestness is touching:

> This book is entirely writing from my own brains I don't want people run away with the idea that somebody wrote it out first, because they didn't and I hope people will believe this little statement, for I am only a kid and just want a start with something where I can earn a bit of dough to repay my master in some way or other for what he has done these past months if he had not come along when he did I could not have carried on no food and hardly a rag to my back.

I have to rely on family history as to how Bill met this man who was to become his unofficial guardian and was to have such a profound effect on him. All his life Bill enjoyed boxing and racing and from an early age he avidly followed the fortunes of his heroes in the sports papers. I still have his old copies of *Sport Pictures* from 1919 (when Bill was only eleven) and *All Sports Weekly*, an illustrated paper which came out on Fridays priced 2d, with pictures of stars such as heavyweight fighters Jack Dempsey and Georges Carpentier.

Bill himself learnt to box at a 'boys' club' – these were an early attempt to keep youngsters off the street and out of trouble, rather like later youth clubs. Bill was small and wiry and a very good little 'scrapper', and I believe it was an interest in watching young boys box, and in sketching them, which took Hugh Blaker to the boys' club where they first met.

Blaker became Bill's mentor, sharing a fascination with boxing and horse racing, but encouraging him to discover other more artistic pursuits as well. But just who was this man, the unlikely saviour from his life as an 'urchin'?

Chapter Three
A CHANGE IN CIRCUMSTANCES

HUGH OSWALD BLAKER WAS an artist and art connoisseur. Born in Worthing in 1873, he went to school at Cranleigh and then studied art in Antwerp and Paris. His own work was accomplished and he exhibited in various galleries – the British Museum bought one of his drawings and between 1927 and 1934 he had a picture in the Musée du Luxembourg in Paris. He was a significant enough figure that in the early 1990s there was an exhibition of his paintings in Wales, curated by Robert Meyrick, which then toured to Bath. The most noticeable quality of his work is the constant experimentation with style, showing the influence of many contemporary artists.

He was best known, however, as an avid collector and a respected expert who identified many previously unknown works by great masters. His first success occurred when he was still young and certainly not wealthy. He saw a picture – a portrait of Isabella Brandt – classed as 'Rubens School' but which he was convinced was by Rubens himself. He decided to trust his instinct and bid for it, paying £60, which was almost all he had. It was sent to the Kaiser Friedrich Museum in Berlin, adjudged to be genuine and purchased by them for £5,000.

According to his obituary in *The Times* dated 7th October 1936:

> His power of discerning the hand of the great masters was born not only of a vast knowledge and experience but even more a deep and unfailing passion for the great and fine in art. While others based their conclusions on a microscopic study of the painted surface, Blaker responded at once to

the spirit breathing through the picture. He trusted to an inborn instinct which rarely led him astray.

Catholic in taste, his interest was not limited to the great masters – he also loved modern work and was one of the first in Britain to acclaim Cézanne. His powers of persuasion led to several examples of Cézanne's work being hung at the Tate Gallery in London, though it took him a while to convince the trustees of the artist's importance. The Tate also exhibited pictures from Hugh Blaker's own collection, including a Modigliani, *The Peasant Boy*, later presented to the gallery by his sister in memory of him. His private collection consisted mainly of modern English and French artists: he owned Whistlers, Sickerts, Gilmans, Gores and paintings by Corot, Pissarro, Monticello and many more too numerous to mention. He was a friend and great supporter of Augustus John, and owned several of his works – some of these drawings were the personal favourites of my grandfather.

Blaker considered, however, his greatest discovery to have been 'the other *Mona Lisa*', a superb version painted in Leonardo da Vinci's studio by his disciples. He believed it was as likely to be the original as the one which hangs in the Louvre, because of the prevalence of the practice of great masters getting their pupils to do some of the painting for them. In February 2013 the issue became newsworthy again with experts still arguing over its authenticity.

According to the same *Times* obituary quoted above, 'his familiar figure will be sadly missed in the sale rooms and galleries', where he spent much of his time. He bought not only for himself but also for the Davies sisters, two Welsh heiresses whose famous collection, which he was largely responsible for compiling, now makes up a major part of the National Museum of Wales. It was the experience gained buying for them which built his reputation and no doubt gave him the confidence to purchase on his own behalf.

He had numerous articles on art published in newspapers and periodicals, and from 1905 to 1913 he was curator of the Holburne Art Museum in Bath. He had a love-hate relationship with this establishment, as he disliked its provinciality and was at loggerheads with the arts committees he had to deal with. He was the first to approach the collection with a critical eye and he condemned many of its purchases, which did not endear him to the trustees. Although removed from display, nothing was actually thrown away and some of the pieces he found fault with have since shown their worth. Nevertheless, he is respected for having sparked a modern reappraisal of its works which was long overdue, even if he went about it in a rather high-handed and self-publicising manner. He was known for being outspoken and even commented in one of his diaries: 'I am art in Bath.'

In 1910 he had a book published by Frank Palmer called *Points For Posterity*, an arrogant title for a work which outlined his views on art, politics and philosophy. It contains a vituperative tirade against the vulgarity of the period, and in it he complains that the beginning of the twentieth century was:

> the age of collecting: the rage was assuming the form of national madness and even copper stew pans, old spectacles and lids of potted meat jars, were being swept into the much abused realm of art, where, it might be remembered, disused postage stamps had long held important sway. In fact, these latter appear to be the only *objets d'art* in which the Royal Family, with the world of beautiful abstractions open to them, took an intelligent interest. That men would spend thousands of pounds on very ordinary and ugly pottery productions, stupid in design, stupid in colour, stupid in decoration – in fact, the very quintessence of the stupidity of the 'art collector' of the period, painted with 'exotic birds' and flowers in a manner too unspeakably childish for discussion – is only another proof that money cannot beget brains or even taste...

What on earth would he have thought of later twentieth-century developments in art? And he did not just reserve his vitriol for 'art-collectors', but poured scorn on the women of the period for their painted faces, false hair and unnatural clothing, along with many other contemporary fashions. The treatise makes him sound like the original 'angry young man'. Perhaps it was a calculated attempt to make a name for himself, as some of the opinions he expressed were deeply hypocritical: he criticised gambling yet he himself indulged; at least he did with my grandfather in later life.

After leaving the Holburne Museum, Blaker moved to Isleworth, to the west of London on the River Thames, and by 1914 he was living at 55 Church Street, later taking over number 57 as well. Church Street runs along the river, and the house had beautiful views out over towards the

Old Deer Park in Richmond. A tall, red-brick Regency building with arched windows, it was situated in an area known for its number of artists, writers and bohemians. He filled the house with beautiful paintings. Some twenty years later, when my grandparents occupied number 57, my mother remembers a Millais hanging in the bathroom, and a dining room so crammed with framed pictures, stacked in rows, that you could hardly enter it. The whole top floor of his house was turned into a studio, where he drew, painted and sculpted. But he was not only interested in fine art: he loved poetry and great literature, particularly Shakespeare, as he expressed in one of his poems:

If I had lived in other time
I might have ear for wanton rhyme.
Three hundred years ago I might
Have grasped faint shimmer of the light.
I might have been an underling
And served, in tavern, on a King.
I might even have heard a phrase
That fired my soul in wild amaze.
I'd sooner been a lackey then
Than nowadays a prince of men.
I'd sooner wait on Shakespeare sweet
Than have the whole world at my feet.

Being taken under the wing of such a cultured gentleman completely changed my grandfather's life. As I mentioned, they shared a love of sport, but Bill was also hugely influenced by the artistic and literary taste of his mentor.

*

After meeting my grandfather, Hugh Blaker was responsible for arranging for him to go on a special boys' club trip to the Isle of Wight, where Bill's interest in poetry was developed. Bembridge School, on the Isle of Wight, was founded in 1919 by John Howard Whitehouse. He ran, for some years, boys' camps for London secondary schools, to give youngsters from inner city areas the chance to spend part of the summer holidays in different surroundings. The school had a magnificent coastal setting and was surrounded by woods and fields. One of the founder's habits was to give boys who attended Bembridge a copy of *The Golden Treasury*, a classic collection of lyrical poetry. I can only presume that he also gave them to those who attended the summer camps, for one of my grandfather's valued possessions was the 1922 edition, published by Oxford University Press, of Palgrave's *The Golden Treasury*, in which he had inscribed his name and 'Bembridge School'. It was such a popular book that it was reprinted more than once every year, suggesting that Bill received his copy when he was fourteen, which fits in with the time he met Hugh Blaker. Bill obviously benefited a great deal from boys' clubs, and as an adult he supported them wholeheartedly.

It was usual to leave school at fourteen in those days, and from what my grandfather says in his journal, he must have left around that age, without a proper job to go to. Although he reveals a melodramatic streak when he writes of how hard it was for him, I believe things were so difficult for his mother that she had to give up running lodgings and take a post as housekeeper somewhere. This meant Bill had nowhere to live, and he talks in the journal of being 'turned out of the house' and of needing a home. Hugh Blaker couldn't have appeared on the scene at a more opportune moment.

Because Bill once again lost the influence of his mother – who had, after all been absent during so much of his upbringing – the relationship with Blaker was *Pygmalion*-like, with Hugh becoming both unofficial guardian and mentor. Bill was desperate for a father figure, and this small man, with an arrogant and cultured manner, was the first person, apart from the policeman, to show much interest in him. Hugh introduced him to a world of which he had never had any experience. Eager to learn, Bill was influenced in many ways. By all accounts, Blaker could rub people up the wrong way in his work – he was opinionated and a perfectionist, and didn't suffer fools gladly – and these are all traits Bill was accused of displaying in later life. Blaker was very combative, and waged wars by letter in art magazines and by personal letter with many in the art establishment of the time. He felt there was a vendetta against him, particularly when various offers of paintings to the Tate were turned down. The Cézannes were only accepted after lengthy heated debate. Blaker's belief that he knew better than anyone else was in some ways justified in that the establishment of the time was conservative and took a long time to acknowledge the contemporary movements in French painting. But Blaker himself was not infallible, and some of his 'great masters' turned out not to be such. Bill's attitude later in life – that he was an actor whose abilities were not fully recognised – and his impatience with those who were not serious about their work, seems to reflect some aspects of Blaker's temperament. The actress Chili Bouchier, who played opposite Bill in a film during the forties, said, 'If I can fault him at all it would be his supreme self-confidence and self-possession which sometimes appeared to be arrogance.' This uncannily echoes descriptions of Blaker.

Blaker's motive for helping Bill is unclear, but he was not the only young man to benefit from the gentleman's assistance, though no one else became a surrogate son in the way Bill did. Blaker had a truly philanthropic streak and is known to have helped several struggling young artists, championing their work, sending them parcels of paint and equipment, and purchasing their pictures himself. He was always keen to lend paintings from his own collection for exhibitions, as he believed that the public should have the chance to see, and become knowledgeable about, great art.

*

Blaker helped Bill secure a job, initially recommending him to Frank Wootton, the owner of the most famous racing stables of the time, in Epsom. Wootton was originally from Australia and was the most outstanding young rider of his generation. He won his first race at Folkestone in 1906 on a horse named Retrieve, becoming champion jockey in 1909 and keeping the title until 1912. He rode 882 winners between 1906 and 1913, by which time he was too heavy to race on the flat. After the war, he won 61 races over hurdles and then turned to training, where he was responsible for more than a hundred winners. Considering how closely Bill followed the racing world, it must have been a thrill to work for a hero such as Wootton.

Bill started as a stable lad. He was a natural: already able to ride well from his time on the farm, he was small and wiry, adored horses and knew all about form. Soon he was training as a jockey, and he actually held a jockey's licence for a year. But the healthy outdoor life agreed with him and made him grow. He joined the stables in 1922 when, by his own admission, he was scrawny and undernourished, but after a year he put on so much height and weight that Wootton said he felt that being a jockey was not for him. At sixteen, Wootton had still been small and used to weigh in at 7st 4lbs, but Bill grew to 5 feet 8 inches and would not have been able to get down to such a weight, even though he was never heavy.

Apart from the horsemanship he had learnt, Bill took away one other memento of his time at the stables – a large scar on his temple, which is actually visible in some of his stills shots even though it was covered with make-up during filming. The story goes that he had a fall and was kicked by a horse, and someone, trying to be helpful, threw disinfectant on the gash – but it was the ordinary harsh stable variety and burnt the skin, causing more blistering than the original cut. However, he kept his enthusiasm for horses and horse racing throughout his life and always hoped to be able to put his riding skills to use in films. In fact, there was actually only one production – *Strawberry Roan* – in which he got the chance to show them off.

*

Bill's other love as a boy was the cinema – the dream of becoming like his hero, Charlie Chaplin, was the only idea that appealed to him once he knew he could not be a jockey. Perhaps this was encouraged or even suggested by Hugh Blaker, who is known to have indulged in amateur dramatics when he was younger. Anyway, Bill's unofficial guardian paid for him to attend Italia Conti, the famous drama school which still exists and whose headed notepaper proudly lists him as an ex-pupil.

The school is now well known for combining ordinary education with acting classes, but when my grandfather attended it simply taught acting, speech, dancing and singing. It was run by two sisters, Italia Conti and Bianca Murray, the latter doing most of the teaching. Italia ran the school, directed and acted as an agent to her pupils. She had a school secretary, an agency secretary and an office at the Holborn Empire, and she supplied children for many films and plays, who were always accompanied by governesses when they were working. The canteen was always packed with students during the breaks from classes, which were all of a practical nature – scenes from plays, audition pieces, singing and dancing. The dancing encompassed everything from ballet to ballroom. Everyone had to partake, even if they had two left feet. The idea was to prepare the pupils to be able to tackle any sort of work when they entered the business. Luckily, Bill didn't have two left feet, and these classes gave him the grounding which enabled him to perform in musical revues, as he did some years later. My mother also remembers him being a good ballroom dancer.

Other pupils there at the same time as my grandfather included Roger, Barry and Peggy Livesey, Jack Hawkins and Freddie Peisley; the latter two he was to work with later in films. Bill started attending when he was fifteen towards the end of 1923, and Italia believed he had real talent for the stage. In a letter to Hugh Blaker, dated 4th September 1924, she said he had been a consistently good boy and very enthusiastic about his work. This sounds so different from the Bill who constantly got into trouble as a boy. He had found his métier. She also says:

> and I consider in sending him to Boarding School you will be giving him the one thing he needs for the development of that talent – polish and refinement of speech and manner – he also needs the discipline a good school will give him. I hope he will work well and do your kindness credit.

Hugh Blaker had the idea of sending him to a public school and had requested a reference for the school from Miss Conti. She also says she would be happy to have him back for finishing lessons before he started his career as an adult actor; but, as we shall see, he preferred to learn while he was working.

The school Blaker chose for his protégé was the Imperial Service College, Windsor. Set up in the nineteenth century as a boarding school and then merged with an army crammer and the United Services College from Cornwall, it was a public school with military overtones. It no longer exists today as it was absorbed into Hailbury College, although in its time it was very grand, rivalling Eton. The school was expensive, costing £41 13s 4d a term, plus extras such as tailors' costs, books, fencing and boxing lessons. Bill was sent during the autumn term of 1924, and we still possess the end-of-term bill, with charges made for pocket money, Christmas cards and other sundries, together with the cost of the spring term payable in advance. It was difficult for him to fit in, given his background. When interviewed as an adult, Bill always mentioned that he ran away from school. It was Imperial Service College, Windsor to which he was referring. The discipline was strict, and for a boy who had run wild in London before working in a stable and then going to drama school, this must have been difficult to cope with.

Probably influenced by his guardian's admiration of Shakespeare, Bill decided he would like to join the touring company of Sir Frank Benson. He would be able to gain his independence and earn money. In an article in a fan club bulletin of the 1940s Bill claims he even prevailed upon his parents to write to the great tragedian to plead on his behalf. For 'parents' I think we should read Hugh Blaker. We do not know how many times he ran away from school to try to join Benson's troupe, but Bill's guardian seem to have been remarkably indulgent, and it is likely that the intercession of his mentor helped him secure a place with this famous company in 1925.

The change in my grandfather's circumstances brought about by Hugh Blaker was immense. Perhaps, without his guidance, Bill would have become a petty thief; maybe on the other hand he would have grown out of shoplifting and mixing with crooked bookmakers; but I am sure his early experiences gave him a great deal to draw on as an actor. He was always able to play a crook with utter conviction. He knew what it was like to be poor and ashamed of his background, he had learnt to be tough to cope with being called names, and now he had the advantage of some private education and the encouragement of a sophisticated and cultured man. He learnt to appreciate poetry and paintings and Shakespeare. Although he would never play aristocrats in films, he was able to move with ease from working man to professional. But perhaps it also meant that he didn't quite know where he fitted in.

Chapter Four

FIRST YEARS IN THE THEATRE
AND FALLING IN LOVE

AFTER MANY ENTREATIES, IN early 1925 my grandfather was finally allowed to stay with Sir Frank Benson's company. Benson was one of the last great Victorian actor-managers, particularly known for his productions of Shakespeare. Born in November 1858, he had been a pupil of the famous actor Henry Irving; by 1883 he was managing his own tours and three years later he produced his first season at Stratford-upon-Avon, where he made his name. Productions of Shakespeare had been mounted in Shakespeare's birthplace for some years, but with his entrepreneurial skill Benson helped make the festivals at the Stratford Memorial Theatre into a national institution. These eventually gave rise to the Royal Shakespeare Company.

During his life Benson was supposed to have produced every Shakespeare play except *Titus Andronicus* – so bloodthirsty that it was out of fashion for years. He usually took the leading role. According to most of his obituaries, he would be remembered less for his abilities as an actor than for the huge impact he had on classical theatre: apart from his works at Stratford, Benson toured the provinces for years with productions of Shakespeare and famous English comedies, even taking some abroad. In keeping with his larger-than-life image, he is the only actor to have been knighted inside a theatre. After a performance at the Theatre Royal on Drury Lane in 1916, George V summoned him to the royal box, where he was knighted with a property sword as there wasn't a real one to hand.

By the time my grandfather joined him in 1925, Sir Frank Benson (or 'Pa' Benson, as he was affectionately known) would have been about sixty-seven and past his prime. Even by contemporary standards, his acting was old-fashioned and mannered (he was certainly too old to be playing some of the roles he took on), but he was still revered by the provincial audiences and he inspired great loyalty in all those who worked for him. Ex-members of his company were known as 'Old Bensonians'. They used to meet for reunion dinners – my grandfather kept some of his invitations – which continued even after Frank Benson's death on 31st December 1939.

According to the obituary in the *Observer*, his company 'became the university of acting. The young men and women who joined him were really put through the discipline in rehearsal, as understudies, and in small parts. Consequently to be an Old Bensonian was to have more than a proud name: it meant genuine qualification.' All through his touring life he had had youngsters turning up at his door begging to be taken on. My grandfather was one of the lucky ones, along with Robert Donat, who joined the company during the same period. They started out as general dogsbodies, worked up to being assistant stage managers, then trod the boards as walk-ons before finally graduating to acting parts.

Although much admired, Benson was also known for his eccentricities, particularly his obsession with the fitness of his troupe. With his sporting prowess, my grandfather would have been useful to the actor-manager. They were expected to rehearse in the morning, play cricket or hockey in the afternoon and perform in the evening. We still have a handwritten team list for a special cricket match on Friday 18th June, between Benson C G and Imperial Co Ltd at Frys Ground, containing the names Claridge, Chisholm, Donat, Hartnell, Hickson and others with F.R.B. (Benson) as captain and Lloyd Pearson as vice-captain. Lunch and tea were laid on and all the company were invited – and no doubt expected – to attend. Benson had a strong sense of public duty and demanded the same from his actors. Bill often mentioned that in 1926 during the General Strike he marched all his actors off and enrolled them as special constables.

Benson was criticised by some of his contemporaries for these oddities, but in his biography of Donat, J. C. Trewin speaks of Donat defending Benson against his detractors. His regime bred well-disciplined, highly professional performers. Both Bill and Donat were later known for their professionalism, which was instilled in them during these early years. Bill was certainly proud of his apprenticeship and always mentioned it when interviewed about his career, even though he did not appear in any Shakespeare after this time. As late as 1965, when he appeared on *Desert Island Discs*, he said rather wistfully that he still hoped to appear in some more Shakespeare.

My grandfather toured with Frank Benson's company for about two years, and during this period he was billed variously as 'William Hartnell', 'Henry Hartnell', and sometimes 'William Henry' (Henry was his middle name). When I saw the first variation, I wondered if it was a misprint in the programme, but when a second turned up, I thought he must have been experimenting to find the most suitable stage name for himself. These variations only appear for his backstage credits, so perhaps he was ashamed of himself for working behind the scenes for so long. Although he admired Robert Donat, it must have been difficult not to feel some jealousy, as the extremely attractive young man with the melodious voice was soon playing good roles on stage while he was still assistant stage manager. But Donat was two years older than Bill, a typical 'leading man' type, and had had far more performing experience before joining Benson. Maybe I'm reading too much into these name changes, as Bill did go on later in his career to vary his first name slightly according to the type of show he appeared in – 'Billy' for comedy, 'William' for anything serious or classical, and occasionally 'Bill' (for no apparent reason).

A permanently touring company like Pa Benson's created a strong sense of camaraderie because the itinerant lifestyle could be very lonely – the constant moving from town to town, living out of a suitcase and staying in theatrical digs. Working different hours from the majority of people meant that the rest of the cast became your family. Although I don't think they were especially close, Bill and Robert Donat worked hard together, touring up and down the country, and they kept in touch for some years. Donat soon went on to be successful in films such as *The Count of Monte Cristo* and *The 39 Steps*, and was praised for his 'natural' acting style on screen, as was my grandfather some time later. It is curious that the over-theatrical style which must have been the norm for the Benson shows in no way turned the two young actors into affected screen performers, unlike some stage actors who went into talkies. Bill always admired Donat and saved various notes from him, including thanks for first-night best wishes. When going through a quiet patch in his film career, my grandfather evidently wrote to him for help, and in early 1936 Donat replied, 'I shall certainly do all I possibly can here at the Studios, but the casting department are rather suspicious of all personal introductions. Can you send me some photographs, and I will hand them on, together with all the "influence" I possess?' This is jumping forward several years, but it shows how important contacts were for those working in such a precarious industry.

Apart from the programmes, my grandfather kept a wonderful old photograph of the company taken at the King's Theatre, Hammersmith, on Friday 30th April 1926. They are assembled on stage after a special gala performance of *The Merchant of Venice*, in aid of the Stratford Memorial Theatre which had been burnt down. Benson played Shylock and the existing company was augmented by many distinguished Old Bensonians. Portia was played by Lilian Braithwaite, one of the best-known classical actresses of her time. She had first performed with Frank Benson's company in Stratford in 1901, and eventually became a Dame in 1943. Robert Donat and my grandfather (at this point known as William Hartnell) had walk-on parts as 'Venetians and Masquers'. These 'Venetians and Masquers' numbered twenty-eight in all and among the names is a certain Italia Conti at whose drama school Bill had studied a few years earlier.

The provincial tours were gruelling as the plays were often performed in true repertoire fashion: this meant several different titles within a week and sometimes even a different play every performance. The schedule for their visit to the Prince's Theatre, Manchester, week commencing 7th June 1926, was as follows:

MONDAY evening	*She Stoops to Conquer*
TUESDAY	*Julius Caesar*
WEDNESDAY matinée	*As You Like It*
WEDNESDAY evening	*Hamlet*
THURSDAY	*The Tempest*
FRIDAY	*The School for Scandal*
SATURDAY matinée	*The Merchant of Venice*
SATURDAY evening	*Macbeth*

The company at this time included Norman Chidgey, Norman Claridge, Henry Fielding, Beatrice Archdale, Molly Sainton and many others, with my grandfather as assistant stage manager. To do so many different plays in a week must have been incredibly demanding. Imagine standing on stage and losing concentration for a moment – you would probably have to remind yourself which day of the week it was to remember the play you were in. Two different Shakespeares on matinée days would have been exhausting: no wonder fitness was a prerequisite of the company members.

*

Bill had a few other jobs between engagements with Sir Frank Benson but finally left the company in 1928 and went to work in repertory theatre. At this time repertory theatre usually meant 'weekly rep', which differed from the above in that the play changed every week and the company had a permanent home. Actors rehearsed one play during the day and performed another one that evening, and any spare time was spent learning the script for the following show. Actors usually stayed with one rep company for some time, and local audiences could see a different play every week and follow their favourite actors in different roles. A facility to learn lines quickly and to forget them as soon as the production had finished was one of the skills which rep theatre encouraged. My grandfather always prided himself on this ability, and it was particularly useful years later when appearing in weekly television shows.

The move from playing small parts for Sir Frank Benson to playing leads in repertory theatre was very swift. By 6th August 1928 Bill was playing the eponymous role in *Good Morning, Bill* by P. G. Wodehouse at the King's Theatre, Hammersmith, the theatre in which he had had a walk-on part only two years previously in *The Merchant of Venice*. The play was billed as a 'Sparkling Comedy'; my grandfather excelled in this type of production and continued to appear in them for many years. He had good natural timing, which he had perfected by watching others; and, not having the physique to play romantic leads, he decided that light comedy was his forte. He was obviously a great success in the role because he played the lead in *Good Morning, Bill* several times during his career. There were countless other opportunities for him to show off his skills. During the twenties there had been a boom in British theatre, and many new comedy writers had emerged including Noël Coward, Ivor Novello, Ben Travers and Edgar Wallace, as well as more serious playwrights such as Galsworthy, Somerset Maugham and J. M. Barrie. Before the Depression hit there was plenty of money around to mount lavish shows, with well-known producers such as C. B. Cochran putting on huge revues and musicals. My grandfather adored watching musical comedies and it was these to which he aspired, despite his early classical training.

*

Shortly after his appearance in *Good Morning, Bill*, my grandfather was cast by Gordon McLeod for a tour of Canada. This was possibly the most important event of his life as far as my ancestry is concerned. The transatlantic visit was announced in *The Stage* (the industry's newspaper, which is still published) on 28th August 1928, and the company set sail in the SS *Metagama* two days later. Gordon McLeod was a celebrated leading man who had toured Canada before. This time, in charge of his own company, he presented two plays for his first season as an actor-manager: a rather melodramatic vehicle for himself, *Miss Elizabeth's Prisoner*, and a contrasting modern piece called *A Bill of Divorcement*.

Miss Elizabeth's Prisoner, by Robert Neilson Stevens and E. Lyall Swete, was billed as a 'romantic comedy' and was set in the United States in 1778. It had mixed reviews which admitted that it was 'good costume fun', even if the piece was somewhat dated. The play was preceded by a prologue, in which, to quote a review, 'T. W. Dunscombe and W. H. Hartnell have much to indicate by their roles of why England lost the war of American Independence'. As I have not traced a copy, I am not sure if that was a compliment or a criticism, but it apparently went down very well with the audiences. In *Miss Elizabeth's Prisoner*, Billy Hartnell, as he called himself at this time, played the small part of Sergeant Carrington (the first of many roles as a sergeant), the rest of the cast comprising Gordon McLeod and leading lady Lilian Christine, Stanley Browne, T. W. Dunscombe, Allen Brooks, Olive Walter, P. Kynaston Reeves and Aubrey Mallalieu. The acting world was much smaller then than it is now and within a few years he was to work with several of them again in films. There was also a certain Heather McIntyre playing Molly Edwards, the maid. Heather, a very spirited and pretty girl of twenty, was to play juvenile lead in the second production of the tour. The first show opened on 10th September

1928 at Her Majesty's Theatre in Montreal, Quebec. The company stayed there for a week; they then toured the play from one side of Canada to the other, sometimes doing one-night stands, sometimes staying a few days. Many long hours were spent in trains, as can be seen from their exhausting schedule:

SEPTEMBER	17th	Capitol Theatre	Cornwall, Ontario
	18th	New Theatre	Brockville
	19th	Grand Theatre	Kingston
	20th	Grand Theatre	Peterborough
	21st (2 days)	Savoy Theatre	Hamilton
	24th (1 wk)	Princess	Toronto
OCTOBER	1st	Temple	Brantford
	2nd	Capitol	Quelph
	3rd	Imperial	Sarnia
	4th (3 days)	Grand	London
	8th	Opera House	Orillia
	9th	Royal	North Bay
	11th (3 days)	Orpheum	Fort William
	15th (1 wk)	Walker Theatre	Winnipeg, Manitoba
	22nd (3 days)	Empire	Saskatoon, Saskatchewan
	25th (3 days)	Regina	Regina
	29th	Capitol	Moose Jaw
	30th	Orpheum	Estevan
	31st	High	Weyburn
NOVEMBER	1st	Lyric	Swift Current
	2nd	Empress	Medicine Hat
	3rd	Majestic	Lethbridge
	5th (3 days)	Grand	Calgary
	8th (3 days)	Empire	Edmonton
	12th (1 wk)	Vancouvres	Vancouver, BC
	19th (1 wk)	Victoria	Victoria

At this last venue, the company played its final three shows of *Prisoner*, then opened *A Bill of Divorcement*, which it toured back to the east coast over the next seven weeks, visiting many of the same theatres. Canada was a favourite country for enterprising British companies. That November, audiences in Victoria were to be treated to a double dose of British acting, as Gordon McLeod's company was followed into the Victoria Theatre by the Stratford-on-Avon Festival Company. They had only visited the town once before, when Sir Frank Benson had brought the company over in 1913, about ten years before my grandfather worked with him.

A Bill of Divorcement by Clemence Dane was completely different from the first piece, and was calculated to shock many of the provincial audiences. W. Graham Allen, in the *Halifax Chronicle*, described it as 'Ibsenish' because it dealt with social issues rarely discussed in contemporary drama. The story focuses on divorce and the possibility of madness being passed down through the generations. This sounds grim, but Mr Allen also said that it was 'not as morbid and stark as one might expect' because of the 'delightfully subtle humour'. The play has not survived the test of time, but it was made into a film in 1932 with the young Katharine Hepburn playing the same role as my grandmother, for which she received an Oscar. Gordon McLeod played Hilary Fairfield, a shell-shocked veteran who escapes after nineteen years of insanity, on the eve of his release from an asylum. He finds his way home to discover that his wife (played by Lilian Christine) has divorced him and is about to marry another man. He then begs her not to desert him. Heather McIntyre played the daughter, Sydney, who was, according to contemporary reviews, the embodiment of 'new youth, gay, flippant, frankly discussing problems that would make your grandmother blush'. She is beset by fears of inherited insanity and the possibility of passing it on to her children. So she decides to send away Kit Pumphrey, the man with whom she is in love and to whom she is engaged, and devote her life to looking after her father.

Kit was played by my grandfather. Although Heather didn't win an Oscar, she did win all the notices, and also got her man. Or perhaps he got his girl. Anyway, they fell in love, perhaps somewhat inevitably, given that they were the only two youngsters on a six-month tour a long way from home, and they were playing lovers on stage. Any actor will tell you what tours are like. It is often very difficult not to let feelings created on stage spill over into real life.

The reviews for *Miss Elizabeth's Prisoner* had been somewhat subdued, but the newspapers raved about my grandmother in *A Bill of Divorcement*. According to the *Toronto Saturday Night*:

> Honors of the piece, of course, go to Heather McIntyre. Here is an actress. Here, more-over may be a theatrical 'find' of the first importance... Miss

McIntyre's work in *A Bill of Divorcement* is supremely fine... in a role which brought Katherine Cornell to the front rank, Miss McIntyre achieves a distinction which should do as much for her. It is not too much to prophesy, or to hope, that the theatrical world will see more of her in the future.

What a wonderful review! There were others: 'The young modern, a strikingly clever part, was taken by Heather McIntyre, a strikingly clever young actress. What more can one say?' (*Calgary Daily Herald*) and 'Miss Heather McIntyre... well deserved the great ovation she received' (*Victoria Daily Times*).

My grandfather did not escape mention himself: 'W. Hartnell as the daughter's sweetheart was a consistently good actor', as he was apparently 'boyish and engaging'. In the play Sydney deliberately antagonises her fiancé to send him away, and this scene was obviously the high point of the drama. The *Daily Columnist* in Victoria wrote:

Act III, in which this episode takes place, is one of the subtlest bits of writing and acting in the whole play, with a measure of suppressed grief on one side and on the other, of incomprehension, anger, thwarted love, which has rarely been more expressively portrayed.

The real-life chemistry between the two of them evidently made their performances particularly intense.

Perhaps Gordon McLeod was peeved at being passed over by the critics – or perhaps he was genuinely ill – but for whatever reason, he was off for several of the performances and his place was taken by one of the other actors. Despite the absence of the leading man, it was definitely the more successful of the two shows. It was seen by over two thousand people in the course of the three performances in St Johns, their second-to-last venue. The final show was in Halifax on 7th February 1929, then they returned to St John and sailed home from there.

Both my grandparents adored Canada and its wide open spaces. They visited all the sights, and although Bill did not keep a diary the picture postcards he sent home to his mother give an effective record of their itinerary. Despite the difficulties of their earlier relationship, Bill seemed close to her, and usually wrote every other day, frequently signing off with 'Tons of love'. Bill had always loved the countryside, and on this trip he saw some of the world's grandest and wildest scenery with someone who could share this passion. On Sunday 23rd September he and Heather visited Niagara Falls and went across the rapids in an 'Aero Cable' – an unstable-looking cable car, completely open on all sides, with nothing but railings round the platform area. On other occasions they saw the Chaudiere Fall Rapids near North Bay, Ontario, climbed Mount McKay, travelled through the Rocky Mountains on a train which ran alongside the Kicking Horse River, and even stood on American soil for half an hour. They covered huge expanses of the country and experienced temperatures unknown to them in England: at the start of the tour it was boiling hot but in January it was thirty degrees below and they had to acquire thick furs to tour from town to town as the trains travelled through feet of thick snow.

Bill was enthusiastic about everything and wrote that he had never felt so well and happy in his life. Reading what he said at this time, and what my grandmother told me later about this period, I realised he had a romantic streak which does not appear to have been revealed to many people. They rode together on the prairies. They took photographs of each other striding out with the wind in their hair. One wonderful picture of Bill, in jodhpurs and lace-up riding boots, inscribed 'Nov 2nd 1928, Lethbridge, Alberta, taken by Heather in the prairie', was sent home to his 'darling Mummie'. By this time his mother was living next door to Hugh Blaker, Bill's guardian, at 57 Church Street, Isleworth, most likely acting as his housekeeper. Bill also sent cards to his Aunt Bessie, who still lived in Bideford, Devon, informing her that they had travelled 25,000 miles around Canada and signing off 'Will', which was what she always called him. His 'Gardy', Hugh Blaker, also received news; one postcard is annotated with two little figures (Heather and Bill) walking hand in hand down the main street of New Glasgow, Nova Scotia. Apparently they both missed home, even though they found the tour thrilling. Other cards talked excitedly about the wonderful girl with whom he was in love. A few months older than him, Amy Heather Miriam Armstrong McIntyre was petite and raven haired, with a strong personality. She was certainly a wonderful catch for him.

*

Heather's background couldn't have been more different from Bill's. Her parents were from the professional classes: one grandfather had been a surgeon, while on her mother's side she was related to a famous acting family, the Forbes-Robertsons. They were also linked by marriage with the Harmsworths, the newspaper magnates. Born in Glasgow, Heather was Scottish through and through. Her father had worked his way up to become the only non-family director of Shanks, the 'sanitary engineers'. When the company transferred to London, he moved the family to a large house near Hanger Lane on the west side of the capital. Money was not a problem: they had a cook and a maid, and my grandmother, along with her brother, Malcolm, received a good education. They then moved, to Findon, Sussex, where she attended a school in Worthing, and then they moved again, this time to Boar's Hill, near Oxford, where she went to Oxford High, a girls' public day school with a very good reputation. Malcolm, who was five years her senior, went up to Oxford and Heather might well have followed him had she not been distracted by acting.

Heather's father was a starchy man and her parents' marriage had not been a happy one; they 'separated' in about 1920, an unusual occurrence in those days. Her mother was romantic and fey in a typically Edwardian style, and she even had some of her own poetry 'vanity' published (when you pay to have your work printed and bound yourself), most of it very sickly by today's standards. The house they had in Boar's Hill was ideal for her: it was next door to the home of John Masefield, the Poet Laureate. My grandmother grew up with musical soirées and poetry readings, and mixed with artists and writers such as Gilbert Murray and Lillah McCarthy, ex-wife of Harley Granville Barker, the well-known writer. She became a good friend of Judith Masefield, the Poet Laureate's daughter. John Masefield had a theatre called 'The Music Room' at the bottom of his garden, and this is where Heather began performing. Her first part was as Lady Macduff's son in Shakespeare's *Macbeth* and she told me how very exciting it was as she had to die on stage. The Oxford University Drama Society (which is still responsible for starting the careers of many actors such as Diana Quick and Imogen Stubbs) put on productions in his theatre and, at seventeen, Heather appeared in *Peer Gynt* and *Henry V* as part of the O.U.D.S. company. She was spotted in the latter by a London producer, Arthur Bouchier, who gave her a little part in a professional production of *Prince's Harem* at the 'Q' Theatre at Kew Gardens. This play only lasted three weeks but her acting career was launched.

In Oxford she had taken singing lessons and attended the Muriel Lane School of Dancing at the Playhouse. She had been friendly with Esme

Vernon and Margaret Rawlings at school, who also became actresses. Now in London with Esme, Heather briefly attended the Rosina Fillippi School of acting, but was soon working constantly in a variety of shows, including *The Beaux' Stratagem* and a tour of *Easy Virtue*, as well as a couple more amateur productions. According to the notes her mother kept, she even did a little film work, and then another show for O.U.D.S., before securing the roles in Gordon McLeod's tour of Canada.

My grandmother was a confident young woman, with lots of intelligence and drive. She had great social ease which came from moving in artistic circles and meeting her older brother's friends. She adored her brother. Malcolm, by this time, raced motor cars, flew aeroplanes and considered himself an inventor; he led a rather glamorous lifestyle which was later halted when he broke his back in a car crash. Heather had many suitors and had received several proposals of marriage; she was even engaged at some point before her tour to Canada. Perhaps she broke it off to go abroad, as she was very ambitious. My grandfather must have been bowled over by her. She had the sophistication and refinement which he longed for, and came from a society he had been exposed to by Hugh Blaker but which he felt excluded from because of his background. They shared a love of poetry, and I can imagine them reading poems together as they travelled across the prairies. Heather wrote quite polished verse herself, and must have inspired my grandfather to do the same, though his poems are heartfelt rather than technically accomplished. Bill, despite his later gruffness, was very charming when he was young. He was entertaining and had the ability to tell amusing stories, and – although not classically good-looking – his boyish looks were always attractive to women.

*

When my grandparents arrived back from Canada in February 1929, they were both just over twenty-one. I believe they intended to get married, but one can only imagine what Heather's family would have thought about her marrying a penniless actor. By the beginning of April 1929, however, they had made a mistake which made marriage an absolute necessity. Heather had fallen pregnant. She kept a journal about how she felt over the following months, but it is difficult to ascertain from this whether they knew about the pregnancy before they arranged the wedding, or whether it was planned in secret because they thought there would be opposition. Whatever the truth, they were ashamed enough never to tell my mother the date of their wedding anniversary, although she did finally guess the situation. Bill and Heather were married at Chelsea Registry Office on 9th May 1929. Their witnesses were Esme Vernon, Heather's lifelong friend from school, who was to be godmother to their child, and a Mr Frank Hayward (possibly a boyfriend of Esme's). The sun was shining and they went punting on the river afterwards with friends.

Their first home together was a tiny rented flatlet in Maida Vale, and they both worried about money as neither of them had a job, although Hugh Blaker did sometimes help out. As actors they had to learn to live with the constant insecurity of not knowing when they were next going to earn anything. Part of them hated that insecurity and part of them found it exhilarating, despite everything.

From her journal, I know that Heather was very upset when she found out about the baby, and there were tears and arguments because they both wanted success so much and a child would be such a responsibility. Heather had been thrilled at the reception she received in Canada and the thought of having to give up work because of a child made her feel bitter. Even though Bill pointed out that she could go on acting afterwards, my grandmother did not want to give up even for a year. Perhaps some of the upsets were due to the hormonal changes, but this probably did not occur to them because she felt very well physically and did not suffer from many of the early signs of pregnancy such as morning sickness. She felt guilty about making her 'Billy' miserable, but she became obsessed with going on stage again before the birth. She prayed for work and her prayers were answered, as they both got parts in July on a tour of a play called *77 Park Lane*. Heather played the lead and they toured together for eight weeks.

All actors tell countless theatrical stories about things that have gone wrong on tour, and one of the funniest ones my grandfather ever told was about this show. It was obviously a dramatic piece in which, at the climax, he was supposed to commit suicide with a revolver. One night, on stage, he realised he hadn't got the revolver in his pocket. He managed to whisper this fact into Heather's ear. She then pretended to faint, and staggered off into the wings so that she could go and look for it. Unfortunately the dressing-room door was locked and by the time she got back on stage it was too late – he had improvised and strangled himself!

Heather loved the fun and companionship of touring, but gradually she woke up to the fact that she was carrying a child and 'then, quite suddenly,' she wrote, 'I was awake. It was just after Whitby, when Billy and I had been so happy with Phyl Pearson [a friend] in Whitby… everything else in the world became secondary… I wasn't an actress any longer, I was a mother.' She didn't want to be sociable any more. Even being on stage every night seemed less important than the baby. Heather became very clingy and wanted to be with Bill every moment of the day. The more she shunned other people, the more she felt her love for my grandfather deepen, but she wrote that she sometimes made them both unhappy because she could not explain how she felt. She resented him doing anything on his own, such as going out for a drink or to the movies, but then because she felt so hurt, she was indifferent to him when he came back. On tour, they also argued about silly things such as breakfast time. Because she was pregnant, Heather would wake up early feeling ravenous, and she wanted Bill to get up with her. But usually he wanted to lie in, having done a show the night before. It was a difficult and emotional time for them both.

They thought of a name early on: Jo (short for John) if it was a boy and Anne if it was a girl. When my grandmother first felt the baby move, she thought it was indigestion, but after a while she learnt how to soothe it. At night, Bill loved to quieten it himself by putting his hand on her stomach. Heather guessed it was going to be a boy; she was wrong, but then my mother *was* quite tall! After eight weeks on tour, Heather decided she should leave, and another actress took her role. She was, after all, nearly six months pregnant. She remarked in her journal that it was a little distracting to feel her baby kick inside her while she was on stage: 'Sometimes I have felt you moving inside me, and then I wanted to laugh out loud, because the stage, the lights and the theatre… mattered so little compared with you!'

Bill continued with the tour and so they were to be apart for quite a while. Heather went to stay in Benson, a village not far from Oxford, so that she could be near her mother. The Benson house belonged to her brother's wife's family, but it was always treated as a family home. Even after my mother's birth, she was to spend some time there with her nanny. My grandparents both wanted their child to be beautiful and healthy. It was more important to them than having a clever or successful child, and

Heather thought being in the country for the last few months would be beneficial to the baby: 'I have come to Benson, where I shall see green fields and trees, instead of mean streets, where I shall breathe the clean air of the hills, instead of the dusty air of towns.' But she missed Billy terribly, craving his warmth and tenderness. He missed her too and wrote her these words:

> Climb to the hills my darling,
> And let the clean fresh wind blow in your face.
> Open wide your nostrils and breathe in mother earth.
> Wander through fields of waving corn,
> And give your baby golden locks.
> Go into the woods and listen to the song of the trees.
> Take the paths that are covered with golden brown leaves
> Then when you are tired, rest awhile on a mossy bank,
> And listen to the humming of the beautiful bees.
> When the day is over, and the sun has set,
> Turn your eyes to the moon,
> Her light will give you rest, long beautiful rest.

His poetry certainly wouldn't win any prizes, being rather clichéd, but his love for Heather and of the countryside was sincere. This part of my grandmother's journal shows an aspect of Bill which of course I could never know about. My image of him, although he was aloof but kindly to me as a child, was influenced by the roles he played in his more famous films, many of which were hard and aggressive. I also knew how difficult their relationship became later on. The journal was not found until long after Heather's death and even my mother didn't really see this side of him. Perhaps it shouldn't have been, but it was a shock to read of the intensity of their love for each other during this time. Heather wrote that after several weeks of separation, Bill unexpectedly grabbed a couple of days away from the tour, and they never felt closer than that particular weekend at Benson.

At the beginning of October Heather wrote the following 'Sonnet for Billy':

> Dear, should I die, let there be no regret:
> Remember that I loved the world, and you.
> And as the time must pass, swiftly forget
> What sadness may have been between us two.

Remember only, we two, hand in hand,
Have climbed the mountains, breathed the mountain air;
Have galloped side by side on prairie land,
Have felt the seas' winds blowing in our hair;
That we have seen wide skies with stars deep set,
And laughed, and sung. Remember we have crept
Into each other's arms; our lips have met;
And we have lain, our bodies close, and slept.
    Remember only happiness we had;
    Remember that I loved you, and be glad.

My grandmother stayed at Benson until the baby was due to be born. On the evening of 20th December, when labour started, she went into the Acland Nursing Home in Oxford. Bill was so wound up that he spent the night pacing round the foot of the Martyr's Memorial in the town centre. It wasn't the fashion then for the father to be at the birth, of course, but a few hours afterwards, on the morning of the 21st, Bill visited with Heather's mother. Heather stayed in hospital for four weeks, perhaps because she had a tendency to anaemia, so baby Anne's first Christmas was spent at the Acland. Bill was thrilled and bought his new daughter a white toy duck with a bright yellow beak as a first present. He was very popular with the nurses who looked after them because he was always telling jokes and doing impressions; his visits had them all in fits of laughter. When Heather left the home with the baby, she went back to Benson for the next few weeks, and Bill visited every so often because they still had no place of their own. My mother was christened Anne on 13th March at the Church of St Philip and St James in Woodstock Road, Oxford (though curiously she had been registered as Heather), and three days later my grandparents moved back up to London to stay in digs in Aberdare Gardens.

*

The first year after my mother was born was a very unsettled period for them. They moved several times, from Aberdare Gardens to a tiny furnished flat at 2 West Bolton Gardens, and then to 50 Redcliffe Gardens, all in west London. Heather was ill for a while and spent time with her mother again. They worried constantly about money. Despite this, a nanny was employed; and paid for, I believe, by Heather's father.

Apparently, he gave her a small allowance for many years. Having a nanny would have been quite usual in the kind of society in which Heather grew up, and she certainly would not have been able to contemplate going back to work without one. The nanny, Joan (who was later employed by the Churchill family), stayed with them for a couple of years, but it is unclear whether or not she lived in permanently, as their first flats were evidently small. Occasionally Anne was left at Benson with her grandmother and the nanny while Heather stayed with Bill in London. This was sometimes necessary when he was in a show so that his sleep was not disturbed; especially as my mother's favourite toy was Bill's drum – the very same one that fascinated me as a child – on which she spent many happy hours banging away.

Bill was constantly searching for work and, with his irregular work pattern, he probably saw more of his daughter than was the fashion for men in those days. He loved playing with her. My grandmother wrote in her journal that Anne used to fight with Bill over her crusts, which usually ended up on the floor, amid laughter and tears.

At the end of March 1931 the family, with the nanny, went for a picnic to Kew, meeting up with Miss Blaker, Hugh Blaker's sister. In Kew Gardens they spent a happy afternoon watching Anne looking at the birds and trees, walking her by the hand, and laughing when she wouldn't crawl on the grass because it prickled. Hugh Blaker himself was like a surrogate grandfather to my mother. He had written a poem for her birth, and it was published in a little bound collection of his verse, which Bill always treasured.

During this period Bill appeared in various shows. In May 1930 he played Duke Meinhard in *The Ugly Duchess* at the Arts Theatre Club, Great Newport Street, near Leicester Square. Although this theatre is in the West End of London, it has never been considered a West End theatre, but it used its status as a 'club' to put on new plays and try-outs. *The Ugly Duchess*, based on the novel by Feuchtwangler, had a cast of twenty-four and was set in the Tyrol in the fourteenth century. It is the story of a hideously ugly duchess who, despite managing to acquire two husbands and indulging in amatory adventures which led her to be named the German Messalina, saw all those whom she really desired going to her rival. In a review of the play in the *Star*, A. E. Wilson praises the leading lady, Esme Beringer, for her performance, but criticises some of the others, ending his piece with: 'Some of the acting was of the "blood and thunder" order. I was impressed, however, by the brief sketch which William Hartnell gave of the weakling Duke Meinhard.' Bill shone even though his part was not large. The appreciation of his natural, untheatrical style of acting was to be echoed throughout his life. There were only thirteen performances of the play scheduled, so Bill was soon searching for work again. The acting profession was very different in those days, and actors did not have individual agents who sought jobs for them. Looking for work meant hanging around the offices of the few agents and producers, trying to be in the right place at the right time. Bill also worked as an understudy to various leading comic actors such as Ernest Truex, Charles Heslop and Lawrence Grossmith. Understudying can be rather soul-destroying, but Bill saw it as an opportunity to learn from other people's methods.

In the spring of 1931 Bill went on tour with a Barry O'Brien production of *The Man Who Changed His Name* by Edgar Wallace, in which he played Frank O'Ryan. Among the dates they played was the Grand Theatre, Wolverhampton, where they performed the week of 9th March 1931. You could get to see this play for 6*d* if you went in at the last minute and took an unreserved seat in the balcony, although the best reserved seats cost 4*s*. Bill was earning only a few pounds a week himself.

Whenever he could Bill would go home for the weekend and take little Anne out on trips. But it was not easy to establish yourself in a difficult profession while worrying about a family. Both Bill and Heather were young and having to spend long periods apart. They needed more space at home and longed to live near a park. At the beginning of May 1931, they moved to somewhere a little more permanent – 2 Brook Gardens, Barnes, in south-west London. This was an Edwardian terraced house in a small cul-de-sac between the railway line and Barnes Common. That summer little Anne was looked after by her nanny while Heather went on tour, as she had finally decided to go back on stage.

Chapter Five

THE MOVE INTO FILMS:
THE 'QUOTA QUICKIE'

THEATRE DID NOT PAY very well even with both Bill and Heather working, and with a young child the need for them to earn good money became pressing. While in Canada, they had discussed the idea of going to Hollywood but decided against it, believing their talents better suited to the film industry in England. Trying to break into films, however, was very frustrating, and initially Bill was only able to get walk-on parts. The first few pictures in which he appeared fleetingly were silent, but the movie business was changing rapidly.

Experiments with sound had been going on for years, but in 1927 a breakthrough was made in the United States: Warner Brothers used Western Electric's Vitaphone system to provide dialogue for the famous film *The Jazz Singer*. Cinemas in America were wired up for sound and the different studios vied with each other to find the best systems. By the start of 1929 there were more than thirty sound films on offer. *The Jazz Singer* had a first viewing in Britain in 1928, although it wasn't properly released here until 1929. Britain was naturally a couple of years behind with the process, and the first sound films made were of a revue type, usually involving music hall stars and with little attempt at narrative.

The technology in the studios outstripped the speed at which the cinemas updated their equipment. During the first eleven months of 1929, 215 of the 599 feature films on offer to distributors had sound of some sort, but many of the cinemas couldn't yet show them. The takeover by talkies was fairly swift though, as the year 1934 saw only two silent films submitted to the censors. Some of the old silent film stars couldn't cope with the dialogue and their careers came to an ignominious end. Directors found that talkies needed actors with different skills and this created many new opportunities for stage performers. Bill always tried to be in the right place at the right time, and he seized every opportunity he could.

No record exists of the films in which Bill was an extra, but an old CV scribbled on the back of a photograph lists the titles in which he played what he called 'small roles'. The earliest of these was *The Unwritten Law*, a short film which opened in June 1929 about a girl sheltering a convict who then discovers that he killed her husband. Next came *School for Scandal* – an adaptation of the famous Sheridan play – produced and directed by Maurice Elvey, starring Basil Gill and Madeleine Carroll. Bill was in illustrious company, as other actors with small unnamed roles in this production included Anna Neagle and Rex Harrison. *Man of Mayfair* was next, starring Jack Buchanan and Joan Barry, released in December 1931. Then Maurice Elvey gave him a part in *Diamond Cut Diamond*, a crime drama in which two international jewel thieves are outwitted by a female crook. After this, Bill appeared in *Say It With Music*, one of the many productions which relied heavily on its musical content, made largely as a vehicle for its star, Jack Payne. Payne, a famous bandleader of the time, played himself in a story about music helping a composer recover after a near-fatal plane crash. This sentimental-sounding story was produced by Herbert Wilcox, who became a very important figure in the industry.

Then Bill got his first real break, with a more substantial speaking part than he'd had before, in a film which starred Robert Donat. Perhaps his old touring mate from Sir Frank Benson's company was in some way responsible for this piece of luck. Donat played a bank clerk who embezzled money and then headed for the bright lights of the capital city. Bill was thrilled to be under the bright lights himself at last. The film was called *That Night in London*.

*

Not only had huge opportunities in film production been created by the emergence of the talkies, but the British government had passed an act in 1927 which further encouraged a burgeoning industry. The British film business has always been overshadowed by Hollywood and the US market is so huge that most successful movies can break even just in their own territory; thus productions have always been easier to finance in the US than here. This was true in the 1920s just as much as it is now. Not content with this head start, even early in the twentieth century the big American distributors had various strategies for ensuring that their pictures filled the British screens. They gained a stranglehold on the exhibitors in Britain by insisting that any cinema owner who wanted to book a popular US film also had to take a considerable number of lesser American films sight unseen – some of them not yet even made. According to Rachael Low in her book *Film Making in 1930s Britain*: 'By the late 20s the American advantage had been reinforced by exploitation methods which had the British market so tied up that British productions had difficulty in finding dates for their films even in their own country.' However, at that time film making was recognised as an important industry for this country economically, so the government of the day tried to give it a helping hand by passing what became known as the 'Quota Act'. This attempted to put a stop to the block booking by distributors through restricting advance and blind booking. It also set a fixed percentage requirement of British films so that renters had to offer, and exhibitors had to show, a 'quota' of British footage which rose annually to reach twenty per cent in 1938.

Unfortunately the government was trying to solve too many problems with one act. It did not really succeed in stopping block booking and the 'quota' resulted in a proliferation of mediocre films being made. There was too little British product to enable the renting subsidiaries of the large Hollywood companies to comply with the act, so several of them proposed to make movies in Britain. However, it became apparent that they would be creating an industry to rival their own, so US giants like Warner Brothers avoided this by setting up subsidiaries, such as First National at Teddington, which rapidly churned out cheap films to fulfil their requirement. Fox had its own company, Fox-British, with studios at Wembley, which did the same. Other small production houses sprang up specifically to feed these big American distributors. The bulk of this work consisted of uninspiring comedies and thrillers made on minuscule budgets, with poor scripts, often in a matter of days. These films became known disparagingly as 'quota quickies'. So although the protected market did result in a doubling of production in the 1930s, it was almost at the expense of the reputation of the industry. When interviewed on *Desert*

Island Discs in the sixties, Bill recalled that if you fluffed during the recording of some of these films, you simply carried on and ad-libbed because there wasn't enough time or money for retakes. However, there was a positive consequence of all this activity: an increase in work for actors and technicians, which in the days of mass unemployment from 1929 to the early thirties was certainly to be welcomed.

Some companies tried to get round the quota in outrageous ways. Rachael Low gives an example of an importer acquiring 11,000 feet of silent Indian film (Commonwealth films counted as British) for less than a shilling a foot, and running it early morning in front of the cleaners. Fat lot of use that was to the British industry. The system was obviously open to abuse, but Bill and many other actors were grateful to gain experience in front of the camera.

Bill's career started to take off. It is difficult to say when he was actually working on each film, as each one was made many months before it reached the screens. *That Night in London* opened in 1932 but it was probably made the previous year. Anyway, Bill moved swiftly from his first small roles to playing leads in some of the typical 'quota quickies'. The first one he starred in, which he often mentioned in interviews, was a British Fox film called *I'm an Explosive*. It was directed and written by Adrian Brunel, who was responsible for many similar films with wildly improbable storylines. This one, a comedy, was made at Nettleford Studios in ten days for approximately £60. It is about a professor who has invented a liquid explosive which he keeps in an old whisky bottle. He returns to his laboratory one day to find some of it missing and he believes that his brother, played by Bill, has drunk it by mistake. In fact no such thing has happened, but Bill's character is chased everywhere by the Secret Service; and eventually the Chemical Warfare Department is induced to pay out a large sum in compensation, with which he marries his girlfriend. Plots like these might have worked for silent movies but were not really sophisticated enough for talkies.

Released a month earlier than *I'm an Explosive*, which was shown in March 1933, Bill's next film was also directed by Adrian Brunel. It was made in the same studios in Twickenham, this time produced by George Smith, who often worked with Brunel. Smith was associated mostly with the company set up in Britain by US giant Fox, and he was one of the most prolific producers of these 'quota quickies'. *Follow the Lady* was a typical example: it was another comedy with a tortuous plot, this time about two bachelors who get involved in a mix-up with a French girl, her boyfriend, a baby, the girl they both wanted to marry, her mother, etc, etc. Bill again played the lead. Always using the name 'Bill Hartnell' in the credits for these films, he was soon making a third for British Fox. *The Perfect Flaw* was a thriller, the other staple fodder of this genre. It involved an ambitious clerk whose get-rich-quick scheme goes awry and leads to a plot to kill a wealthy stockbroker. D. A. Clarke-Smith headlined, having also been in the previous two films. Actors would frequently find themselves working with familiar faces as the 'quickie' directors tended to use people they knew would produce the required performances with little fuss and bother. Although not under contract to particular studios, a nucleus of actors was used over and over again.

British & Dominion was another company which produced quota films in Britain for one of the American corporations, this time Paramount. Bill made several films for them. The first – a rather feeble thriller involving stolen gems, love affairs, murder and fake suicide – was called *The Lure*, and was produced and directed by Arthur Maude. The second, *Seeing is Believing*, was a comedy which came out five months later in February 1934. Bill starred as an aspiring detective, Ronald Gibson, who mistakes two real detectives for jewel thieves. He accuses a beautiful girl of stealing a bracelet and then inevitably falls in love with her. All is then sorted out by Gibson's father, Sir Robert, played by an actor with the wonderful name of Fewlass Llewellyn. The following year saw Bill in another British & Dominion production, *While Parents Sleep*, again directed by Adrian Brunel. British & Dominion were typical of the companies which threw films together as quickly as possible (in their case allegedly one a month), keeping costs down by adhering to the 'Norton Formula'. This meant that if more than three takes were required, permission had to be sought from Anthony Havelock-Allen, who was in charge of all production at British & Dominion. If more than four were required the director had to go to the very top man: Richard Norton himself. With these kinds of restraints it is not surprising *Kine Weekly* commented that although casts were reasonably good, the lack of care taken over production showed, and scripts often entailed complicated, improbable stories with endless dialogue.

Because of the change from silent movies to talkies, much new technology had to be invented. The old cameras used for silent films made whirring noises and lights often hissed. These problems were overcome somewhat clumsily at first. Cameras were encased in soundproofed booths which made them cumbersome and tended to restrict their manoeuvrability. This, together with as yet fairly unsophisticated microphones, meant that location work was difficult and so most films of the time were shot entirely in a studio.

Yet despite all these shortcomings, the 'quickies' must have been fun for the actor to make. Eric Cross, who as cinematographer later photographed Bill in several pictures in the 1940s and fifties, had a job early in his career on camera for one of the few 'quickies' which were shot on location. It was filmed mostly on a yacht in Poole harbour, on the south coast, and the speed at which it was all done rather shocked the inexperienced Cross. In a letter to me, he wrote:

> During the rest of the week it dawned on me that the whole reason for the film was to have a supply of pretty girls for the yacht owner. We all stayed at the Antelope Hotel in Poole, and Billy Hartnell kept me amused and my mind off the doubtful film. Apart from other gifts, he was great on comedy and a wonderful practical joker. He removed a standard lamp at the foot of the stairs in the hotel one evening and stood with the large lampshade on his head and played havoc with some of the cast and a few of the guests coming down for dinner. He also made himself up as a clown and went walking up the main street – we all gave him a few coins – and when he came back we couldn't stop laughing.

Bill got the opportunity to play all sorts of roles, from romantic lead to crook, upper-class twit to detective. He was continually improving his comedy timing, but began to get a little frustrated about not getting the chance to appear in better quality films.

In 1935 Bill starred in another comedy about an inept gang of crooks, *Swinging the Lead*, and then featured in two more George Smith productions: *Old Faithful* and *The Shadow of Mike Emerald*. He also appeared in a different type of movie. Based on an Offenbach operetta and produced by Paris Nero Films, *La Vie Parisienne* was made simultaneously in French and English with slightly different casts. Such films were made to overcome a problem which was never encountered in the days of silent movies. Without dialogue, movies were international and could be shown in any country merely with a change of captions. Talkies reduced the potential audience of a film, so making two versions back to back, using the same set and technicians for both, was one of the methods used to keep costs down.

*

As Bill's ability to find work in films improved, so did his profile in theatre. At the end of 1931 he played the lead in Noël Coward's *The Young Idea* at the King's Theatre, Hammersmith, where he had already appeared several times. As Sholto, the precocious youngster who, with his sister, plots to reunite their divorced parents, he had a wonderful role for showing off his energy and wit. It was the part that Noël Coward played at the age of twenty-one, both in America and the UK. Bill himself was only twenty-three, and already beginning to build up a good resumé. Both he and Heather adored Noël Coward as a writer and over the years went to see his shows whenever they could. *The Young Idea* was followed a few months later by his first proper West End appearance in *The Man I Killed*, an over-emotional war play by Maurice Rostand, which opened on 2nd March 1932 at the Apollo Theatre, Shaftesbury Avenue. It starred Emlyn Williams and Celia Johnson, with Bill taking the role of Erik. Unfortunately, it didn't please the audiences and closed very quickly. In his autobiography, Emlyn Williams records that after the first night a camp friend said: 'What a depressing show, French indeed. Well, ducky, it's got what we in Angleterre call longeurs… oh, la la.' Then Williams adds, 'The run of the play, though, had no longeurs. We lasted till Saturday.' But at least Bill now had a West End credit.

Later on that year Bill appeared in another high-profile production: a new George Bernard Shaw play called *Too True to be Good*. This had premiered in America, then played the Malvern Festival in August 1932. It opened at the New Theatre in the West End in September with a fresh cast, but despite quotes extracted from the notices – 'I foretell for this piece a very long run since nine-tenths of it goes as merrily as an Aldwych farce' (James Agate, *Sunday Times*); 'It is by way of being great literature' (*Evening News*) and 'I found it deeply interesting, even at times an absorbing work' (*Daily Mail*) – it baffled the audiences and did not run for long. The tone of the reviewers' remarks suggests that they also found it a somewhat difficult and patchy piece. Anyway, it went out on tour immediately, presented by Barry Jackson of the Birmingham Repertory Theatre, with yet again a slightly different cast, this time starring Donald Wolfit and Greer Garson. Bill may well have been understudying in the West End, but for the tour he played the part of Sergeant Meek, an enigmatic character who knows everything. It is a very good role in what is perhaps one of Bernard Shaw's less successful works. The play has little plot, beginning in the sick room of a spoilt girl simply called 'The Patient'. A burglar climbs in her window, followed by his accomplice, the maid. They end up in a strange land with the roles reversed; the girl pretends to be a native slave, the burglar reveals himself as a sophist, and the ex-servant, passing herself off as a lady, dallies with a colonel. As he so often did, Shaw uses the characters as mouthpieces for airing his views, and during the second half the speeches become long philosophical treatises. Nevertheless, it was a prestigious tour, visiting Manchester, Leeds, Sheffield, Blackpool, Edinburgh and Newcastle among other venues.

George Bernard Shaw was known for being pernickety, and detailed essays about his plays were published with every script. He took great interest in the productions and showed the same attention to detail in his notes to actors. In Leeds, my grandfather received the following letter, dated 18th October 1932 and sent from Shaw's now famous home in Ayot St Lawrence:

> Dear William Hartnell,
>
> I have altered the part of Meek slightly – mostly in the description of him. The propitiatory smile was a mistake of mine. Meek's smile is *invisible*: the joke that he is an ex-colonel is there all the time; but he expresses it by an iron face, not by a smiling one. I am cutting the colonel's line accordingly.
>
> I also made a mistake in one of the speeches. He should say, not 'It was part of my duty sir,' but 'It was the duty of the intelligence orderly, sir. I'm the intelligence orderly.'
>
> With the smile off the part will be perfect. I enjoyed the performance, which is a lot for an author to admit.
>
> Faithfully,
> G Bernard Shaw

High praise indeed from a man as fussy as Shaw.

It was an experience touring with Donald Wolfit (the inspiration for Ronald Harwood's 1980 play *The Dresser*) and a temptation to tour with

Greer Garson. Family history has it that Bill tried to seduce Miss Garson but she rebuffed him with a comment that he had a very beautiful wife so why on earth was he looking elsewhere? His response to that was never recorded.

A couple of years later he did a second production of *Too True to be Good*, and this time he merited third headline billing. It was presented at the 'Q' Theatre, opposite Kew Bridge Station, a well-respected theatre run by Jack de Leon, a well-known impresario. Although the 'Q' was quite near to where they lived, Bill was away on tour a great deal during this period. In 1933 – I have been unable to confirm the exact date – he was on the road again with yet another show, called *Just Married*.

*

Being away on tour gave Bill ample opportunity to be unfaithful, and Heather was obviously aware of this from the first years of their marriage. But the early thirties saw upheaval in other areas of their personal lives. Each had to cope with the death of their mother. Lucy Hartnell probably died in 1931 – a slight mystery surrounds the event as there doesn't appear to be a death certificate for her, but this must simply be an administrative omission rather than anything more sinister. She was certainly alive in 1930, but had died before Heather's mother, whose death was registered on 21st April 1932. Although they were relatively young, neither had been in good health for quite a while. Heather was close to her mother and terribly upset. However, she was glad that Minnie had lived long enough to see and appreciate her granddaughter Anne. Heather's father was still alive and living an austere life in a flat above his office. Shortly after his estranged wife's death, he remarried and went to live in a big house in Iver, Buckinghamshire, where the family sometimes visited. Heather was never completely at ease with her stepmother, although she was a jolly woman who loved the theatre and adored Bill because he made her blush and giggle with his jokes.

Bill never talked about his own mother or her death. Despite his cheery postcards to her, his overwhelming feeling was that she hadn't loved him, but he had tried to be a dutiful son and her death must still have been a blow. Apart from his Aunt Bessie who still lived in Devon, Hugh Blaker was the only person he now regarded as 'family'.

Sometime after Lucy died, Heather, Bill and little Anne moved into Hugh Blaker's house in Isleworth, by the River Thames. He was now the tenant of both 55 and 57 Church Street. My grandparents lived in number 55 and the houses were linked on the top floor by Hugh's studio, where he painted and sculpted, both Bill and my mother sometimes sitting for him. Bill also tried his hand at painting and modelling up there. The drawing room, in the Edwardian manner, was on the first floor. The dining room on the ground floor couldn't be used because it was so crammed with pictures. The double garden at the back was wonderful for Anne to play in, and she had a pet tortoise attached to a very long ribbon so it wandered free but couldn't get lost. They also had a stroppy wire-haired terrier called Dickie, who was very mischievous and a bit of a fighter. Staying there made things easier for Bill and Heather financially, as their work patterns were still very irregular. There was no dole system in those days, and they would probably have been far too proud to claim. Heather's father still gave her a small allowance and Hugh probably helped out sometimes if neither of them was working. If he was feeling broke, Bill would go to Brentford market at the end of the day when they were selling things off cheap and pride himself on bringing home a chicken at a bargain price.

The house stood opposite a pub, the London Apprentice, which in those days was rather run down but still the haunt of many artists and writers. Bill's cultural education was continued here, for he met many of Hugh's friends and associates, several of whom lived close by. Number 59 Church Street was occupied by the Pentys. Arthur Penty was an architect and also well known for his political views. He was a Guild Socialist, following the opinions of people such as William Morris and John Ruskin. He wrote a book about his views, which was more to do with embracing a way of life than simple politics – Blaker himself had a similar socialist outlook, as did many of their circle. The Pentys had three children, and my mother, although she was very young, remembers going round for wonderful Christmas parties where as soon as any child entered the front door he or she was blindfolded and given a stick to bash at a big bag of toffees hanging from the ceiling. They were allowed to keep all the toffees they managed to knock down with two or three swipes. Other exciting games for the children included pinning the tail on the donkey, and sardines. Bill was great fun and loved fooling around with the kids and making them laugh. He liked children and he and Heather intended to have another baby. Heather became pregnant while they were living there but tragedy struck. When rushing to answer the telephone one day she fell down the stairs and the fall caused a miscarriage. Although she was nearly full term, the little boy didn't live, and Heather was so ill afterwards that she was warned not to have another child.

On the other side of the house lived Adrian Bury: he was a poet, author and artist. Bill was given copies of works by his circle of friends, and he read avidly to make up for his early lack of education. One of the books Hugh gave Bill was called *The Tremulous String* by Monk Gibbon. A collection of prose poems, ten of which had been published in *The Fortnightly Review*, they were very 'modern' and experimental in style. This was in keeping with Hugh's belief about always being at the forefront of artistic thought. The first one is called 'Invocation':

Who gave a few words of truth to one man and
Song to another and an undying saying to a third;
Who gave beauty, that is not touched by season and
Knowledge, that time has yet to overthrow. Unknown,
Unknowable, blown down whatever road thou listest,
Breathe into my heart also, even one chance phrase.
Do to me as to these. Give me also something to
Speak; touch my lips lightly if only for a moment;
Make me also a whisperer of unchanging things.

Bill sometimes annotated the backs of photographs with comments reminiscent of these spiritual longings.

Another artist called Bobbie Maynard was also part of this circle. Hugh was responsible for him being appointed to run the printing press set up at Gregynog in Wales, which had been purchased by the Davies sisters, whose art collection Hugh had been so instrumental in creating. Originally intended to be a craft village, a centre of artistic excellence for Wales, it ended up simply as a private printing press, where Maynard specialised in woodcuts to illustrate the books.

Although to outsiders Hugh sometimes appeared taciturn, this was probably just shyness. The actor David Langton, who appeared in *The Shadow of Mike Emerald* with Bill and became a good friend, working with both Heather and Bill frequently, remembers him as a small and rather introverted man. But on his own ground he was fun and my mother remembers many evenings at home when Bill and Hugh played cards in a smoky room full of noisy men. Richard Penty, Arthur's son, recalls hearing Bill and Hugh singing: 'No money in the bank, No more children we can spank...'

The only person that was a bit of a spoilsport was Hugh's sister, Jane (Jennie) Blaker, who spent some time living with him, and even after she had gone back to Wales, visited frequently. She didn't really approve of all her brother's artistic antics, although it was through her that Hugh had met the Davies sisters, since she had been their companion and governess. My mother was always slightly in awe of the dour woman she called 'Aunt Jane'.

Heather was, on the other hand, completely at home among these artistic people: she had grown up in a similar, if slightly more refined, circle in Oxford. Bill, who some years later attempted to write plays with Heather, would never, I'm sure, have tried his hand at writing if it had not been for the influence of Hugh's acquaintances. While they were living in Isleworth, Hugh was himself composing a play, called *Woman Triumphant*: set thirty years in the future (the early 1960s) when women have taken over the world and are in charge of everything. Could Heather, the 'striking young modern', have been an inspiration for this? Throughout their lives, Heather and Bill's closest friends were often writers, and their book collection contained countless editions given to them and signed by the authors.

Chapter Six

THE MID THIRTIES UNTIL THE WAR: THE LIGHT COMEDIAN

FEELING MORE AT HOME in Isleworth and more settled than they had ever felt anywhere before, Heather and Bill spent a large part of the mid 1930s working locally at Richmond Theatre, only a few miles from Church Street. Still a popular theatre, it has an elegant, ornate red-brick façade looking out over Richmond Green and a traditional stage and auditorium. Situated in an area which has always been affluent, it then seated approximately 1,300 people and was run as a weekly rep with a resident company, showing a different play every seven days. Mr Arthur Rees was manager of the theatre when Bill and Heather joined. He had taken over in 1932, after having been a singer with the D'Oyly Carte company, and soon became producer and leading actor at Richmond, eventually taking over the lease at the beginning of 1935. When interviewed by A. E. Wilson for an article in *The Star* a month later, Rees described his policy: he favoured comedy rather than melodrama, but liked 'strong' plays. Then he said:

> I believe in building up a company not of the old barn-storming type, but
> of players of the modern kind, capable of acting with finesse and polish.
> They should not necessarily be young artists, but they must be young-
> minded. I want creative players as distinct from script players.

Bill and Heather were both 'players of the modern kind' and were always praised for the naturalness of their performances. The drama critic Wilson seemed to approve of them as he concluded this same article with:

Billy Hartnell is a lively and resourceful comedian with an engaging humour, and he should go far. Jane Whatley [Rees's wife]... has already made herself a great favourite in Richmond, and so has Heather Hartnell, who has been associated with the Playhouse, Oxford.

Weekly rep was exhausting. The plays were performed twice nightly, at 6.30 and 8.40 p.m., and during the day the actors rehearsed the next one. The casts were comparatively large, usually with eight to fifteen characters, and no one ever doubled. Sometimes even the stage manager and the designer, Sarah Greenhalgh, had to take small roles. How she managed to find time to paint a new set each week – her budget per show was £5 – and rehearse is a mystery. With so little time to prepare, the productions relied heavily on the actors' natural talent, energy and ability to learn lines quickly.

Bill's first engagement with the Arthur Rees Players was in September 1934. As Neville Hammond in *While Parents Sleep*, he gave 'a good representation of a young man torn between his official duties and his emotional desires', according to the *Richmond & Twickenham Times*. The playwright turned his own work into a screenplay which was made as a 'quickie' by British & Dominion, directed by Adrian Brunel, one of the many in which Bill appeared. The film version came out in September 1935, with Bill actually playing a different role from the stage production.

At the rep, *While Parents Sleep* was followed by another serious play called *Behold We Live*, and then the P. G. Wodehouse farce *Good Morning, Bill*, in which Bill had already played the lead six years previously at the King's Theatre, Hammersmith. At least it made learning the lines easier! This was also one of the plays in which, very early in his career, he understudied and learnt his craft by watching its star. When interviewed by Roy Plomley on *Desert Island Discs* in the 1960s, Bill described his first experiences after leaving Sir Frank Benson's company:

> I had to take a job on tour and earn my living the best way I could, which I did. I was on tour doing once-nightly and twice-nightly shows for fourpence a week and living in back rooms... and [my first West End appearance]... was a very modest entrance on my part I think. I was understudy when I first appeared... I understudied such personalities as Ernest Truex in *Good Morning, Bill*, which was a Robert Courtneidge production, and Ralph Lynn in his light comedies and farces; Charles

Heslop who was in musicals, and also a farcical actor; and Bud Flanagan…
and a well-known actor when I was a boy, Lawrence Grossmith.

Bill didn't keep programmes – or perhaps they have been lost – for most of these shows, but Ernest Truex played the lead in *Good Morning, Bill* at the Duke of York's Theatre in the West End in 1927. Lawrence Grossmith was also in this production, so it is likely that it was Bill's job to understudy them both, and that this had been his 'modest entrance' in the West End (as opposed to his first proper credit in *The Man I Killed*).

The hard work he put in then was paying off now that he was playing leads himself. The critic at the *Surrey Comet* obviously thought so, as in his review of 3rd October 1934 he comments:

> Undoubtedly the outstanding performance is that of Bill Paradene by Mr Billy Hartnell, who has many of the mannerisms which Ernest Truex introduced when he so successfully created the role. Throughout the play Mr Hartnell is bobbing about the stage, feverishly lovesick, his nerves on edge at even the sound of the woman (Miss Jane Whatley) he adores. Amongst the funniest parts of the play are the love scenes between him and Miss Whatley, as a very practical doctor who tells him to take powders and have more control of his facial muscles when he excitedly proposes to her.

The next show, *The Brontës*, saw Heather joining her husband on the Richmond stage. She played the timid Anne Brontë, with Sheila Raynor and Jane Whatley as the other sisters. According to the local Thames Valley paper: 'The very difficult part of the dissipated Branwell – the darkest tragedy in the Brontës' lives – is played with remarkable realism by Billy Hartnell. He exploits the role to its fullest extent.' Heather didn't appear in the next production, *Eliza Comes to Stay* (in which Bill got another chance to show off his comic ability as the lead, the Hon. Sandy Verrall), but they were both in the one after – the dramatic *Counsellor at Law*. My grandmother had already captured the hearts of the local audience, for the *Richmond & Twickenham Times* called her 'one of Richmond's most popular players' in its review that week. Her role was that of devoted secretary to the famous New York lawyer around whom the story revolves, played by Arthur Rees himself. Because he also had to produce and direct, it was by now rare for him to play the lead, and he usually took the older character parts. Bill, meanwhile, had firmly established himself as the juvenile lead in the company, although because of the tightness of the schedule, every three to four weeks he would play a smaller role to relieve the pressure slightly. Heather started to alternate juvenile female lead with Jane Whatley, who was pregnant. So both Heather and Bill had a lot of lines to learn. At least they could test each other at home. *Apron Strings*, the next production presented at Richmond, gave them the chance to play husband and wife on stage, which they did with great success, taking 'advantage of the full scope offered them'. Bill is again praised for his outstanding ability in the *Richmond & Twickenham Times*. Although only a local paper, the reviews were not completely uncritical and certainly commented on any production or performance which didn't work.

The week beginning 5th November 1934 saw a costume comedy set in America called *The Pursuit of Happiness* at Richmond, in which Bill blacked up and played a servant. There was no sense in those days of it being politically incorrect, and Heather had to black up in *White Cargo* the following year, in which she played a native girl called Tondeleyo. They both thought it fun (despite having to cover themselves in a lot of extra make-up) and saw it as a chance to play a completely different kind of character. For many people half the enjoyment of performing is the dressing up and pretending that you come from a different world. The actors actually had to provide their own costumes in weekly rep, although they may have had some help from Sarah Greenhalgh (the designer) for *The Pursuit of Happiness*, as it was a period piece. Having a 'good wardrobe' was one of the requirements of an actor, and was particularly important for a leading lady, who would be expected to be able to look glamorous in show after show. Providing your own clothes was the rule for many years and in fact still happened in some of the very smallest two-weekly summer seasons even into the twenty-first century. From having been a scruffy child through lack of money, Bill had now begun to take a great interest in his appearance; whether this had anything to do with the influence of Hugh Blaker or Heather, or whether it was simply in reaction to his early years is impossible to say, but almost everyone I have interviewed commented on how fastidious he was about his dress. In a theatrical family, clothes were never thrown away, as they could always be used or adapted for a production. So, not only were the actors performing at night, rehearsing for the next play during the day and learning a new part every week, but they also had to find time to organise costumes and clean and iron them. They really did eat, sleep and breathe theatre.

Bill could start to think of himself as a local celebrity because, at the beginning of November, one of the 'quickies' in which he played the lead was screened at the Richmond cinema. The film, *Seeing is Believing*, was second feature to the Marx Brothers' crazy film *Duck Soup*. Meanwhile, there were only three more shows by the Arthur Rees Players before the Christmas panto, which was presented by an outside management, giving the actors two weeks off. Bill played the lead in another comedy, *Nothing but the Truth*, but didn't appear in the following show, *Sixteen*. Heather did, however, getting rave reviews for acting 'so beautifully and with such poignancy that it is difficult to believe that she is only "playing a part"'. As the Richmond Operatic Society were performing there for the succeeding week, Bill had seven days free. They must have been very welcome. Both Heather and Bill appeared in *Indoor Fireworks*, the last production in December.

The first night, on 7th January 1935, of *Lord Richard in the Pantry*, the show which opened the new season, celebrated the tenancy of Arthur Rees, who had taken over the lease from Joseph Mears. At the time you could see a show from the gallery for 6*d*, the pit for 11*d* and the stalls for 1*s* 10*d* (approximately 9p). Even the most expensive seats in the circle cost a mere 2*s* 5*d*. Although it was a popular theatre, they were constantly in competition with the cinemas, and felt the pinch when a new Odeon opened locally that March. Bill again received brilliant notices for his lead role as Lord Richard, a young aristocrat who attempts to do the work of a butler while trying to avoid the brazen pursuit of a young society girl, played by my grandmother. Two weeks later he was playing the eponymous hero of *Mr Faintheart*. This was the first production in which he appeared with the actor Basil Langton, who became a good friend and with whom he was to work often. Basil changed his name to David Langton when he left the army after the war, because he discovered there was another Basil Langton who was a conscientious objector. David had been a major and didn't want to be confused with him. But the name 'Basil' stuck with my family and 'Uncle Basil', as my mother always called him, visited the Church Street home on many occasions. He, of course, became well known in later years for *Upstairs, Downstairs*.

Heather, Bill and David appeared in the next three shows together. The first, a 'modern, spicy and far-fetched' comedy about a crazy family, was called *The Maitlands*. Bill then had 'the time of his life' as Rodney Martin in *It Pays to Advertise*, the part in which Ralph Lynn made his name at the Aldwych in 1924. Ralph Lynn was a great hero of my grandfather's, being one of the three farce kings of the British stage. Along with Robertson Hare and Tom Walls, he was responsible for the huge success of the 'Aldwych Farces', most written by Ben Travers, which started with *Cuckoo in the Nest* in 1925, and had their heyday in the late twenties and early thirties. Plays included *Rookery Nook*, *Thark*, *Plunder* and *Dirty Work*. Lynn specialised in playing upper-class twits, the type of role Bill revelled in at Richmond. He may have understudied him early in his career, but was certainly proud to do so in 1940 in another farce at the Aldwych called *Nap Hand*, which also starred Charles Heslop, a leading musical comedy actor.

The Ghost Train by Arnold Ridley (later well known for his role in *Dad's Army*) was the next show. The comedy ghost story was a very popular rep play which was turned into a film starring Arthur Askey in 1940, and as a play has been produced occasionally ever since.

Having played the lead in these three productions, my grandfather then took a break from the company until April, when he returned to play Lord Fancourt Babberley in the wonderful comedy *Charley's Aunt*. Most of the plays performed at Richmond haven't stood the test of time, but *Charley's Aunt* is a classic, and is still popular today. Heather played Kitty and David Langton played Jack Chesney, two of the young leads who are in love. To help out Jack and his college friend Charley in their romantic schemes Lord Fancourt dresses up in women's clothing and pretends, not particularly successfully, to be Charley's aunt from Brazil ('where the nuts come from'). Bill adored the role, which involved lots of speedy costume changes.

Indeed, Heather, Bill and David all spoke with great affection of their times at Richmond, even though it was hard work. Bill took time off to do some filming, but Heather continued to appear in most of the shows that season, often with David and an actress called Dorothy Galbraith, who also became a great friend. However, they were all upset that spring by the death of Arthur Rees's wife, Jane Whatley, in childbirth. Heather and Bill sent their own tribute of flowers in addition to the wreath, shaped like a proscenium arch, sent by the whole Arthur Rees company. Complications in childbirth were much more frequent and could easily be fatal in the 1930s. Having had such a difficult time herself, this event no doubt reinforced the advice Heather had been given by her doctor not to try for another child, though I know it saddened her.

After *Charley's Aunt*, Bill didn't perform again at Richmond until that September, when he and Heather appeared in *White Cargo*, the show about the Gold Coast in which Heather blacked up. Five weeks later (November 1935), the farce *A Little Bit of Fluff* was to mark Bill's last appearance with the Arthur Rees Players. Heather, however, was to continue with them for some time. In February 1936 Arthur Rees celebrated his 125th play and 1,500 performances at Richmond with *Maria Marten* and interval entertainment which included The World's Strongest Man and the Terry-Bull Male Quartet. But running the theatre financially and artistically, as well as appearing on stage, was proving a strain. The tenancy was beginning to experience financial difficulties. Later on that year various strategies were tried, including two seats for the price of one on Mondays, reduced price seats, and then an increase in prices, all to no avail. At the beginning of 1937 the theatre closed for a month and reopened under new management, Circle Theatres. Bill was to make one return visit to Richmond Theatre for this company when, in April 1937, he played the lead in a comedy thriller called *Someone at the Door*. As he was by now appearing in more films and his profile was rising, this merited a photograph and special article in the *Richmond & Twickenham Times*.

*

In between stints at Richmond, Bill was making more 'quota quickies'. *The Crimson Circle*, another thriller involving blackmail and murder, was followed in September 1936 by *Nothing Like Publicity*, one of Bill's favourite 'quickies'. He played the lead, Pat Spencer, a freelance press agent who befriends a young actress and takes her with him when he goes to interview a publicity-shy American heiress, played by Moira Lynd. They are mistaken for the heiress and her solicitor, and end up being presented to the Wharncliffe family, whose diamonds she had travelled from America to receive. At the last minute, the supposed heiress turns up, and Spencer and his friend are unmasked; but before the jewels are handed over, the real heiress appears and the other one is shown to be an impostor and notorious jewel thief. All turns out happily in the end as Spencer gets his exclusive interview and decides to team up with the young actress. Another tortuous storyline from George Smith for Radio Pictures. Whether Bill particularly enjoyed making it because the script was better (I hardly think so, given the plot) or the company was especially good or the girls in it were extra pretty, I don't know; but it did reunite him with Gordon McLeod, the actor-manager who organised the tour to Canada on which my grandparents met, playing Sir Arthur Wharncliffe.

Midnight at Madame Tussauds, which came out three months later, was directed by George Pearson, who had been considered one of Britain's top directors of silent films between 1915 and 1925. By now, however, he was in decline, and this was one of the last productions he worked on. Although some of it was actually shot on location in Madame Tussauds itself, the thriller in which a financier bets he can spend the night in the Chamber of Horrors and finds himself an intended murder victim was very much a B movie. That was the problem. They all had been. *While Parents Sleep* was showing at the Richmond cinema in February 1936, but it was second feature to Fred Astaire and Ginger Rogers' *Top Hat*. Hollywood still had the upper hand.

There were of course some better British films being produced, but the only one Bill had been in was *The Guv'nor*. This was made by Michael Balcon, who along with Korda was one of the few top-class producers of the period working in Britain. *The Guv'nor* was a vehicle for the comedian George Arliss, and is a rather sentimental comedy of mistaken identity, where a tramp called Rothschild is taken in by a bank and made director because of his surname. In fact, the bank tries to use him in a plot to swindle a girl out of a valuable mine; and, after thwarting this scheme, Arliss decides he doesn't like the high life and goes back on the road. Bill plays a cameo role of a car salesman who attempts to sell the newly appointed director a flash car to go with his new-found wealth. He only has a couple of scenes, but his enthusiasm and charm make it an eye-catching performance.

The next better-quality feature he appeared in, *Farewell Again*, came out in May 1937 and starred Flora Robson (who was related by marriage to Heather). This was about life aboard a troop ship just before active service in the Far East. Again, Bill only had a small role in it, and this was the pattern for the next few films. He had played leads in the 'quickies', but in the more prestigious films he was relegated to cameos. In *They Drive by Night*, an atmospheric thriller starring Emlyn Williams and Ernest Thesiger, he played a sympathetic bus conductor who gives a ride to Williams' fugitive. Bill's frustration with the situation spurred him on to write to Robert Donat, who was now doing so well, to ask if there was any help he could give. Although I'm sure Bill sent Donat his photo and CV as requested, nothing seems to have come of it.

Meanwhile, the film industry itself was going through a crisis. Movies were big business. According to the film statistician Simon Rowson, by the mid-thirties approximately eighteen and a half million people were going to the cinema every week and nearly sixty per cent of them went more than once during the seven days. Even a small place like Richmond had several cinemas, and then managed to support an Odeon as well. Odeons, with their familiar art deco style, were the success story of the thirties, and rapidly became a huge chain. Some cinemas were real 'picture palaces', with wonderful décor creating a fantasy world with palm trees or an abundance of ornate gilding. With so many to choose from, you didn't have to go far to see several different pictures in as many days. But the main features were still predominantly American. The Quota Act of 1927 had not succeeded in stopping the domination of Hollywood, and there were many complaints by unions, MPs and those in the business about the standard of the films being made in Britain. A departmental commission on film was set up by the Board of Trade under Lord Moyne, but while it heard representations from all sections of the industry, unhelpfully there were no film makers on the committee, and it did not really grasp the conflicting views put forward to it. Added to the lack of confidence in quality, there was a decline in production due to sources of money drying up. There had been a couple of scandals involving financing where companies had not sufficiently insured themselves, and the City became alarmed at the indebtedness of certain production houses. Pressure was put on the Films Commission to come up with a bill which would improve standards but not put the smaller producers out of business. Unfortunately, the Cinematography Film Act which was passed in early 1938 did not succeed in this aim; there were even bitter suspicions that the

Americans had put pressure on the Board of Trade. Whatever the truth, the 'quickie' was killed off by it. This does not mean to say, however, that all the films Bill made after this were brilliant, though most of them were of the longer variety, the average length of the 'quickies' having been only sixty minutes.

They Drive by Night had been made for Warner Bros by First National, the subsidiary Warner had set up at Teddington. This was one of the better-run studios, and was well resourced with staff having been trained by the Americans who then returned to Burbank. Doc Soloman, the highly efficient studio manager, was very helpful to my grandfather, and the next two films he made were also for First National/Warner. These were *Too Dangerous to Live* and *Murder Will Out*. The first starred Sebastian Shaw and Greta Gynt, a beautiful blonde starlet, on whom Bill had quite a crush, while the second headlined John Loder, Jane Baxter and Jack Hawkins (with whom he had been at Italia Conti). Although better than 'quickies', both crime thrillers still had rather implausible stories.

Too Dangerous and *Murder Will Out* were made in 1937/8, well before hostilities broke out, though not released until 1939. The period from 1936 to the war was a lean time for Bill as far as film was concerned, as he appeared only in these two and two others (in 1937 and 1938), and his roles in each were unspectacular. The tone of the films he was making had changed as well. His earlier success on celluloid had been founded on his charm and comedy timing, but the later films were more often thrillers. Perhaps this reflected the general trend in cinema during the thirties – a move away from the light-hearted note of the 1920s – but Bill had thoroughly enjoyed his lead comedy roles, and at least he continued to play them in theatre.

*

In April 1936, just over a year after playing the part of Teddy Deakin in *The Ghost Train* at Richmond, Bill again took on the role, this time at the Victoria Palace Theatre, which was being run as a weekly rep by Martin Sabine. Today, the Victoria Palace usually carries large musicals, but at that time it was too far from the Leicester Square area to be considered a West End theatre. Here, he was reunited with his friend David Langton, who in fact spent the whole season there; Bill himself also appeared there in *The Greeks Had a Word For It*, *The Late Christopher Bean* and *Family*

Affairs, all directed by Geoffrey Norman. Then, after his brief visit to Richmond Theatre under the new management, Bill's career took a slightly different direction. It has been mentioned that he loved farce and musical comedy. He could sing and move well. In 1937 he appeared in an operetta produced by C. B. Cochran. He was so proud of this that he kept the contract, and a subsequent one from Cochran, annotating it gleefully:

My first contract with C. B. Hooray! The ole piss pot!

Charles Blake Cochran was possibly the most important impresario of the first half of the twentieth century. He was knighted for his services to the business in the late forties and was also awarded the highest of French accolades, the Legion d'Honneur, for introducing French artists and plays to England. He started out as an actor in America, then became an agent. In this role he was responsible for introducing Houdini to Britain. In the early years of the century he was involved in promoting boxing and other 'acts' such as the 'Wonder Zoo' at Olympia. He seems to have had truly catholic tastes: in the US in 1897 his first theatrical production had been the far more highbrow *John Gabriel Borkman* by Ibsen. His first production in the UK was in 1902. Then in 1914 he took a lease on the Ambassadors Theatre in London and produced many shows there during the 1920s; he also managed the Empire, Leicester Square for a while and rebuilt the Oxford Playhouse. Next, he took over the London Pavilion and in the twenties put on a huge number of musical entertainments. The first of his own 'Cochran Revues' opened in 1926, followed by *Blackbirds,* which was hugely successful. He was a man of boundless energy and seems almost to have taken over the West End: he had an interest in, either as lessee or licensee, the Apollo, the Aldwych, the Garrick, the New Oxford and the Princes, in addition to being the managing director of the Palace and the general manager of the Royal Albert Hall (from 1926 to 1938). He did not restrict himself exclusively to musical work and was responsible for mounting the original productions of Noël Coward's *Bitter Sweet* and *Private Lives* – Coward having previously appeared in at least one Cochran revue. Cochran went on successfully producing right through the forties, until his death in 1951. It's not surprising Bill was proud to work for such a legendary figure.

The first contract with Cochran was to play 'as required' in *Paganini*; in fact taking two roles – Richardo and Foletto – for which he was paid the princely sum of £8 per week. Richardo was an inhabitant of the village and Foletto a smuggler and, although he had no solo songs, Bill sang as part of the ensemble. Rehearsals started on 20th May 1937 and the show, staged by Tyrone Guthrie, opened on 4th June. It starred Evelyn Laye and Richard Tauber, and the music was written by Franz Lehár (who wrote *The Merry Widow*), though it was not one of his most successful works and has faded into obscurity.

Next, Bill appeared in a musical comedy called *Take it Easy* at the Palace Theatre, and then afterwards played the first journalist in *Power and Glory* at the Savoy Theatre, which didn't last long. He secured his second engagement with C. B. Cochran almost exactly a year after the first one. This time it was to understudy another hero of his, Bud Flanagan, in a 'show with music and dancing' called *Many Happy Returns* at the Adelphi. Bud Flanagan was one half of comedy duo Flanagan and Allen, who had paired up in 1924. In 1932 they took part in a *Crazy Week at the Palladium*, where they joined comedians Nervo and Knox, Naughton and Gold and 'Monsewer' Eddie Grey. This was the genesis of The Crazy Gang, whose first joint show in 1935 was *Life Begins at Oxford Circus*. The most famous comedy group of the time, their humour was anarchic and knockabout, and they did a number of productions at the Palladium and several crazy films including *Underneath the Arches* and *Alf's Button Afloat*. Bill adored The Crazy Gang and went to see their shows whenever he could.

It might appear strange to go from playing leads to understudying, but he considered understudying such a star as Flanagan to be prestigious – after all, he did see himself as a comedian. In the 1936 edition of *Spotlight* (the actors' directory which contains a photograph and contact details) he entered himself as comedian, then character and juvenile as secondary. He was so proud of understudying Flanagan that he kept a photo of the pair signed, 'To Bill – Many Thanks – Bud 1938 – & Ches'. With drawing-pin holes in it, it looked distinctly as if it had been proudly put up on his dressing-room wall.

Many Happy Returns co-starred Flanagan's partner Chesney Allen, naturally, with Beatrice Lillie as the female lead, together with a huge cast of singers and dancers. The show consisted of sketches and songs by a variety of different people, including Gershwin, Moss Hart, Lorenz Hart and Richard Rodgers. Numbers included 'Down and Out Blues', 'Rhythm' and 'The Rival Hamlets'. Bill must have had a reasonable voice because Flanagan was the one who sang the melody in the partnership, though the songs were comic rather than lyrical. Unfortunately, as understudy Bill was paid even less than he had been by C. B. Cochran the previous year, and received only £7 per week. But at least he got the chance to go on for his hero (probably owing to Flanagan being ill). On the back of the contract is written: 'My second contract with C. B. Should be a third the old Barskit!' There does not seem to have been a third, however, as the approaching war began to affect the type of role Bill was to get.

*

Heather, meanwhile, had been working perhaps more continuously than her husband during most of the mid-thirties; first of all at Richmond and then in October 1936 she was cast in a West End show called *All-In Marriage* by Emile Littler and Aurania Rouverol. It starred Harcourt Williams and Cora Goffin, who was to stay in touch with Heather for many years. I'm not sure who looked after Anne during this busy period. The doctor had forbidden Heather to send her to school until she was nearly six because of a serious illness when she was very little. At two and a half, Anne had TB glands and had to spend some time in hospital, which upset the family a great deal. Luckily she made a full recovery. Once my mother was old enough, she was sent to a local convent school called Gumley House, where she became a weekly boarder. She loved the nuns who ran the school and was very happy there. Every Sunday Heather would arrive to take her home for the day.

With Bill getting only sporadic film work, money had been quite tight, though somehow he always managed to find enough to have a bet on the horses. This was a bone of contention for many years between Heather and Bill. While they were living in Isleworth, however, he had a fellow conspirator in Hugh Blaker. Their friend David Langton recalled that the second time he met Hugh Blaker, with Bill, Bill also produced a 'pal' he had met at the racecourse. He was called Sid and looked like a ferret, and apparently he subsequently took Bill and Hugh for a ride very easily. Bill was rather a soft touch; when he had money he was very generous with it, and he was sometimes taken in by people who swore they had a good tip for him. One tip proved to be very good, however. In 1936 Bill and Hugh took a special trip up to Liverpool to watch the Grand National at Aintree. They had been told to back a horse called Davy Jones – which was a hundred-to-one outsider – and they placed large bets. The horse was several lengths ahead towards the end of the race, much to the amazement of most of the crowd, and looked certain to romp home, but at the penultimate fence Davy Jones' rein broke and although the jockey tried to guide him with his whip, the horse ran out of the course into a group of spectators. Bill and Hugh returned home crestfallen, having come so close to making a great deal of money.

But Bill was very happy at Church Street; he lived in a nice house, met many interesting people, and in Hugh he had someone who was both friend and father-figure. Sadly, Hugh Blaker died suddenly in October 1936. He was only sixty-two, and Bill was deeply upset. Although he and Heather continued to live at 55 Church Street for at least another six months, this period of stability came to an end. It took a while to sort out all Hugh's belongings, and Bill discovered that as his mentor had believed that making a will was bad luck he had not made one since 1919 (before Hugh and Bill had met). Everything went to Hugh's sister Jane, despite the fact that Hugh had promised to give Bill some paintings. Most of Hugh's collection was later sold off by his sister (there were two large sales in late 1936 and 1948 at the Leicester Galleries), and the majority of his own paintings ended up in Wales, for Jane returned to live with the Davies sisters. When Miss Blaker died she left my mother a few hundred pounds' worth of shares in her will, but nothing to Bill and Heather. It seems strange she left them nothing. Was she perhaps jealous of Hugh's relationship with them? Or did she think Bill, although so much younger, was a bad influence on him? The family would greatly have preferred to have had a painting, particularly one or two of Hugh's own (Bill only had a couple of little sketches of his), but not being artistic herself, Jane probably didn't understand this. As it was, Heather and Bill had to go to one of the auctions and buy a couple of the cheapest Augustus Johns. These were all they could afford. They were but two of the paintings which had hung on the walls of their beloved home in Isleworth. Even these were sold during Bill's long illness in later life.

Chapter Seven
THE WAR YEARS: THE BIG IRONY

LEAVING CHURCH STREET MARKED the start of an unsettled phase during which Heather and Bill moved several times – they alternated between London, the south coast and the north of England. Family life wasn't particularly easy as they spent weeks and weeks apart, and Anne went through a rapid succession of schools. With the film industry going through a slump, Bill experienced several spells of unemployment between theatre contracts, though Heather's career was going quite well. But obviously it wasn't just their own lives which were unstable. From 1938 there was a sense of insecurity in Europe as Hitler was in expansionist mood. Then, after Chamberlain had been to Germany and returned full of the Führer's promises, came the false hope of appeasement. War was of course declared in September 1939 and so everyone's life was disrupted.

The first place Bill and Heather moved to after Isleworth was 9 Randolph Avenue in Maida Vale, north-west London. Bill spent some time out of work; however, inspired by all the authors he had met through Hugh Blaker, he began to occupy himself by writing. Heather had always enjoyed putting pen to paper and so together they started to write plays. While they were in Maida Vale they finished their first draft of *Broken Glass* – now the title of one of Arthur Miller's late plays, a very different piece from Heather and Bill's – which was a thriller about a murdered grandmother. They continued to write together for many years, completing several plays which they would send off to theatres and directors in an effort to get them produced. With titles such as *Mail Baggery*, *Captain's Case* and *No Body at Home*, they were mostly thrillers or comedies. The latter was read by Andrew Melville at the Palace Theatre, Watford in 1951. He turned it down in a letter to Bill with the comment:

> At the moment I find our audiences will not come to anything of a macabre nature and I am afraid this quality is so strongly marked in your play that I cannot take the risk at the present time.

Heather was the more disciplined writer, and completed several plays on her own, culminating in a successful production in 1955 of *Treble Trouble* (or *Home and Away*) at Richmond Theatre, which transferred to the West End. Bill also did some solo writing, mainly later in his career when he was making regular television appearances. He tried his hand at scripts for the various shows he was in, such as *The Army Game* and *Doctor Who*, remarking in several interviews that he was always disappointed the BBC hadn't liked his ideas about the Doctor having a wicked double.

Heather didn't stay at Randolph Avenue for very long. In March 1938 she went to visit her great friend Esme Vernon (with whom she had been at school) at Sheffield Rep, in south Yorkshire; Heather herself had performed with the company a couple of years before. According to a newspaper article a few days after she arrived, Esme broke her arm in a riding accident. My grandmother took her place in the company and stayed on as leading lady for over a year. This may of course have been invented by the publicity department of the theatre to add a little excitement to the departure of one actress and the appearance of a new one; nevertheless, it made a good story. Heather had to live in digs and this meant that she and Bill were apart for some time. She became great friends with two of the other actors at Sheffield Rep, Anthony Marlowe (whose real name was Fernando Perredita) and his wife Merelina Watts. During the Christmas break, when a pantomime was playing at the theatre, Heather came back to London with them and they all spent the festive season together, with Anne and Bill, at Fernando and Merelina's flat in Chelsea. They did their Christmas shopping along the King's Road, and my mother vividly remembers the lamps shining along the street. But it was to be the last winter with blazing street lamps for some years.

After Christmas Heather returned to Sheffield, taking my mother up north with her. With the threat of war, the authorities at Anne's convent had decided that, being near the Thames, they might be a prime target for bombing raids, so had relocated to Broadstairs, in Kent. Heather thought this a ridiculous idea as it was right on the south coast, which logically was just as likely to be bombed. So after one term there she took Anne away and put her in a sister convent, near Skipton in Yorkshire, which was not only perhaps safer, but also closer to where she herself was in Sheffield.

Bill appeared in a couple of shows in the West End of London and then joined Heather briefly for a 'special week' at Sheffield Rep in July 1939. One of the regular actors fell ill, and he rushed up to save the day. Playing the lead in a four-hander, his ability to learn lines quickly was tested to the limit. The review in *The Star* carried a pencil sketch of him and gave him full credit:

> The production of S. N. Behrman's comedy *The Second Man*, at Sheffield Playhouse last night, was a personal triumph for Billy Hartnell, who gave an exceptionally capable performance in a difficult role, which he had learned in less than 48 hours.

Shortly after this play, Heather and Bill returned south and took a flat in the seaside town of Worthing in Sussex. It was in Warwick Road, just off Spa Point, and consisted of a ground floor and basement with garden. Perhaps they moved to Worthing because Heather had already got a job at the local rep (or perhaps she was given work there after arriving), but as Hugh Blaker originally came from Worthing it had an attraction for Bill anyway. There was a large theatre community in the area around Brighton (the neighbouring town) and, although Bill had to endure another spell out of work, summer 1939 was great fun as new friends were made and old acquaintances renewed. Bill had already encountered Guillen Hopper in film circles; he was a larger-than-life character who had built roads in South America, was a sometime reporter, script writer and had pretensions to being an agent. He lived in Shoreham with his wife Elsie and stepson Terry, who was about a year older than Anne. Terry Carroll (he reverted to his real father's name) became a writer, television reporter and regular presenter of a programme called *Day by Day* in the sixties. He remembers that summer well. Guillen was out of work and he and his family often took long walks along the sea front. One day Terry's stepfather did a double take and shouted, 'Good God, there's Billy Hartnell!' He rushed over to say hello and was immediately invited back to tea. Anne and Terry were introduced; they quickly became firm friends and ended up like brother and sister, each having suffered the loneliness of being an only child. They spent hours playing together – creating exhibitions in the basement and charging friends and family to visit them, making up songs, including one about Bill (who had a propensity to break wind) entitled 'Billy the Farter They Call Me' to the tune of 'Big Hearted Arthur They Call Me'. As Terry recalls, 'I'm not sure that it was very skilled as we weren't exactly experienced lyricists – but it made us laugh.' Terry became a surrogate son for Bill.

They laughed a good deal that summer; Bill was wonderful at impersonations and especially adept at taking off The Crazy Gang since understudying Bud Flanagan the year before. He would go into a shop with them to buy sweets and ask for 'Licolish Alsolts' in a funny voice and they would all dissolve into giggles. He used to impersonate his other great hero, Charlie Chaplin, as well, twirling a cane and doing funny walks. One of Bill's favourite Chaplin routines, which he himself had perfected, was from the early film *The Gold Rush*, and involved sticking forks into two bread rolls and manipulating them like feet, doing a dance routine on the tablecloth. Before the war Bill was a great practical joker, and so full of fun that Anne and Terry would sometimes laugh until they cried.

*

However, there was always the nagging worry about finding a job. Heather had been working constantly in theatre and had also been doing some radio broadcasting. Although Bill wasn't overtly jealous of the fact that she was working and he wasn't, sometimes he was a little bad-tempered as it did affect his pride. Guillen was also unemployed, so the two of them would drown their sorrows at the pub and try to think up various schemes to make money. One day they came up with a plan after talking to a fisherman in a bar. The fisherman had obviously decided, with war looming, he wouldn't be able to make a living any more as fishing would be restricted, so he tried to sell them his small boat. How they imagined it would be profitable for them, when it wasn't for the fisherman, I don't know, but Bill and Guillen thought it was an excellent idea. Why not make money out of doing something they enjoyed as a hobby? There was the added advantage that if war did break out, then as fishermen they would not be drafted. (Not that Bill was unpatriotic – people such as farmers, butchers and fishermen were considered vital to the country in their own capacities as they provided food.) The only problem was that neither of them had the funds to buy the boat. They decided to enlist the support of their friend David Langton, who was in a show in Brighton and consequently was less broke than they were. Bill and Guillen thought they would try a bit of emotional blackmail and engaged the help of Terry, assuming it would be harder to turn down a request from a child.

Terry was given strict instructions to get on his bike, cycle to Brighton – no mean distance for an eleven-year-old – go to the theatre and insist on seeing 'Uncle Basil', and to extract money from him at all costs. Terry was a very obedient child, so he cycled madly to Brighton and impressed on the stage doorman that it was imperative that he see David Langton. He went up to his dressing room and repeated his message: 'You've got to buy a boat, Uncle Basil, Guillen says so and so does Uncle Bill. The boat's ready, they just need the money. Please, you've got to give me some money; they are expecting me to come back with it.' Terry couldn't remember whether it was before or after the show or during the interval, but whenever it was David cannot have been very pleased to be interrupted by a demand for money to finance a crackpot scheme. Terry literally had to get on his bike and pedal back to Worthing with bad news. In the end the boat was never purchased and the whole plot, no doubt hatched over several pints of beer, fizzled out.

Guillen also had vague plans about being Bill's agent, but this didn't come to anything either. In fact Bill began to be represented by Eric L'Epine Smith. Securing work had always been a question of finding a casting agent who was looking for actors for a particular production, and the idea of personal representation, with an agent doing the slog of finding out what work was going on and promoting his own clients, was in its infancy. Everything was much more casual in that an actor would be given an outline of a film, asked if he wanted a certain role which would be so many weeks' work, then if in agreement the two parties would simply shake on it. Actors would be expected to work all the hours necessary. Even though the performers' union Equity had been set up in the thirties (both Bill and Heather had joined), it took a while for terms and conditions to be regulated.

Eric, however, after being an agent for a short while, decided at the beginning of the war to become a casting director for Warner Brothers. Bill was furious and said to him, 'You can't go there, you've got to look after me!' Bill always wanted his own way and was liable to get angry if someone didn't do as he wanted. To pacify him, Eric introduced him to Al Parker, who was to be his agent until the early fifties. Al had a lot of actors on his books, and was perhaps not the most perceptive of agents, as he managed to overlook an eager young actress who came to work in his office for a while – Audrey Hepburn. But he was well known in the business and had offices in Park Lane. Eric L'Epine Smith, meanwhile, was to have a hand in Bill's career in other ways, until he reverted to being an agent in the early fifties. He had co-written with Brandon Fleming a play called *Faithfully Yours* which went out on tour in late autumn 1939; both Heather and Bill were offered roles. The flat in Worthing was closed up and they went off to such places as Southsea, Eastbourne (both rather sleepy resorts on the south coast) and Swansea, in Wales.

My grandparents took a companion with them, having just acquired a new dog, an Irish terrier called Jolly. He became very used to being trailed around different theatres and the following year (in Harrogate) he was even to appear on stage. They had no option but to take the dog on tour, as, although they all spent Christmas together in Worthing, there was nowhere they looked on as a permanent home. Anne had spent the autumn term farmed out with local people in Amberley, near Worthing, while she attended the village school. There were periods when she didn't see much of her parents, though she was always good at writing to them, and Bill fondly kept many of the letters she sent to him at various theatres. But there were times which made up for this, such as the summer holidays of 1939, when they all spent weeks on end together. Anne's parents were back from the tour just in time for her birthday (four days before Christmas) and they proudly watched her play the mayor in the school show. Anne was so nervous about them being in the audience that she was ill the night before, and although harbouring secret desires to follow her parents on to the stage, nerves always got the better of her and she never did become an actress.

After the tour of *Faithfully Yours*, Heather went up to the north of England again, this time to join the White Rose Players at Harrogate as leading lady, replacing Sonia Dresdel. After the fall of Dunkirk, she took Anne away from school on the south coast, believing once again that their daughter would be much safer in Yorkshire with her. As weekly rep meant Heather was busy all day and all evening, it wasn't feasible for Anne to stay with her in digs in Dragon Parade. So at the suggestion of the box office lady at the rep, Anne went to live on a farm, with the woman's cousin Dorothy Johnson and her husband Len. They already had an evacuee staying with them, but no children of their own. The evacuee, Margery, was from the centre of Leeds and, unused to the countryside, she was rather frightened of the animals, but Anne loved Yorkshire, the freedom of the woods and fields, and the wilderness of the scenery in comparison with the south-east of England. She learnt how to milk the cows by hand, and used to ride round on the back of the big old black pig. Heather enjoyed her time at Harrogate as well She made many good friends at the theatre, where she was in illustrious company: Trevor Howard acted opposite her for several shows before he was called up, playing Rochester to her Jane Eyre, among other roles. My mother had a huge crush on him. Dulcie Gray joined the company, and so did Terence Alexander, first as acting assistant stage manager, then as young male lead. Terry Alexander went on to become best known many years later as Charlie Hungerford in the series *Bergerac*.

*

Bill, meanwhile, after understudying Ralph Lynn at the Aldwych had attempted to volunteer for the RAF. Not that he could fly, but the RAF was always seen as the most romantic of the services and he was influenced by Heather's brother, Malcolm, who, with a partner, had his own plane and of course volunteered immediately. Malcolm, with his Oxford education, went straight in as an officer, but was non-combatant because of his damaged back (the result of a racing-car accident), and Bill was told they were only taking men under thirty at the time. So he went to stay with Heather in Harrogate while waiting to be called up for the army. He joined the White Rose Players for a few shows, including *What Anne Brought Home*, in which Heather played the title role and Bill the rather awkward young man she brings home. My mother, aged eleven, was in the audience watching with Dorothy Johnson. At a point when the young man was wandering around not knowing what to do with himself, and Heather's character was signalling vainly for him to sit down, my mother got so excited that she jumped up out of her seat and shouted, 'Daddy, do sit down!' The whole theatre erupted with laughter and Bill was so taken aback that he just plonked himself down on a seat. Later my mother was terribly embarrassed by what she had done, but everyone thought it so funny that nobody told her off.

Bill was finally called up and joined the army on 10th October 1940. He was assigned to the Royal Armoured Corps 22nd Dragoons, spending some of his training time at Durham, and some in Devon. He was very patriotic, and did his best, but he hated the army. Many men did, of course, but perhaps those with an 'artistic' temperament found it particularly hard. The discipline of the regime was tough and the thought of killing someone was difficult to cope with, even though he was a good shot and there was talk of him getting a stripe. However, he was never particularly physically strong and the rigours of training affected him badly: he succumbed to bleeding piles, and then a knotted-up stomach. Later called spastic colon, and now irritable bowel syndrome, this condition is usually caused by emotional stress. Several actors have admitted to having experienced similar problems during the war: Sir John Mills in his autobiography describes how badly he suffered from stomach trouble, and Sir Peter Ustinov also mentions similar symptoms in his life story.

Bill spent his Christmas leave at the farm with Heather, Anne and the Johnsons. He had visited before, of course, and both he and Heather felt very welcome there. Dorothy adored Bill, especially when he turned his charm on, as he always did for women. And he was good at making her laugh. Bill loved the homeliness of the place, but one thing annoyed him. It is a typical example of his exacting nature, his need to have everything just so. Dorothy liked her meat overdone, whereas Bill, who was very pernickety about his food, preferred beef (when they had it) underdone. He would always try to take over the cooking when they had a joint, much to the amusement of Dorothy, who naturally knew the vagaries of the old farm range far better than he did. The Christmas break was all too short, and Bill was distressed at the thought of going back to training – he even went absent, sneaking an extra day or two of leave. Somehow he got away with it – perhaps by pleading illness.

He tried hard for the next six months, but began to suffer from dermatitis, presumably a nervous reaction to his distress; he was also told it could be an allergy to the khaki dye in the clothing. In the end he suffered a minor nervous breakdown and was discharged from the army on 1st July 1941, having served only 258 days. The discharge papers show that his rank was trooper, his conduct had been 'good', and he was 'a reliable man, clean, honest and sober'. However, he was deemed to be permanently unfit for any form of military service. What an irony that he was to spend so much of the rest of his career in army uniform, often bullying young recruits in a way that he would have resented himself, giving some of the best performances of sergeants that the screen was ever to see. Many years later Terry Carroll overheard someone in a bar who claimed to know all about Bill Hartnell, saying to a companion that of course Bill wasn't really an actor, he had been a genuine army sergeant and had been pulled in specially to appear in *The Way Ahead*, and that was what had started his career. The fact that he was so convincing as a soldier was a huge compliment: Bill was always meticulous about detail in his performances, and this was based on his close observation of the type of person he was to play.

*

Bill was out of the army, but very run down, and he needed somewhere to live. As they had no permanent home now, a friend of Heather's from the theatre company, Hugh Rennie, suggested that they rent his bungalow on Thames Ditton Island, in the Thames to the west of London. There were about forty wooden houses on the small island, built off the ground on stilts to avoid possible flooding. Although they had initially been constructed as holiday homes just after the First World War, a number of people actually lived in them all year round. Hugh's house, number 23, had a large veranda, two bedrooms, a sitting room, kitchen and bathroom, and garden. Facing the main stream, it had beautiful views out towards Hampton Court Palace. The island was attached to the mainland by a small footbridge with a toll gate, so if you didn't have the necessary penny on you, you had to scramble precariously up the bank to avoid the massive metal turnstile. The only other way on to the island was by ferry and the old ferryman, Painter, would bring furniture and other necessities over in his flat-bottomed boat. With only one path down the middle there was no other form of transport, and everyone used a rowing boat to get around. Bill and Heather's dinghy was moored at the landing stage, and was even used to walk the dog. Jolly Dog would be rowed across to the mainland and deposited on the towpath which ran from Hampton Court to Kingston. He could run around to his heart's content and Bill, Heather or

Anne would row to keep up with him. Occasionally he escaped from the garden on his own, and would find his way over the little footbridge and down on to the towpath; the first my grandparents would know of it would be when they heard Jolly barking at them from the other side of the river, demanding to be rowed home.

Bill loved the island, but his nerves were still in a terrible state and it was perhaps not the best place to recuperate. Being on the outskirts of London he could hear the bombing and air-raid sirens, and there were big guns situated in Bushey Park not far away. The roofs of most of the houses on the island were made of corrugated iron, and so when any shrapnel fell it made a terrible din. The wooden structures did not offer much protection, so they had to dive for cover under a strong table if any bombs came close. Anne, on holiday from school, remembers her father clutching her in terror when they heard bombs dropping.

Bill's skin trouble continued for some while. He tried various doctors, one of whom painted the rough areas with a purple-coloured dye, but that didn't work either. To top it all he somehow managed to contract scarlet fever. He was very ill with it and was put into isolation in hospital. Eventually, recovering enough to go home, he decided to go down to Bideford, the small town in the south-west of England where his Aunt Bessie still lived, and stay at the local pub run by the Penningtons, whom he knew well. Getting away did him good, and it was in Bideford that he finally found a doctor who could cure him of the eczema-like skin complaint.

To occupy himself in Devon, Bill put together a stand-up routine. He also had his first go at producing a show: called *French Mustard*, it was described as 'a crazy, spicy, piquant revue' and was put on in aid of the Soldiers, Sailors and Airmen's Families Association. 'Billie', as he was billed, starred, but there were other artistes and the band of the Royal Air Force (Northam) provided music. His stand-up routine featured in other entertainments as well, including an event mounted by Warner Bros/First National at Teddington Studios on November 22nd 1942 in aid of the Merchant Navy Comforts Service Fund. This comprised the Reco Bros Empire Circus with Famous Variety Acts; so Bill appeared between 'The Four Sensations – Aerial Trapeze' and 'Reco & May – Britain's Comedy Wire Act'. The actor Norman Mitchell remembers seeing Bill's act elsewhere in London during the war as well. Bill was serious about his comedy: in one article later he was quoted as saying that if he hadn't got his big break in films, he would have turned to being a professional stand-up comic.

Subsequently Bill returned to the island at Thames Ditton and Heather came down from Harrogate and started work in a local munitions factory, making shells. The company, called Martin Walters, had been well-known boat builders before the war. Terry Carroll, who spent some time living with them while he was a cub reporter on the *Richmond & Twickenham Times*, thinks she enjoyed herself on the shop floor and – always a great organiser – had a tendency to boss about all the other women in her section. She was proud to help the war effort, and both she and Bill were very public spirited, although he must have been carrying round a certain amount of guilt about having failed to cope with the army. They registered as fire wardens for the island. Since they enjoyed living there so much, when number 30 came up for sale they decided to buy it. It had a bigger sitting room than Hugh's bungalow and was on the backwater. This was used mainly by rowing boats belonging to local people and so was much quieter than the main-stream side. Although there were few pleasure craft going up and down the Thames during the war, air-sea rescue boats were often to be seen, and everyone used to rush out of their houses and cheer as they went past.

*

Bill tried valiantly to pull himself together so that he could rebuild his career. Eric L'Epine Smith and Doc Soloman at Warner Brothers helped him back into the film industry, which was churning out patriotic movies as quickly as possible. Sadly, Doc Soloman was killed before the end of the war when a doodlebug landed on one of the Warner Brothers offices where he was working late. The first film they proposed Bill for was made in 1941. He was given a small character role of a cabby in *Flying Fortress*, which starred Richard Greene. Bill was almost unrecognisable in it: he was heavily made up with a big bushy moustache. It has occurred to me that perhaps his skin was still bad at this point, hence the makeup and hair. Sadly, his character comes to an untimely end in an air raid. Next he secured a small role in *They Flew Alone*, a Herbert Wilcox film about the famous flying pioneers Amy Johnson and Jim Mollinson. A well-made film with lots of aerial feats, it was let down by the fact that Anna Neagle and Robert Newton were not ideal casting as the leads. It is probable that Bill knew the real Jim Mollinson before the war, through Heather's brother's connections with the flying fraternity.

Within a short space of time Bill made several more films; 1942 was a record year with six films in which he appeared being released. But they would all have been shot some months earlier, as it takes some time to edit and complete the films, and organise publicity for the opening. Although there are no family records about it, a man who worked on *In Which We Serve*, the famous Noël Coward/David Lean-directed movie, has said in an interview that Bill was fired from this by Coward for turning up late and keeping everyone waiting on the first day. His role was apparently given to a unit production manager. He was normally such a stickler for time keeping and I can only speculate that it could even have been his first job back after his illness (I have been unable to find out the exact shooting date of the film) and, with his nerves still bad, perhaps he was still not really in a very fit state to work. There may have been some other reason, but it was very uncharacteristic. He may well have put a good face on things to hide how he was feeling; but whatever caused this incident, it can't have helped his confidence.

One of the other films from that period was *Sabotage at Sea* – an undercover story about sabotage and murder aboard ship made for British National (a different company from First National, which was associated with Warner Brothers). British National was the company which later put Bill under contract to star in several productions; but they seem to have been unaware of his potential at this stage, and it took his success in *The Way Ahead* for them to appreciate his ability. He also made several more pictures for the First National/Warner Bros stable, including *The Peterville Diamond* – an amusing comedy about a neglected wife who is bought a large diamond by her business-obsessed husband, and the attempts by a jewel thief to relieve her of it – in which Bill played a butler. Around this time my grandfather made a conscious decision not to be made up heavily for film roles, as he had been in *Flying Fortress*. Always praised for his natural style of acting, in *Suspected Person* he gave a very naturalistic performance in a role which was similar to many he was to be cast in from now on. The film was a good thriller in which Bill, as Detective Saunders, right-hand man to David Farrar's Inspector Thompson, helps to track down the proceeds of an American bank robbery carried out by gangsters Robert Beatty and Eric Clavering. Also starring was Patricia Roc, who tries to persuade her brother to return the money which he has unwittingly ended up with. Using Canadian/American actors helped with box-office appeal in the US, and Beatty was to work in Britain again, several times with Bill, who always got on well with him.

Next, Bill appeared in two films made at Ealing Studios, produced by Michael Balcon and directed by Basil Deardon. Ealing has always been known for its classic comedy pictures, and both these war films were vehicles for their well-known comedy stars, Will Hay and Tommy Trinder. *The Goose Steps Out* is a daft story about a schoolmaster (Will Hay) who teaches German, finding himself sent to Germany because he is the double of a captured German, also played by Will Hay. He causes havoc teaching trainee spies – including Charles Hawtrey and Peter Ustinov – about England while trying to find out details of a secret bomb the Germans are developing. The film ends with ridiculous fun in the cockpit of an aircraft, with Will Hay becoming a hero. Bill played a very small part – he doesn't even get a credit at the end of the film – as a German officer sent to meet the high-ranking officials off a train, but we have a publicity still from the film and as usual he looks immaculate, medals sparkling and boots shining. It is possible, however, that he would have preferred the role of the comic Führer in the film. Among the many photographs he left is one of him made up to look like Hitler. It's a very good likeness, and my mother said that he had an ambition to play the German leader – but he never did. He loved to play characters in which he could immerse himself totally.

The Bells Go Down was another wartime propaganda movie from Ealing, starring Tommy Trinder and James Mason. Set in the East End of London, it glorified the community spirit during the Blitz. Having become a fire warden in real life, Bill now played a volunteer in the Auxiliary Fire Service, an old hand who gives the green and foolish Tommy Trinder advice about what it all entailed. There is a slightly bitter quality discernible in his characterisation not present in his pre-war work. The film is filled with shots of bombed and burning houses; in the end Tommy Trinder's character dies heroically, but life goes on despite the tragedies.

Although Bill appeared in two consecutive comedies made by a major studio, the roles he played in each of them were straight – a great contrast to what he was doing away from films with his stand-up comedy routine. Both film parts were also comparatively small. It took a return to the theatre to give him the break he needed.

Chapter Eight
PICTURE STEALER NUMBER ONE: THE WAY AHEAD

IN LATE 1942 BILL was cast by the director known as 'Dickie Bird' (Richard Bird) in a stage adaptation of Graham Greene's famous novel *Brighton Rock*. The play toured the provinces before going to the Garrick Theatre in the West End in February 1943. It merited a double spread of photographs in the fashionable magazine *The Tatler and Bystander* on 17th March 1943:

> … It is a sensation, a strong story of the machinations of Brighton's race gangs and of the sordid lives and distorted mentalities of the men and women who make up these gangs. It may come as a shock to many theatregoers, seasoned as they are on the unfortunate Miss Blandish, to learn that such gangs have, and do exist, in this country. The play provides a strong part for Hermione Baddeley, who as Ida Arnold, a warm-hearted, dominating frequenter of saloon bars, finally tracks down the chief gangster, a ruthless, thwarted, embittered youth of seventeen, played by Richard Attenborough.

Richard (now Lord) Attenborough was only nineteen when he played the unpleasant young crook, Pinkie. Dulcie Gray (who had worked with Heather in Harrogate) played the other juvenile lead, a waitress who comes upon evidence which could implicate Pinkie in murder; when he meets her, intending to frighten her into silence, she falls hopelessly in love with him and he callously decides to marry her to invalidate anything she might say in court. My grandfather played Dallow, Pinkie's henchman

– according to *Punch*, 'a quietly done but perfectly observed study in human sliminess' – but even he, shocked by Pinkie's increasing ruthlessness, deserts him in the end.

The play was, again according to *Punch*, 'slangy, ruthless and hard as nails', and the comments in *The Tatler* suggest that people weren't used to the realistic depiction of razor slashing on stage, though the horrors of the war perhaps made the play more acceptable to audiences, surrounded as they were by bombs dropping, than it would have been in the thirties. Hermione Baddeley – a well-known character actress of the time – says in her autobiography that at the curtain call on the first night in London she stepped forward to say how good the two youngsters had been when there was an almighty crash. Everyone was convinced that a bomb had made a direct hit and the roof would cave in, but luckily for the theatregoers it proved to be a nearby building which had been destroyed.

Lord Attenborough remembers Hermione Baddeley as a larger-than-life character, but recalls that Bill was very different: he kept himself to himself on tour and was a consummate professional, very serious about his work. He brought a sense of total reality to what he did and yet his performance was meticulously judged; everything was worked out in extraordinary detail, and then he used his theatre technique to project his interpretation from the stage. Attenborough felt that this was the antithesis of much contemporary West End acting, which could be very theatrical. It was this realism which made Bill such a good screen actor, and one of the few of the period who understood the different requirements of stage and screen. 'Dickie' Attenborough, as the family always called him, was to work with Bill again, firstly in the screen version of *Brighton Rock* and then in several further films, so he was well placed to assess Bill's abilities. His skill, he believed, was something innate, rather than something which could be learnt from drama school. Attenborough thought Bill more like the 'angry young men' of the profession who emerged later, actors such as Albert Finney, Peter O'Toole and Tom Courtenay. Bill certainly made no bones about resenting the old school tie set-up which accounted for most of the leading men of the time. Was it that Bill, despite his meticulous preparation, had a quality of danger which made him exciting to watch? The danger wasn't to do with being unpredictable – he never fluffed (i.e. tripped over a line of dialogue) or changed anything during performance, which made him a very dependable actor to work with – but more to do with the intensity with which he did things. He sometimes tended, though, to be impatient and irritable with those who were less of a perfectionist than himself.

This doesn't sound much like the pre-war Bill who was such a practical joker, although since meeting Hugh Blaker he had acquired a fastidious side to his nature. Was this focusing on the minute detail of performance his way of dealing with the guilt of being unable to cope with the army, and his fears about the war? Some contemporary articles refer to him coming out of army hospital with a stutter, enough to frighten any actor. Although my mother does not remember a stutter, she says that his nerves were certainly never the same after his breakdown, and that he became more bad-tempered. His drinking increased, though it was generally social drinking and never interfered with his work. However, there was also probably an element of identification with the part he was playing. Several people who worked with him say that Bill always became very wrapped up in the role of the moment, and as Dallow in *Brighton Rock* wasn't a particularly pleasant character, this was perhaps reflected in his offstage persona during the tour. He was also still insecure about his background, which seemed so different from that of many of the upper-class stars of the time (such as David Niven, with whom he was soon to work), and in a short while he found it necessary to invent a family history for himself to cover the shame he felt.

*

It was to be a few years before the film version of *Brighton Rock* was made, partly because Dickie Attenborough was called up by the RAF – indeed, the show only had a limited West End run because of this. But in the audience one night was an influential director who was so impressed with Bill's performance that he cast him in his next film. This director was Carol Reed, supposedly the illegitimate son of the Victorian actor-manager Sir Herbert Beerbohm Tree. Reed had early on assisted well-respected director Basil Dean, and had then directed several notable pre-war films himself. His work was known for its gritty realism, as in the film *Penny Paradise*, about a Liverpool tugboat captain who thinks he has won the pools. The film he cast Bill in, which was to signal a change in status for my grandfather, was *The Way Ahead*.

The genesis of *The Way Ahead* lay in an army recruitment film which had been very successful because many well-known actors, such as Robert Donat, had appeared in it. The army had always been seen as the poor relation of all the forces, and the Army Council wanted a propaganda film which would do for them what Noël Coward's *In Which We Serve* had done for the navy by glorifying the courage of those who fought at sea. Sir Peter Ustinov, attached to the Army Kinematograph service in Wembley Park, had already met both Captain Carol Reed and Gunnery Major Eric Ambler, and in his autobiography he describes how the film came about under the aegis of Two Cities Films. Conveniently, Lieutenant-Colonel David Niven was also available and on hand at the time, and the four of them set up and wrote the film from an office at the Ritz. Ustinov, having consistently failed to get promoted, was only a private and had a few problems in collaborating with the other three, who were all officers, so for their trip to locations in North Africa he was made a temporary civilian. However, his low rank helped to give him a good view of the reality of being in the army, and the film was consistently praised for its depiction of the many different characters who find themselves thrown together as new recruits. The film shows how this disparate group, including characters played by Jimmy Hanley, Stanley Holloway and John Laurie, are put through their paces by a tough sergeant, played by Bill, until they become a dependable and close-knit unit under the command of David Niven. The film was shot at Denman studios and on location in Algiers, where US 'sappers' assisted by blowing up buildings, and then played practical jokes on all and sundry. Peter Ustinov not only co-wrote the film, but appeared in it as well, as a rather bad-tempered bar owner.

Although it would have had an industry screening earlier, the general release of the film was held back for a while and it finally opened just in time for 'D' Day, the landing in France of Allied troops in June 1944. It was a film that captured the feeling of the moment and most of the critics described it as one of the two most important films of the war. According to the *Sunday Graphic* of 11th June 1944:

> *The Way Ahead* is concerned with something more fundamental – how there comes to be an army at all, how shopkeepers and professional men, farmers and artisans and sportsmen can challenge the professional armies of militarist nations and hold their own, and eventually win. They are not all heroes by inclination. Some of the characters answer the call-up

reluctantly, with many a misgiving about business or wife or family... It is all very human and extraordinarily funny. The little group of characters whose fortunes we follow are etched so skilfully that in no time you feel you have known them all your life.

Bill's portrayal of Sergeant Ned Fletcher was finely judged and gained much praise. He managed to combine a hard, tough exterior with sensitivity, using his eyes so expressively that he was able to dominate a scene even without any lines. Ernest Betts, the reviewer in the *Sunday Express*, described the role:

> The Regular Army sergeant of Billy Hartnell, a tough implacable hunk of beef with the chesty voice of a Guardsman, nothing human in his face, [is]... a pain in the neck – until trouble starts. Whereupon a gleam of humanity melts him down and his heart begins to beat. This is the finest study of a soldier I have seen on the screen – better than Gary Cooper's *Sergeant York*.

Bill prepared for the role by visiting the army training camp at Pirbright in Surrey. He spent a long time watching the sergeants in action, and talking to them in the sergeants' mess. After two or three weeks he was allowed to take some new recruits for their first training session, and no one guessed he wasn't a proper sergeant. Terry Carroll, who was living in the bungalow at Thames Ditton during this period, said that Bill's voice wasn't naturally deep, and he had to work hard to achieve the 'chesty voice of a guardsman' described above. Bill received a letter after the release of the film from his ex-sergeant in the Royal Armoured Corps, saying:

> I scarcely recognised the cheeky rookie who used to curse me softly under his breath when I got out my little black notebook and said 'Hartnell – spud peeling'.

Although the film has dated somewhat, the battle sequences are good and my grandfather's performance still looks powerful because it was so truthful, and not coloured by any period mannerisms. Lord Attenborough believes it was 'one of the great cinema performances – whether seen now or in a hundred years – a magical performance'. The producer Guido Coen, who used to run Twickenham Studios, said that Bill should have received an Oscar for it. One reviewer, writing an article on actors who stole pictures from the main artists, called Bill 'Picture Stealer No. 1' for his role in *The Way Ahead*.

*

Two films in which Bill appeared had come out in the months before
Carol Reed's picture. The first, *The Dark Tower*, another Warner
Bros/First National offering, was notable for being Herbert Lom's first
film. It also marked the beginning of an association between Bill and the
director John Harlow which was to last for several films. They were to
become good friends, drinking regularly at the Savage Club and the Green
Room Club, and even spending Christmas together, with their families, at
Boscastle. *Headline*, the other film before *The Way Ahead*, was also
directed by John Harlow.

With the release of *The Way Ahead* Bill succeeded at last in thoroughly
impressing people in his own profession: on the strength of this
performance, he was put under contract by one of the studios to star in
four films. British National Films had been set up in 1934 during the
studio boom, by Lady Yule (a patriotic millionairess widow) and J. Arthur
Rank, an industrialist who had made his millions through flour milling.
The latter, a strict Methodist, had started out by buying projectors for his
local Sunday school and then came into the movie business via religious
films. He was first and foremost a financier, and he soon moved into
distribution and studio ownership, buying a huge country house at
Pinewood in Iver Heath, Buckinghamshire, and building the most up-to-
date studios in the grounds. Rank in fact resigned from British National in
1937 and thereafter it was run by John Corfield. Unfortunately its output
was not notable. However, the four films my grandfather did for them
showed he could carry a movie, and gave him some varied and enjoyable
roles.

The first, called *The Agitator* (*The Biter Bit* was its original title),
directed again by his friend John Harlow, cast him as a young socialist
agitator, angry that his father had been cheated of money he deserved for
an invention. When he is left the factory in compensation on the death of
the old owner, he finds that being managing director isn't as easy as he
thought and alienates those he used to consider his friends. According to
one of the impartial reviews to which cinemas could subscribe: 'Billy
Hartnell subtly suggests the man who is gradually brought to the
realisation that he cannot live up to his convictions'; the reviewer believed
that, though rather laboured, it was 'a film which should appeal to the

masses and prove a good proposition for industrial and most popular halls.' Cinema owners relied on these reviews, weekly *Film Reports* from the Cinematograph Exhibitors' Association, and the monthly *Film Bulletins* from the British Film Institute, to counteract the publicity material, naturally biased, from the distributors, and to help them decide which films to rent; it also gave them some idea as to the type of audience a particular film would appeal to. *The Agitator*, also featuring actors such as John Laurie and George Carney, my other grandfather, was considered good, populist entertainment, but its release was held up while censors considered whether the subject matter was too inflammatory.

The month in which it finally came out, January 1945, also saw the opening of Bill's next film for British National. It was very different from any other film he was to appear in, and apart from the early 'quickies' was the only one in which he was to have a 'romantic lead' role, though the story ends in tragedy. In *Strawberry Roan* he plays a farmer infatuated with a show girl, Carol Raye. When he marries her she turns out to be most unsuitable as a farmer's wife. He neglects his work and her extravagance helps to ruin him, and then she is killed riding off after an argument. Bill's character is devastated and in despair sells his farm. My grandfather enjoyed portraying a different type of character from usual and loved filming in the countryside. Most of it was shot around the village of Wishton, near Salisbury in Wiltshire. The writer of the book from which the story was taken, A. G. Street, lived not far from there in Wilton. As it was such a lovely place to spend the summer, Heather joined her husband and Anne came down from Yorkshire for the holidays. It was a long journey involving several changes of train, and Anne, being only fourteen, was entrusted to a young sergeant by Dorothy Johnson (whom she was still staying with in Yorkshire), as the country was swarming with soldiers. Heather went to Bristol to collect their daughter, and they had to spend the night in a small hotel; it was here that they witnessed what they considered one of the strangest sights of the war. Owing to rationing, the management were strict about the hours when food was served. While Heather and Anne were in the lounge a gentleman came in and asked for tea and cakes as he was evidently very hungry. On receiving the information that there were no cakes, he asked for toast, but was again refused. He had to make do with a cup of tea, and to the utter amazement of Heather and Anne he sat there muttering into his cup about the lack of anything to eat and then proceeded to tear off strips from his newspaper and shove them into his mouth. He chewed and then washed the paper down with his tea. They giggled so much that they had to move tables and dined out on the retelling of this for years; even Bill, who loved telling comic stories so much, could not top it.

Bill also enjoyed having to ride in *Strawberry Roan*. 'A lovely little filly – with plenty of spirit' was the way he described his horse on the back of a photo he kept. The local hotel at which the family were staying in Wishford supplied some of the horses used as they also ran a small stables. It was here that Anne learnt to ride properly, though she had always loved the animals because of her father's great interest in them. At last Bill was getting a chance to employ the skills he had acquired early on at the racing stables, but it was to be the only time he was able to use them on celluloid. In his way of getting wrapped up in the part of the moment, for some time afterwards he strutted around proudly in his riding breeches and jacket, made especially for him, which he had been able to purchase from the film company.

Later on in 1945 *Murder in Reverse* was released. In this Bill plays a stevedore, Tom Masterick, contentedly working at Limehouse Docks, until a fellow worker, Smith, runs off with his wife. The two men fight, starting in a bar and ending up among the cranes in the dock. Smith falls into the water from a great height, and although Masterick swears he saw him alive after their brawl, he disappears and Masterick is subsequently tried for Smith's murder. Condemned to death, Bill's character is reprieved when a newspaper takes up his case. After serving fifteen years in jail he comes out and attempts, with the help of a reporter friend, to track down Smith, eventually taking revenge by shooting him, challenging the authorities to convict him twice for the same murder. Masterick's wife was played by Chili Bouchier, who remembers getting on well with Bill and admiring him as a good strong actor. The cast also included Jimmy Hanley and Dinah Sheridan (who were in the process of planning their own wedding). Bill has to age more than fifteen years in the film, ending up grey-haired and broken. Dinah Sheridan played his daughter as an adult, while a young Petula Clark played the daughter as a child. Heather and Bill always thought Petula delightful; she had also been in *Strawberry Roan* and looked up to Bill as an 'uncle' figure.

Bill now started to get a lot of coverage in the newspapers. *Murder in Reverse* was well received – on 19th October 1945 the *Evening Standard* called it 'a quietly distinguished little film', and in the Scottish *Sunday Express* Isabel Sinclair recommended it as follows: 'The film has technical excellence – the tense excitement of dockside and legal wrangles, and the playing of a fine team of British actors – especially Billy Hartnell.' Bill began a whirl of personal appearances to publicise the pictures, and was given a particularly warm welcome in Glasgow when he told the audience that he had had the sense to marry a girl from Glasgow; there was even greater applause when he plugged the British film industry by saying, 'Once British studios get really under way [after the effects of the war] there's no reason why our productions shouldn't compete with the best Hollywood can send us' – a comment reminiscent of Colin Welland's cry ('The British are coming!') at the Oscar ceremony many years later in 1982, heralding a supposed renaissance in British film making. *Plus ça change.*

Picturegoer of 26th May 1945 devoted a full-page article to Bill which started with Lady Yule saying at a press conference that her company, British National, intended to combat the star shortage by discovering and developing new talent. Bill, it implied, was that new talent: not an overnight sensation, but someone who had worked his way up from the ranks of the extras. This was the first time he had really had his life story told in an article, and it made the most of the difficulties he had gone through. The press loves a Cinderella story. Bill was attracting attention nationally and many reviewers felt he had been unjustly neglected. 'Why don't British producers make better use of the acting talents at their disposal? What is the reason for the failure, for instance, to make the best use of such a fine character actor as Billy Hartnell?' asked *The Times* in October 1945. Unfortunately British National films mostly played as second features, though reviewers seemed to believe Bill's talent was worthy of better. A. E. Wilson was a great fan of Bill's and in *The Star* he berated British National for not having a big West End opening for *Murder in Reverse*, which he considered ingenious, dramatic and well directed. His only complaint was the unreality of the scenes set in a newspaper office. The film was also dubbed and did very well in France as *Meurtre à Crédit*, Bill making several personal appearances there.

A. E. Wilson was even more annoyed that Bill's fourth picture for British National, *Appointment with Crime*, opened at the Astoria Cinema in Charing Cross Road, which he did not consider a top-rank picture-house. He criticised the exhibitors for their timidity:

> Why is it that a British film of such unusual quality as *Appointment with Crime* has been denied the advantage of showing at one of the leading West End shop windows?... It gripped and excited me throughout – an effect due among other things to the rapidity of the action, the ingenuity of its story, and the strength of its acting.

Wilson asks whether this timidity is because William Hartnell was not considered a top West End draw; but he insists that stardom depends on exploitation, and that the quality of Bill's performance in *The Way Ahead* and *Murder in Reverse* suggested that he had all the toughness worthy of his being developed into a British Cagney or Bogart (Bill was called 'Britain's Humphrey Bogart' by Raymond Leader in his book *Cinema Close-Ups* in 1947).

Jimpson Harman in the *Evening News* believed that the monopoly of the Americans and the Rank Organisation in the West End of London was responsible for him nearly missing

> the best of the week's releases... With, I suppose, about one third of the money an American director would have been given to spend on the job, Mr Harlow has turned out a fast-moving, realistic, amusing and ruthlessly thrilling underworld drama which kept me on the edge of my seat the whole time.

Appointment with Crime, the 'breezy little thriller' which was written especially for Bill and directed by his friend John Harlow, was a tough, uncompromising story about a smash-and-grab man who is caught during a raid when a grille slams down on his hands and he is abandoned by his accomplices. After a prison sentence he vows revenge on the men who let him down, killing one of them and framing the other. Herbert Lom plays a rich and crooked art connoisseur whom he blackmails, then shoots. Bill's character, Leo Martin, uses a dance-hall girl who has fallen for him as an alibi, but she is eventually persuaded by Robert Beatty's police inspector of Martin's true nature, and at the end of the film Martin is caught once again by the wrists, this time by the train window as he tries to escape. Bill's role has no redeeming features: he never shows remorse and even

perjures himself on the Bible; and the amount of violence in the film –
tame by our standards now but shocking then – meant that it was banned
by certain local watch committees. The picture, which started out being
called *999*, was made quickly – John Harlow was a very efficient director –
but some of the sequences had to be refilmed because Bill wore a leather
jacket: when he moved the microphone picked up the rustling noise and it
sounded like a hurricane. The leather had to be specially oiled and
stretched before retakes.

Most of the reviews approved of the film: the *Sunday Dispatch* praised
'each scene hitting you smack between the eyes till it reaches its howling
climax'; but it is particularly worth noting what Dilys Powell, one of the
most respected film reviewers of all time, said in the *Sunday Times*. She
believed that the British film industry was starting to make use of local life
and that a number of new stars were emerging. One of the problems, she
believed, was the lack of star actresses, all of whom had little chance to
play other than well-bred parts, and thus someone like Joyce Howard (the
dance-hall girl whom Leo Martin uses) was not convincing as an
unsophisticated Londoner. Although the number of murders in the last
third of the film made it a little melodramatic, 'William Hartnell, as the
thief released from prison and bent on revenge, gives a performance of
compact savagery and grim cunning.'

This last role completely killed off Bill's early image as a comedian, and
in view of this he was always now billed as 'William Hartnell' rather than
'Billy'. According to an article in the *Evening News*, this was at the behest
of British National who thought his serious roles deserved a more serious-
sounding name. Bill apparently said he didn't mind what they called him
as long as he got good pictures. For a long while he would be seen as a
British tough guy: in *Reynolds News* Milton Deane wrote:

> A young man who is quietly and unobtrusively doing a lot of good work in
> British pictures and who, in my opinion, could go right to the top of the
> tree if given a real chance is to be seen in one of the new pictures this week.
> His name is William Hartnell and he might be called the British James
> Cagney. He gave a fine performance as the Sergeant in *The Way Ahead*,
> and you have seen him in *Strawberry Roan* and *Murder in Reverse*. In these
> films, and in the new one I have just seen, he proves that he is of the stuff
> of which stars are made. But he needs a little grooming and developing,

and there are rough edges that call for a little grinding and polishing. And above all he needs his Big Break.

Deane believed the British National films didn't quite give Bill this 'big break'. Was Bill not as successful as he could have been because the British National films tended to depict him as a loser? Hollywood nowadays believes audiences like upbeat conclusions. Even when playing an essentially 'nice' or innocent character, as in *Strawberry Roan* or *Murder in Reverse*, Bill tended to end up broken, suffering huge humiliation. There is no way he could have played his role in *Appointment with Crime* to elicit any more sympathy from the audience: Leo Martin was written as a bad character through and through. Anyway, the contract with British National was not renewed, neither was he taken up by another studio, and thereafter he always remained a freelancer. This meant that although Bill was not tied down – he didn't in fact particularly like the contract system because of its restrictions – he did not have a studio promoting his career and he had to work hard to improve his own status.

*

Even though he was not put under contract by another studio, the next three or four pictures Bill made were all top quality films and he had co-star or lead supporting role status. In *Temptation Harbour* he co-starred under Robert Newton and Simone Simon, playing another unpleasant crook who, while killing a man in a fight, loses a suitcase full of stolen money. Robert Newton's railway signalman picks it up, and instead of handling it in, he leaves town, pursued by Bill's character. In a fight the signalman kills the crook accidentally, and finally decides to turn the money in to the police. Bill's character again had no redeeming features. *Temptation Harbour* came out in February 1947, as did *Odd Man Out*, in which Robert Newton was again one of the stars, along with James Mason, Kathleen Ryan, Cyril Cusack and another familiar face, Robert Beatty. It reunited Bill with director Carol Reed, and was an atmospheric and well-made film about an IRA man who escapes from prison; while on the run he meets several colourful characters, including Robert Newton's mad artist and Bill's fiery publican, Fencie, who hides him for a while.

Finally the film version of *Brighton Rock* was made. Rather than base it on the stage adaptation, Graham Greene worked together with Terence

Rattigan on the screenplay from Greene's own novel, and the picture was made by the Boulting Brothers, with Roy as producer and John as director. Shooting took place in studios at Welwyn and on location in Brighton, using some of the original cast from the stage production four years previously. Dickie Attenborough and Hermione Baddeley reprised their roles as the young gangster Pinkie and the nosy concert artiste, Ida Arnold, who hounds him. Bill played Dallow again, and Harcourt Williams the crooked lawyer Prewett. Dulcie Gray, who had played Rose on stage, was under contract to a different film studio and so the role was given to newcomer Carol Marsh. The character Phil Corkery, who is Ida Arnold's friend, was played on stage by Ernest Borrow, but the Boultings cast my other grandfather, George Carney – the second time he and Bill were to work together. Ironically, George died later that year at the age of sixty from a thrombosis, long before my parents met, so he was never to know about the connection between the families. All the cast seemed to enjoy making *Brighton Rock*. We have many photos of them entertaining themselves by playing cricket and other games when not shooting – there is always a great deal of waiting around on a film set. Attenborough told a lovely story about Bill being reprimanded for upstaging him in a particular shot. Bill was sitting in the foreground in the sordid room where they meet, silently eating from a plate of food. Attenborough was on the opposite side of the frame discussing something with the two others in the background, but Bill was fiddling with the food so intensely that it was distracting. The director told him to do less fiddling. Bill did so, but it was still too much. In the end the director threatened that he would be cut out of the shot if he couldn't be more invisible while he was eating.

*

Was all this success going to Bill's head? Chili Bouchier, who worked with him on *Murder in Reverse*, said that the only fault she found in him was a 'supreme self-confidence and self-possession which sometimes appeared to be arrogance'. Was it arrogance, or simply that he was desperately keen to impress and was getting good at hiding his insecurities? Many actors are deeply insecure people, and once they get to star status they are often more nervous about keeping that status. Of course Bill was flattered by all the attention: he was now receiving a large amount of fan mail and a fan club was set up. The first edition of the 'William Hartnell Bulletin' was issued in July 1947 while he was finishing shooting *Brighton Rock*. The eight-page leaflet had a photo on the front and a letter from him inside. There was a 'pen pals' section and a couple of pages of movie gossip, together with a potted life history of my grandfather. It was here that he first claimed he was the son of a professional soldier turned stockbroker, a claim that was sometimes changed to son of a farmer. He did, however, admit his debt to Hugh Blaker:

> Among his hobbies he lists primarily picture and antique furniture collecting. In his boyhood he was at one time placed in the care of a guardian who was a world renowned authority on the subject of art, whom people came from all parts to consult. Of a naturally enquiring nature, Billy picked up most of the inside information, and the precise yet aesthetic judgement of the expert became to some extent his own. His greatest admiration is reserved for his friend Augustus John, closely followed by Whistler and Sickert.

The fan club bulletin, of which there were to be several editions that year, and a 'new series' the following summer in a large format which also answered readers' letters, was probably organised by Don McFadden, who was a publicity agent also providing a cuttings service and promotional articles which he would place in magazines. Bill was popular with reviewers partly because he was so good at making personal appearances and was always willing to meet fans and journalists. We have many publicity photos of him attending autograph-signing sessions and visiting cinemas and civic functions all round the country to promote his films. He enjoyed the film parties and always attended the National Film Award presentations. In 1947 this ceremony was held at the Dorchester Hotel and was attended by anyone who was anyone in the business, including many of the people Bill had worked with. Guests included Korda, the Boultings, C. B. Cochran, Laurel and Hardy, Margaret Lockwood (who won the award that year for most outstanding actress), Michael Balcon, Richard Attenborough and even Bill's own agent, Al Parker. Bill would take Heather with him, or Anne once she reached the age of eighteen. He liked to have a pretty girl on his arm, though he was very protective of his daughter.

Anne had left school just before her sixteenth birthday, and after working in a friend's stable for pocket money, she trained for six months to gain her Institute of Horse certificates, which meant she would be able to teach riding. She spent some of her teens away working with horses, but while at home often had to accompany her father when he went out. Although Bill in many ways loved his new-found celebrity, he was a very private person and did not always want to be recognised. He often dragged Anne to the cinema with him, even if she didn't want to see the film. Anne would be dispatched to buy the tickets and Bill would loiter anonymously in the shadows, fiddling with a cigarette, and then slip in quietly next to her.

Bill also loved the local social life in Thames Ditton, and some of his favourite evenings were spent at one of the two local pubs: the Swan, a well-known beamed riverside pub frequented by the 'in-crowd' just over the footbridge, or the Red Lion, which was a little further up into Thames Ditton and more of a 'village local'. Both Bill and Heather played darts regularly and were in the local teams – even Anne began playing as soon as she was old enough.

They met someone at the Red Lion who was to stay a close friend until he died in the sixties. Arthur Jeffrey Northcote lived in Thames Ditton and worked at the Aircraft Design Department at Weybridge. A brilliant man, he was always known to the family as 'Little Arthur' because of his height: tragically his legs had been broken when he was a very small child and had not been reset properly, so he always wore leg irons. Bill and Heather even named their cat 'Jeffers' in his honour, and he often spent time at the bungalow keeping Heather company when Bill was working; the two of them were obsessed with doing the *Observer* Ximenes crossword together. It was considered the most difficult of all crosswords and Bill couldn't join in this pastime. Terry Carroll thought Bill was always slightly jealous of Little Arthur's cleverness. It was another thing which made him somewhat defensive, since he already believed himself to be less intelligent than Heather. He had not, of course, had the same advantages educationally as either Heather or Arthur. Little Arthur amused everyone because he used to drive around in an old banger which didn't have a hooter, so he would shout *toot-toot* out of the window. There were of course comparatively few cars on the road then, and during the war there had been even fewer, as petrol was so severely rationed. Although Bill owned an MG then, it spent most of its time in the garage. Living on the island meant that his car had to be kept on the mainland. The local taxi-driver (who was obviously allowed more petrol than a private car owner) became known as the 'Hartnell Shuttle' as he was always having to drive Bill up to the studios, or to the station at Surbiton. While shooting *Brighton Rock*, however, Bill purchased a 1936 Alvis which was his pride and joy.

Bill loved living at Thames Ditton. He was not far from many of the west London film studios and he could get into the centre of town in twenty minutes by the direct train from Surbiton – a bus ride from home but on a more direct route to Waterloo than the local station – yet the bungalow was far enough out for them to be surrounded by trees, and for the area to have a real 'village' feel to it. The island had a few disadvantages, though. During the winter of 1947 – when there were power cuts due to industry being run down because of the war – it was particularly cold (the most severe winter since 1894), and they froze as the bungalows were all-electric. Without any form of heating they simply had to go to bed with a hot water bottle and stay there. The big thaw that winter caused flooding and Anne and Heather (Bill was filming) had to be rescued by boat from the veranda by a burly man rowing across the garden. The house was under two feet of water for ten days which caused quite a lot of damage to their belongings – and, unfortunately, their theatre memorabilia. All the inhabitants had to stay with friends on the mainland until the flooding subsided. When they returned, the council provided a bar of soap and disinfectant and didn't turn the electricity back on until everything had been inspected.

Heather and Bill were friends with several people who lived on the island, many of whom were also involved in the arts. Gordon Landsborough, a writer who ended up with his own publishing company, lived a couple of doors away and Heather and Anne frequently played the Chinese game of mah-jong with him and his wife when Bill was away filming. Val Valentine, a larger-than-life character who owned one of the few stone bungalows, was a well-known scriptwriter of such films as *Waterloo Road* and *The Rake's Progress* and was later to co-script one of Bill's films. He would stride down the central path shouting for Bill to join him at the pub, but when in a real drinking and partying mood he was too much even for Bill – no one could keep up with him on those occasions. Parties near the river could sometimes get a little out of hand. A bigwig in the film industry who lived opposite on the mainland once went to get into his boat when drunk and missed his footing. His wife had to hang out all his pound notes on the line to dry. And slightly further up the bank was a man who, when he'd had too much alcohol, used to believe he could walk on water.

Not all Bill and Heather's social life revolved around drinking. Sonny and Renee Jenks were a variety couple who also lived on the island, and Heather and Bill would always go to see them when they played the Kingston Empire in variety or pantomime – Sonny was a leading 'dame' at the time. Although Bill wasn't playing comedy himself any more, he still loved watching it. It was at one of these variety shows that Bill and Heather first saw Wilson, Keppel and Betty, whom they considered one of the funniest acts they had ever seen. (They used to do an Egyptian 'sand dance' which defies description on the page!) Another friend of Bill's was inevitably the local bookie, a man always referred to as 'Monkey', an ex-RAF officer who had a metal plate in his head because of a war wound. Cyril Monk (his real name) and his wife Clare were great fun and everyone used to be very amused – in a kind way – as he would lose his balance after only half a pint of beer owing to his injury. To outsiders it looked as if he couldn't hold his drink, but friends knew that he often bumped into the doorpost. He was very unlike a traditional bookie, but he probably made a lot of money out of Bill, who continued to bet regularly and visit Sandown and Kempton Park racecourses whenever he could.

Bill and Heather were very sociable and often kept open house; although the bungalow wasn't large, they would put people up in the living room. An actor called Sydney Bromley, whom they had worked with at the Richmond Theatre, used to stay sometimes. He was an eccentric little man who became more and more like a pixie as he grew older; his swansong was a wonderful character, Diddler, in the Roman Polanski movie *Pirates*. If Sydney didn't have any work on he would just hang around until Heather got fed up with him under her feet and sent him packing. Terry Carroll also lived with them for some time; his mother and stepfather had gone out to Africa, so in many ways they were more tangible than his own family. During the war Heather and Bill had held an embarkation party for him, then when he was demobbed they threw him another one. After Terry had divided his time between Shoreham and the island for a while, Bill said in his usual abrupt manner, 'You've got to stop buggering about – either you live here or you don't,' so he moved in.

Just as Bill had been hugely influenced by his surrogate father, Hugh Blaker, so Terry was hugely influenced by Bill. Bill was always extremely well turned out, and once he could afford it he spent money on the very best clothes. He liked handmade shirts and his shoes always shone to perfection. His hands were always immaculate, and he often fiddled with his cuffs or his jacket or the purple signet ring he wore. Terry said, 'He always spent ages getting ready to go out – you could swim around the island waiting for him. Once he was ready, though, he would be impatient if he had to wait for anyone else.' Bill liked his family to be well dressed, and when he had money he would turn up with an expensive item of clothing for Heather or Anne. Smart gloves or suchlike were always welcome, but once he bought Anne a fur jacket which she neither wanted nor felt suited her. She would have much preferred the money to buy something she really needed. But it was the gesture which was important for Bill. One day he took Anne to meet his second cousin, the couturier Norman Hartnell, famous for his royal commissions, in order to try on some designs. Although Anne attended first nights and other occasions when she had to dress up, they decided Hartnell's clothes were too grand for her, and even too expensive for Bill to splash out on, so they came away empty handed. Terry tried to emulate Bill's sense of style, but didn't really have the funds. On leaving the army Terry used all his discharge money to have a suit made along the lines of Bill's, which were always slightly different from usual. It had two vents at the back, narrow cuffs and narrow trousers, and was the most expensive suit he ever bought. As Terry got older, however, his role slowly changed from that of surrogate son to drinking partner, which brought with it a few problems of its own.

Bill and Heather had married very young, and over the years they had spent long periods apart while working, so there had always been plenty of opportunity for him to be unfaithful. But Heather was getting fed up with his womanising – she knew of his philandering as it was often signalled by an extravagant present to her – and one day she simply packed her bags and went to stay with a friend in Brighton. Anne was working but living at home at this time, and she became fed up with Bill expecting her to cook him a meal when she got in, especially as he wasn't working at the time and could easily have done it himself. In protest she started staying out late with a boyfriend, so after two or three nights of her returning at eleven o'clock (terrible for an eighteen-year-old then) Bill telephoned Heather and demanded that she 'come home and control your daughter!' Heather felt she had no option but to return. However, when Anne was safely away working at a stables in Scotland, Heather finally decided she wanted a divorce, although in those days that meant she would have to prove Bill's infidelity. She needed evidence that would stand up in court. Terry found himself in the uncomfortable position of piggy-in-the-middle. Heather wanted him to be her spy and report to her any instance when he actually witnessed Bill being unfaithful. She was asking him to take sides. He tried to protest because, after all, he cared for them both; but at her most theatrical she tried to get him to swear to her request, demanding: 'You must give me an undertaking, you must promise me.'

Within days Bill, accompanied by Terry, went to the Swan pub where two pretty girls asked for his autograph in return for which he asked for their phone numbers. This was apparently his standard practice, but when subsequently a date was made, it had to appear to be Terry's arrangement. The two men went to Surbiton and boarded the train to the centre of London to meet the girls. Bill treated them all to champagne cocktails at a club near the Dorchester – he was very grand and generous on these occasions and behaved like the star he was. Terry was then quietly told to disappear with one of the girls while he took the other one out to dinner, arranging to meet up again at the girls' flat. So Terry whiled away the time rather awkwardly with his date, and when he arrived at the flat to fetch Bill to catch the train home, he found him completely inebriated and in a state of semi-undress; not sufficient to prove anything, as Terry thought he was probably too drunk to have succeeded in the seduction he had obviously tried. In attempting to get Bill dressed and organised to leave, Terry realised they had missed the last train back. So they were stuck. The girls lived in rooms in a boarding house, and luckily there were vacant rooms in the building to which they were summarily dispatched for the night. They had no blankets and had to sleep directly on the metal springs of the bed, but Bill was oblivious to all this. In the morning, when he had sobered up, he was horrified, and they dashed off in a taxi to Waterloo, catching a very early train home. Two bedraggled figures were caught walking up the path to the house on the island by Heather, who must have been looking out for them; she shouted with almost Shakespearian relish, 'I want neither of you in this house.'

Bill in best christening clothes, with his mother, 1909

Bill aged 5 with his mother

The first page of Bill's journal, 'The Life of a London Urchin', written at the age of 15

An early portrait photo

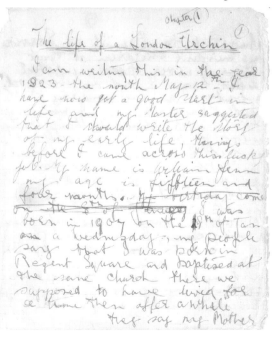

Bill with Hugh Blaker, the unofficial guardian who influenced his early years. This photograph was taken in 1935, by which time Bill had married Heather McIntyre and they were living in Blaker's house in Isleworth

Sir Frank Benson's company in a special performance of *The Merchant of Venice* at the King's Theatre, Hammersmith, 1926. Robert Donat and Bill are in the top right hand corner

Bill and Heather in *A Bill of Divorcement* on tour in Canada, 1928-29

'Myself and Heather McIntyre, she is a darling. We are very much in love with each other'

A postcard sent by Bill to
Hugh Blaker while on tour
in Canada

'Nov 2nd 1928 Lethbridge, Alberta.
Taken by Heather in the prairie.'

Posing for the camera while on board ship

Publicity photographs
of Billy Hartnell and
Heather McIntyre
from 1928

Bill often experimented with costume
and make-up; here, he is dressed as
a biblical character

Hounslow 0167.
William Hartnell,
57, Church St.,
Isleworth
Middlesex.
Miss Conti.
Sir Frank Benson (two
years).
Lead in "The Man Responsible".
Lead in "Good Morning, Bill".
'Jimmy' in "the Lad".
Canadian Tour.

An early
handwritten CV

Bill (far right) in a scene from the 1935 film *The Shadow of Mike Emerald*

With Dorothy Hammond and Max Adrian (far left) in a scene from the 1936 film *Nothing Like Publicity*. Max Adrian would later make a guest appearance alongside Bill in the 1965 *Doctor Who* story 'The Myth Makers'

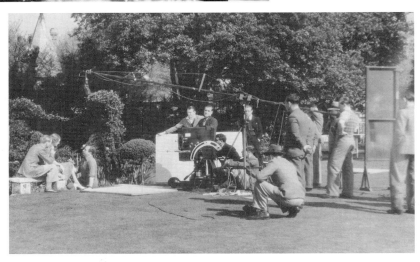

Making films in the 1930s; Bill is on the far left

Murder Will Out, a film from 1939

A poster for *Take it Easy*, a musical comedy in which Bill appeared in 1937

As Joseph in *The Peterville Diamond*, 1942

Two stills from *The Way Ahead*, in which Bill appeared with David Niven, Jimmy Hanley, Stanley Holloway, John Laurie, Hugh Burden, James Donald and Raymond Humphrey, 1944

(Photos copyright © Rank Organisation)

With Mary Morris and George Carney (the author's other grandfather) in *The Agitator*, 1945

Bill (right) with Jimmy Hanley (centre) in *Murder in Reverse*, 1945

With Carol Raye in a still from *Strawberry Roan*, 1945; and a photograph of Bill on horseback taken during the shooting of the film

Appointment with Crime, 1946

With Robert Newton in
Temptation Harbour, 1947

The first issue of the 'William Hartnell
Bulletin' produced by Bill's fan club, July 1947

A film party in 1947 attended by, back row from left to right: Bill, Griffith Jones, John Mills, Pat Roc, Jack Warner; middle row: Jean Kent, Dulcie Gray, Margaret Lockwood, Michael Denison; front row: unknown, John Howard Davies, Petula Clark, Julia Lockwood

Playing cricket on the set of *Brighton Rock* with co-stars Richard Attenborough and Carol Marsh, 1947

Bill as Dallow in *Brighton Rock*

Bill and Richard Attenborough take a break during filming of *Brighton Rock*, 1947

Signing autographs at the Regent Theatre Portsmouth on a promotional tour for the 1948 film *Escape*

Bill with his daughter Anne in 1948

On set for *Now Barabbas Was a Robber*, 1949

Sharing a drink with Alfred Hitchcock and Dennis Price during the production of *Cockpit* (later retitled *The Lost People*), 1949

Enjoying a game of table-top cricket during a break in the shooting of *The Lost People*, 1949

The cast of the play *Seagulls over Sorrento* in which Bill (second from left) toured from 1950 to 1954

Heather and Bill at the wedding of their daughter Anne to Terry Carney

The Ringer with Dora Bryan, 1952

Bill (second from left) in the first production of *Home and Away*, a play written by Heather Hartnell, Richmond Theatre, 1955

In uniform are Ian Carmichael, Thorley Walters, Bill, Richard Attenborough and Terry-Thomas during the making of *Private's Progress*, 1956. With them are the Boulting brothers who produced and directed the film

Richard Attenborough and Bill in *Private's Progress*. The dedication by Attenborough reads: 'Why are you always so unkind to me Bill? Oh well! Maybe someday I'll have the stripes!! Yours ever, Dickie'

A poster for the play *Ring for Catty* in which Bill appeared in 1956

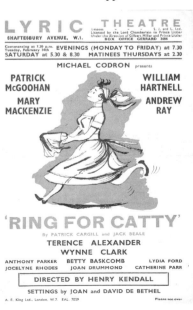

Bill and Heather, with daughter Anne and son-in-law Terry, at the christening of their granddaughter Judith (the author, Jessica Carney), 1957

Bill and a young Patrick McGoohan in *Hell Drivers*, 1957
(Photo copyright © Rank Organisation)

Bill with Stanley Baker in
Hell Drivers
(Photo copyright © Rank Organisation)

Yangtse Incident,
1957

Bill stars in the first of
the 'Carry On' series: *Carry
On Sergeant,* 1958

Bill as a bogus vicar in the film
And the Same to You, 1959

With Brian Rix in *The Night
We Dropped a Clanger*, 1959

Piccadilly Third Stop, 1960

Bill and the rest of the cast of Granada Television's *The Army Game*, 1957-60

Bill with his second cousin, the fashion designer Norman Hartnell

A still from the 1963 film *The World Ten Times Over*, which featured the young Sylvia Syms

Bill and Heather's
cottage in Mayfield, Sussex

Heather and Bill with Stumpy the dog in
their cottage in Mayfield, 1964

With Richard Harris and Rachel Roberts in *This Sporting Life*, 1963 (Photo copyright © Rank Organisation)

Heather and Bill play with their grandchildren, Paul and Judith (the author, Jessica Carney)

As the first Doctor in *Doctor Who*, with
Carole Ann Ford as his granddaughter
Susan, 1963 (Photo copyright © BBC)

At the TARDIS console during the
recording of the 1965 story 'Galaxy 4'

At the TARDIS console with Jacqueline Hill, William Russell and Carole Ann Ford
(Photo copyright © BBC)

Bill with his *Doctor Who* co-stars William Russell, Maureen O'Brien and Jacqueline Hill
(Photo copyright © *Radio Times*)

The Doctor meets the emperor Nero (played by Derek Francis) in the
Doctor Who story 'The Romans' (Photo copyright © BBC)

Vicki, Ian, Barbara and the Doctor return to the TARDIS after experiencing life
during the crusades (Photo copyright © BBC)

Bill arriving in style for one of his many personal appearances as the Doctor, at Pembury Hospital, 23rd May 1965; and (below) addressing fans at the opening of the Pembury Hospital fête
(Photos copyright © *Kent and Sussex Courier*)

A copy of the autograph card sent out to *Doctor Who* fans by Heather during Bill's time as the enigmatic time traveller

Heather and Bill examining some newly arrived Dalek models in their hallway

A poster advertising Bill's appearance in *Puss in Boots*, winter 1966-67

ODEON THEATRE - CHELTENHAM

ON THE STAGE

Manager: E. A. GISLINGHAM   Tel. Cheltenham 24081

Commencing **MONDAY JANUARY 9th** for **ONE WEEK**
MON. at 7.15   TUES. & WED. at 2.30 & 7.15
THURS. & FRI. at 5.0 & 8.0   SAT. at 2.0, 5.0 & 8.0

PRICES OF ADMISSION: 8/6, 7/6, 6/6, 5/- (All Seats Bookable) Book Now
O.A.P.'s 3/- Tues. Mat. only Box Office open 10.30 a.m. - 7.30 p.m. Sun. 4.30 - 7.30 p.m.

Malcolm A. Rose and Donald Auty present

TELEVISION'S ORIGINAL

DR. WHO
WILLIAM HARTNELL
in the Magnificent Christmas Pantomime

PUSS IN BOOTS

with

**SONNY FARRER   .   LIZ MOSCROP
TOMMY OSBORNE & ROY TIERNEY
PADDY GLYNNE   .   VALERIE VYNER**
AND BIG SUPPORTING COMPANY

MEET THE MONSTERS FROM OUTER SPACE
SUPER WIN-A-DALEK COMPETITION

Bill takes a turn behind the bar in a pub in Cornwall

Bill's final stage appearance, in *Brother and Sister* at Bristol Old Vic with Sonia Dresdel, 1967

Heather collared Terry after a while, demanding that he tell her what had happened so she could get on to her solicitor. Terry protested that there was nothing to tell. She was furious: he was the only one who could prove anything and now he was reneging on his promise. But Terry insisted that Bill had spent the night with him in very uncomfortable circumstances, and that what he had witnessed would not stand up in court. Heather would not believe it, called him every name under the sun and ordered him out of the house. Terry packed his suitcase and left with his tail between his legs to the sound of Heather saying, 'Don't even think of coming back.' Poor Terry. My grandmother did love the grand theatrical gesture.

Terry Carroll didn't see Heather and Bill for several years. But he called Heather when he was about to get married. You normally call your mother when such an event is about to happen, but as his real one was in Africa, he rang his surrogate mother, Heather, instead. All was forgiven and forgotten, even though Heather had never obtained her divorce. Terry wore for his wedding the expensive suit he had bought to keep up with Bill.

*

During this period Bill made probably the biggest career mistake of his life. One day the telephone rang; it was his agent, Al Parker. Carol Reed was offering him the role of the sergeant in *The Third Man*. It was to star Trevor Howard, Orson Welles and the American actor Joseph Cotton, with music by Anton Karas. Bill had of course heard that the film was being made. Orson Welles was Orson Welles, and Trevor Howard was riding on the crest of a wave after *Brief Encounter*, but Bill had dearly wanted the Joseph Cotton role. Cotton was not yet that huge a star, but he was American. Bill had just co-starred in *Brighton Rock* and was second lead in *Escape* with Rex Harrison: he was protective of his position. His pride was hurt when Al rang to offer him a smaller role. Neither Al nor Bill were particularly diplomatic in such circumstances, and the phone was slammed down in a huff. Al also represented Bernard Lee. He obviously thought, oh well, if Bill is going to take it that way, I'll get Lee to do it. Bill did have a couple of other films in the offing, and he wasn't to know that *The Third Man* would turn out to be such a seminal film.

119

Chapter Nine

TYPECASTING CONTINUES: BRITAIN'S LEADING SCREEN MENACE

IT WAS NATURALLY ONLY with hindsight that Bill regretted his hasty dismissal of the job offer in *The Third Man*. Perhaps if he had taken it, he would have been bankable in America and would have gone to Hollywood. Many of his films had, after all, already been shown in the US, though sometimes under different titles. But there were more roles for him in England, and he didn't always have to play the crook.

Escape – which incidentally had an American producer and director – was a taut thriller with Rex Harrison playing an ex-RAF officer who escapes from Dartmoor while serving a sentence for accidentally killing a policeman. Harrison's character, Denant, is depicted sympathetically since the policeman was manhandling a prostitute, and Bill's portrayal of the police inspector who tracks him down – which could have been a deeply bland part – manages to convey both a sense of duty and compassion. There is a certain mutual respect between hunter and foe, for the inspector knows that Denant is no ordinary crook, but someone to whom fate has dealt a cruel blow. C. A. Lejeune reviewed the picture in the *Observer* on 28th March 1948: 'To my mind, Mr Hartnell's is the acting triumph of the film.' For *Doctor Who* fans it is of interest in that it's the only film he ever worked on with actor Patrick Troughton (playing a shepherd), who was to replace him in the television series many years later.

Bill played a couple more tough characters on the right side of the law in his next two films, *Now Barabbas Was a Robber* and *The Lost People*. In the former, a Warner Brothers drama about a group of criminals in prison, as Warder Jackson Bill is in charge of murderers, IRA men, thieves and a bigamist, played by actors such as Richard Burton, Richard Greene and Kenneth More. The film received mixed notices, but once again Bill's performance was picked out for praise. In *The Lost People* – originally called *The Cockpit* after the play it was taken from – Bill reverted to the role of experienced army sergeant. The film is set in Europe in a dispersal centre for displaced persons just after the war, where an inexperienced captain takes control and is warned by Bill's sergeant how hard it is to keep the peace between different nationalities sheltering there. The movie is a plea for tolerance, showing the evils of extreme nationalism and bigotry, and although it has dated, its message unfortunately seems as relevant to Europe today as it was then. Bill was once again working with Dickie Attenborough, along with Dennis Price and Mai Zetterling.

Bill was starting to feel typecast. All the characters he was given now seemed to be so humourless, and he missed being able to use his comedic skills. He must have felt the need to remind the public that he could be funny. In an article in *Film Illustrated Monthly* which came out at about the same time as the release of *Now Barabbas*, the writer mentions Bill's dry sense of humour and repeats a story which he told about himself. During the shooting of the film there was thick river fog near the studios at Teddington. Bill was driving with a friend to Twickenham when they found themselves at the head of a convoy of buses. Bill got out of the car and walked along the road with a white handkerchief to lead the way. When they got to the depot, a conductor got out to thank him. Bill then overheard a conversation between the driver and the conductor:

DRIVER: Hey, d'you know who that was?
CONDUCTOR: No, who?
DRIVER: Bill Hartnell.
CONDUCTOR: Who?
DRIVER: Bill Hartnell the film star. Recognise his mug anywhere.
CONDUCTOR: Blimey, never knew film stars came out in the fog!

All Bill's roles in the late forties and early fifties seemed to swing from one side of the law to the other. In *Double Confession*, a very confusingly plotted thriller, Bill is a thoroughly nasty piece of work once more, though in *The Dark Man*, released in February 1951, he plays another policeman.

In the March 1950 edition of *Film Illustrated Monthly*, coinciding with the opening of *Double Confession*, a large picture of Bill was captioned somewhat facetiously:

> On your right Britain's leading screen menace, the Prince of Spivs, Haunter of race-tracks and low dives. The bow-tied dandy with a voice like sandpaper. In one film he crossed over to law and order to play a prison warder. He was so tough that Scotland Yard dubbed him the best crime deterrent of the year. In another film he played an army drill sergeant, and the recruiting figures shot up – for the navy! Who else could it be but William Hartnell?

Did 'Menace Hartnell', as some articles now called him, research his crooks and policemen as carefully as he had his sergeant role in *The Way Ahead*? He had certainly seen the less pleasant side of London life as a boy, and knowing his way round all the horse and greyhound racecourses he had observed some of the less salubrious types who hung out there. He did study famous cases to try to work out what motivated the criminals psychologically; and a friend of his, Arthur Cook, a crime reporter for the *Daily Express*, no doubt furnished him with the grisly details of various crimes. To understand the mentality of the law enforcement characters he played, he cultivated the acquaintance of several CID men; he enjoyed drinking with them and was guest speaker at several police 'dos'. At some point he persuaded them to show him their 'black museum' with its particularly gruesome exhibits, believing this would give him further insight into the workings of the criminal mind. By the time he was working regularly in the play *Seagulls over Sorrento*, the transport police would occasionally hijack him on the way home after the show and take him off to drink at their private club, sending him back absolutely pie-eyed on the last train, with instructions to the guard to make sure he got off at the right station. He had been well disposed towards the police ever since the kind policeman who had been his mother's boyfriend showed interest in him as a child. In most of his performances he manages to imbue policemen with a certain amount of humanity, despite scripts which often gave them very one-dimensional characters.

*

Around 1950 Bill's frustration at being typecast led him to try to alter the course of his career by having Don McFadden, his publicity agent, place a few articles in film magazines expressing his dissatisfaction. How much control he had over the content of these articles is not clear, but perhaps they were ill judged in that he ends up sounding a little ungrateful for his success. In one of them McFadden quotes him:

> I'm tired of being the eternal 'tough guy' of British films. Asking me to play this type of role in the first place was about as practical as asking Danny Kaye to play Napoleon on Elba! Somehow I've managed to scrape through, but after five years of it I can clearly see the danger signal ahead. I'm certain picture-goers are sick and tired of seeing me pull horrid faces before the cameras, and if I don't change my style very soon I shall soon find myself a has-been!

'Somehow I've managed to scrape through' sounds a little like false modesty, considering the reviews he had been getting, and perhaps he was simply too good at playing 'hard men'. Although the article goes on to outline all Bill's earlier comedy experience, it also says that when he pressed for a funny role again, film producers reminded him that it might be dangerous to change tack as audiences identified with him as the 'tough guy'. It is always difficult for actors to break the mould and most become known for one type of character. Few have the luxury of being able to pick and choose, and often if a leading man known for action thrillers tries his hand at playing a comedy lead, reviewers can be very unkind.

Perhaps Bill was his own worst enemy. He seemed so serious about what he did and, being such a perfectionist, sometimes his sense of humour was not much in evidence. His intense professionalism would not have readily suggested comedy to producers and directors (though many comedians are very single-minded about their work – Ken Dodd and the late Bob Monkhouse are just two examples of great experts on the theories of comedy). Not only did Bill look on the preparation for a part as vitally important, but he was also interested in the technique of acting and was fascinated by how this varied from one country to another. Chili Bouchier, who worked opposite him in *Murder in Reverse*, remembered Bill stating emphatically that he wanted to go to Russia. She was mystified by this as it was shortly after the war and the world was in turmoil. I suspect that my grandfather's reason was that Russia was the home of acting theory, famous for such people as Stanislavski. The biographical note about Bill in his fan club bulletins states that his ambition was 'to spend a considerable

JESSICA CARNEY

time in Hollywood and Russia'; but he was always thrilled that two of his films had gone down so well in France, as he was also a big fan of French film acting. The French have always had an understated style which relies less on action and effects and lays greater stress on what can be said with the eyes. Bill never hankered after more lines in any role – in fact he was known to cut speeches he felt were unnecessary. He was good at reacting and knew how important small details could be on the screen. For example, in *Brighton Rock* he used a toothpick (a very un-English habit, and one he had picked up in Canada, where they supplied them on the table) as a noticeable piece of business for his character. Great Hollywood actors such as Steve McQueen would later find that mannerisms such as playing with a baseball helped them create well-defined personalities. Much later, even during the shooting of *Doctor Who*, Bill would outline his views on acting technique to a chosen few.

One of the films from which Bill did cut lines was *The Ringer*, the 1953 directorial debut of Guy Hamilton, a protégé of Carol Reed to whom he had been assistant on *The Fallen Idol* and *The Third Man*. Some of the producers must have been listening to Bill's requests for a more light-hearted role because this film, adapted from Edgar Wallace's amusing thriller *The Gaunt Stranger*, marked his return to comedy on screen. The *Picturegoer* of 10th January 1953 even remarked that Bill had been cast against type as the 'comedy relief'. Bill's cockney burglar is employed by disreputable lawyer Herbert Lom as his butler-cum-minder, but does not succeed in protecting him from the notorious master of disguises, 'The Ringer', played by Donald Wolfit. The film, shot at Shepperton, also starred the beautiful Greta Gynt, with whom Bill had worked previously. The lines my grandfather wanted to take out occurred at the end when he is caught by a policeman. Bill believed the scene would be much more effective without stuttered explanations, and that his thoughts were self-evident.

The Ringer wasn't the only film where Bill asked the director to cut his lines. The *Sunday Graphic* even wrote on this in December 1952:

Cast as the detective inspector in the new George Cole comedy *Will Any Gentleman?* he took one look at the dialogue in his scene and said to the director 'I can convey all this in mime'.

The columnist approved of Bill's action and said he'd like to see much more speech-pruning à la Hartnell. He believed, as Bill did, that in many cases screen dialogue is an annotation of the obvious. Unfortunately, I think the policeman in *Will Any Gentleman?* is one of Bill's few misjudged performances, as he seems to be trying a little too hard to get humour out of an essential humourless role. But it was rare for him to do this.

*

Over the previous few years Bill had taken occasional theatre engagements. As 'a star' he was a draw in the provinces, and in January 1950 he did a 'special' week at the Royal County Theatre in Bedford, a charming little venue with a rococo plaster interior of which the town was very proud. The play was well known to him – he had appeared with Heather in *What Anne Brought Home* at Harrogate Rep during the war. He took the same role as before – the awkward young man whom the heroine, this time played by Rosemary Harris, brings home. She was a juvenile lead then and remembers that 'film stars' were viewed with some awe by the provincial Rep players, but that Bill proved to be very approachable and easy to work with. He was generally charming to actresses anyway. Twice nightly weekly Rep allowed very little time for rehearsal – less than twenty hours per show – and the actors tended to live on Dexadrine to stay awake. Although the work was hard – actors still had to provide their own clothes and were paid only about £7 per week – Rep actors often didn't leave one job unless they had another to go to because at least it presented a regular source of income. For this reason Rosemary Harris stayed for some while at Bedford before going on to make a name for herself. Later on that year Bill was himself to go back to the theatre for what turned out to be the longest run of his career.

In *Seagulls over Sorrento*, Bill took his hard-nosed sergeant persona on to the stage, this time in naval uniform. The play, by Hugh Hastings, was little concerned with seagulls and nothing to do with Sorrento, but was about a group of ratings who had volunteered for a dangerous experimental mission being carried out on a lonely rock in Scapa Flow. Bill's pleas had again been answered in that this was a comedy. However, he was to play the straight character, Petty Officer Herbert, the martinet who finally gets his comeuppance. The show had started out as a one-off Sunday-night performance mounted by 'The Repertory Players', a group of actors who rehearsed a new play and put it on for no money as a showcase, a precursor of today's fringe. It went down so well at the Comedy Theatre that there was instant enthusiasm from the well-known company H. M. Tennants for a full production. However, various delays meant that by the time the show was up and running there was only one member of the original Repertory Players group in it. That was Robert Desmond (Bobby), my father's cousin. Bobby and my father, Terry Carney, were almost like brothers as they had been brought up together.

During the time Bill and Bobby were working together on *Seagulls* my parents met. However, their meeting was not at the theatre and had absolutely no connection with the fact that their respective relatives were acting in the same production. My father had indeed visited Bobby at work but had never even bumped into my grandfather, let alone his daughter. If truth be known, after everything he'd heard about Bill he was rather apprehensive about meeting him. By some strange twist of fate, Terry first saw Anne in a pub in Horsham in Sussex, and once he managed to get chatting to her soon discovered that they had very close acquaintances in common.

The first cast of *Seagulls* included Bill's old friend from Richmond Rep days, David Langton, as the telegraphist, and Ronald Shiner, with whom Bill had already worked in several films, as Able Seaman 'Badger'. The person whom Bill perhaps had the most reason to feel uneasy about working with was Bernard Lee, the actor who had played the part of the sergeant in *The Third Man*, which Bill had turned down. If he did feel any envy, he didn't let it show. There were no women in the play, which was largely about the various private reasons each of the men had for being on the naval base. According to the *Tatler*, which gave it a full-page spread with thumbnail sketches, 'the ratings talk as sailors presumably do talk in the absence of women, mainly about women and rather freely. But it is excellent talk from a theatrical point of view – quarrelsome yet wonderfully good humoured, querulous yet chirpy, racy, sentimental and tough.' It went down well with the audiences (receiving ten curtain calls on the first night), and the *Tatler* also reported that: 'As the final curtain fell, applause, shooting rocket-like up to the roof, signalled a winner.' And it was, running at the Apollo Theatre in the West End for nearly four years, after the customary short pre-London try-out. It transferred to the Duchess Theatre for a while and was also taken to the Continent to entertain the troops stationed abroad. On Sunday 29th April 1951 the actors trooped out to Germany and gave a special performance for the US Seventh Army in Stuttgart, and later on in the run it was taken to the Suez Canal Zone (though Bill didn't go on this trip). There were several cast changes over the years, but both Bill and Bobby stayed with it the entire time, even going on the provincial tour after its stint in the West End.

Bill received universally good reviews, one saying: 'His performance is as immaculate as his jacket.' The *New Statesman and Nation* on 24th June 1950, while finding some of the characterisations a little broad, said:

> Mr Hartnell, as the petty officer, is, quite simply, perfection; his arrogant stance on the back of his heels, his assertive little back stiff as a stanchion, the hands coming up backwards on the hips, the devastating pause before the bark, these give him a fully documented history – the solid years of service in which he has learned his own methods of dealing with the recalcitrant.

As usual, Bill's careful preparation for the role paid off. It was, however, physically hard going doing such a long run, as he had to be knocked to the ground every night (when he got his 'comeuppance'), and although an actor learns how to do this without hurting themselves too much, Bill did manage to strain his back. There were also a lot of stairs to run up and down backstage. The doctor told him he had to rest, but Bill replied that simply wasn't possible, so he went to an osteopath, a practitioner then considered very 'alternative'. But it apparently did the trick.

Being a comedy, there was a certain amount of rivalry over who got the biggest laughs, resulting in a number of backstage arguments. Bill wasn't really involved in most of these jealousies because his character was so stern it wasn't an issue for him. But in 1952 he did have a row with Bobby Desmond over what started out as a ridiculously minor misunderstanding. Bobby had borrowed a dinner jacket from Bill to go to a 'do'. The next day, he went into Bill's dressing room to return the DJ and left it on a hanger. For some reason Bill was furious. The crux of the argument was that he felt Bobby should have done it up neatly in a parcel so he could carry it home; Bobby didn't see what was wrong with putting it on a hanger. In the end Bobby lost his temper as well, shouted something rude, stalked out of the dressing room and slammed the door. They didn't talk for six months, even though they went on stage together every night. Although previously Bobby had appreciated Bill's sense of humour and had generally got on well with him, the incident meant Bobby was banned from my parents' wedding – even though my father wanted him as his best man. The air was only cleared during an anniversary performance; something like the thousandth show, when Bobby went up to Bill and 'goosed' him (pinched him on the backside). They shook hands and neither of them said any more about it.

The actors often used to goose each other at the curtain call. Bill hated it, and was, therefore, the prime victim – he did laugh after a fashion when it happened, and so whoever did it felt they'd won a point. It was an achievement because it was almost impossible to 'corpse' Bill (deliberately make him laugh on stage – something that actors particularly try to do to each other during a long run when they are a little bored!). Bill, so serious about his work, thought it unprofessional to corpse. But he nearly did once. He had to say to Ronnie Shiner, as all the men were standing to attention in line: 'Well, it happens, Mr Jack Strop, I've forgotten it. Do you mind?' One night, of course, he did the classic thing and transposed the vowels in the words: 'Well, it happens, Mr Jock Strap, I've forgotten it. Do you mind?' Everybody on stage was shaking with hysterics, but Bill managed to carry on with only the merest shudder, and didn't miss a beat. In the four years of the show Bobby never saw him corpse or come out of character once.

On stage the other actors might not have had much fun with Bill, but offstage they liked to take the mickey. He always talked about food and took it very seriously. The others used to tease him because he would get so worked up about the idea of a good meal. They'd ask:

'What are you going to have for lunch on Sunday, Bill?'

'I'm having pork.'

'What are you going to do with it?'

'I'm going to put it in the oven and roast it. Pour myself a whisky, open the oven and baste it…'

Bill liked to think he was sophisticated about food, and in the generally competitive atmosphere between the men in the play he probably showed off his knowledge when they went out for lunch during rehearsals or after the show. Nigel Stock, who played 'Sprog', decided to invent a dish. He asked Bill if he had ever tried Tasmanian Duck.

'Tasmanian Duck?' Bill didn't like to be bested.

'Yeah,' continued Stock, 'in fact there's a restaurant near here where it's the speciality.'

Not wanting to be outdone, Bill went to the restaurant on his own and tried to order it, telling them all when he returned he'd had some wonderful Tasmanian Duck. Even though he had realised by then that they were sending him up, he was good humoured enough to keep up the joke.

He didn't mind being teased by the other actors, as he was receiving accolades for his performance from people within the industry, and that was what mattered. The following letter from Peter Cushing arrived after he had been to see the show:

> May I just send my most sincere congratulations on your *excellent* performance on Wednesday evening – it was an evening of joyous excitement – and your contribution to the general success was very great indeed. It was possible to see the P. O.'s mind working! Everything was so true and authentic. Thank you for another faultless performance and for a most unforgettable night in the theatre.

Although Bill fitted in a few film roles during this period, he stayed in the show for four years. A long-term commitment like that would be almost unheard of now, but perhaps he enjoyed the relative security of a regular salary: by 1953 he was earning £75 per week (ten per cent of which, of course, went to his agent, Al Parker). I'm sure Bill would have bowed out of the show had he needed to for a good enough film role. Perhaps Al Parker didn't bother promoting him once he was sure of a reasonable income from his client. Anyway, for whatever reason, at this point he left Al to go to Bill Watts' agency, where his son-in-law, Terry Carney, who had given up being an actor, was now working. Then, in 1954, when Terry went to join his old acquaintance Eric L'Epine Smith, who had once again set up as an agent, Bill moved with him and stayed there ever after, confident in the knowledge that his daughter's husband would give him the best attention possible.

*

My father by that time got on well with Bill, although he had been very nervous and in awe of him when they first met. Terry was at that time still an actor, and his parents had both been on the stage, so they had much in common; but Bill had a reputation for being prickly, and even Anne had a tendency to be wary of her father because of his impatience. Bill was, ironically enough, just as apprehensive about encountering his prospective son-in-law as Terry was about meeting him, especially as no one had much chance to get used to the idea. It had been rather a whirlwind romance: my parents remarkably decided to get married only a few days after meeting. When my father was first introduced to Bill the two of them stood on the veranda at Thames Ditton not knowing what to say to each other. Bill coughed and cleared his throat a lot as he did when he was agitated. Eventually the ice was broken and they got on well – with a few lapses. During my parents' engagement, at the time Bill was in *Seagulls* and before Terry had given up acting, my father found himself broke and out of work. Bill had been thinking of having the bungalow painted, so he asked my father if he wanted to do it. Terry started one morning and Bill went out for most of the day, returning home just before going in to do the show. Terry was by this time packing up for the day and had just got out of the bath. Bill came in and the exchange went something like this:

'What do you think you are doing? You haven't finished!'

'I realise that, but I'll finish it tomorrow.'

'Well, what are you going to do now?'

'Strangely enough, I'm going to see your daughter.'

'Why do you want to do that?'

'In case you've forgotten, we are engaged, and we've arranged to meet this evening.'

Bill was furious and began ranting and raving at my father who stuffed the paintbrush into his hand and shouted, 'Well, if you're so particular about it being finished now, you do it,' and then retreated into the garden. The window was flung open; out came the brush, the paint pots and a torrent of abuse. It ended with Bill and my father chasing round the garden like two little boys, spraying water at each other with the hosepipe.

Bill was, of course, very proud of his daughter Anne when she and Terry got married, which they did on 21st October 1952, at Caxton Hall, the smartest registry office in London at the time. The reception was held at the Mayflower Hotel in Cobham, Surrey, a few miles from Thames Ditton. Since my father wasn't allowed to have Bobby Desmond with him, Leslie Phillips was best man. As there were so many theatre people invited, by early evening several of them, including Bill, had to leave to do their respective shows. The marriage featured in the papers, partly owing to the fact that Bill was starring in the West End, and partly because of the link being made between two acting families.

Shortly after the wedding, when my parents were living in a basement flat in Notting Hill Gate, west London, Heather and Bill went round for Sunday lunch. While the women prepared the food, Bill and Terry popped out to have a drink at the little theatre club just round the corner called the New Lindsay Club. Meeting up with a few people they knew, they each had half a pint of Merrydown special strong cider, which they had noticed was on sale. Then they had another half-pint, then, despite the warning of the bartender, another, and so on. Finally they set off for home, about an hour and a half late. As soon as the cool air hit them, their legs turned to jelly and, giggling helplessly, they had to clutch the railings to help themselves along. When they eventually arrived, they were met with stony silence because the food was ruined and they were in such a terrible state. Lunch was started, and soon Anne and Heather were giggling themselves as the two men looked so ridiculous – they couldn't even find their mouths with their forks. Both Bill and Terry fell fast asleep and woke with the most terrible hangovers: my father never drank cider again for the rest of his life.

*

Among the films Bill made during the run of *Seagulls* was *The Magic Box*. Like almost everyone else in the business he had a little cameo in the biographical history of William Friese-Greene who, although he invented the movie camera, died unrecognised and penniless. It was the film industry's offering for the Festival of Britain, with Robert Donat playing Friese-Greene, and so many famous people in it, including Richard Attenborough, Robert Beatty, Joyce Grenfell, Sybil Thorndike and Laurence Olivier, that they all agreed to alphabetical billing. Bill's contribution was one of the sergeant roles which were becoming so typical.

He played another soldier – this time a company sergeant major with a wonderfully twizzly moustache – in *The Holly and the Ivy*, an illustriously cast film with Ralph Richardson as a widowed reverend who gathers his family about him at Christmas. His children, played by Celia Johnson,

Margaret Leighton and Denholm Elliott, have not turned out quite as he expected and a complicated family drama ensues.

As both these parts were small, Bill was able to shoot the films during the day and appear in the show at night, but his little role in *The Pickwick Papers* was shot during a brief holiday from the play. The Dickens story was turned into a wonderful movie full of brilliant British character actors, and it happened to be shooting in Sussex, where Bill was going for a week's break. According to the *Evening News*, the telephone rang a short while before he was due to go away, and he was offered the role of the cabman with whom Mr Pickwick has an argument, so five days of his holiday were spent in front of the cameras – a 'cabman's holiday', as the newspaper called it.

After finishing in *Seagulls over Sorrento*, Bill made five more films before his next major theatre commitment. *Footsteps in the Fog*, in which he played an inept blackmailer, was a costume drama starring Jean Simmons and Stewart Granger, but in *Josephine and Men*, another Boulting Brothers production, he was again playing the police inspector. *Doublecross*, which was shot under the title *Queer Fish*, a comedy thriller about Soviet spies trying to get across the Channel, was filmed in Fowey, on the coast in Cornwall. The film unit virtually took over the village and the harbour, as much of the action took place at sea. The coxswain from the local lifeboat was at the helm of the converted fishing boat which they had been lent, and the local cinema was used to look at the rushes every evening. Most of the villagers seemed to want to get involved and many were used in crowd scenes, but at other times they were so enthusiastic that they had to be kept back to give the crew enough space to shoot in the narrow high street. The actor Kenneth Cope had a small part in it as a customs official – there was smuggling going on – and he remembers arriving at a very old beamed hotel with a reception area on the first floor. The room had a dado rail all around it, and a large wooden panel with a number of bells in it. All the actors were sitting there with scripts waiting to do a read-through and, having travelled some way to get there, they were hungry and thirsty. One of them pressed a bell to call for service as they wanted tea and sandwiches. Nothing happened. They were chatting and it was mentioned that Dickens had stayed there. Someone pressed another bell. Still no one appeared. Eventually my grandfather lost his

patience and started pressing every bell, shouting 'I'll give them f******
Dickens' at the top of his voice. This seemed to do the trick.

In March 1956 Bill appeared in another Boulting Brothers picture. This
was the highly successful comedy *Private's Progress*, which again reunited
Bill with his old sparring partner Dickie Attenborough. The film is set
during World War II and centres around Ian Carmichael's bumbling
undergraduate who, called up for the army, gets accidentally involved in
all sorts of disreputable schemes, which he pulls off more by luck than
judgement. Bill played the strait-laced sergeant out to get the scoundrel
Cox (Attenborough), who manages to be at the bottom of every scam.
Attenborough gave a photo to Bill of the two of them, signed: 'Why are
you always so unkind to me, Bill? Maybe someday I'll have the stripes.' Ian
Carmichael said that it was the most convincing performance of an NCO
he had ever seen: 'Bill really was that sergeant, not an actor playing a
sergeant.'

Ever since Bill's amusing role in *The Ringer* in 1952, he had again been
featuring in comedies, though not always in a humorous role. The same
month that *Private's Progress* was released, he appeared in *Tons of Trouble*,
a real old-fashioned farce, with Richard Hearne in his familiar silly 'Mr
Pastry' role. Over the next few years Bill was to appear in several films
with some of the major comedians of the time, such as Brian Rix and Peter
Sellers. But as in *Private's Progress*, he was to find that directors usually
relied on him to provide a straight foil for the lead comedy actors.

*

While Bill was still in *Seagulls over Sorrento*, Heather had also gone back
to the theatre: in 1953 she spent some time in rep at the Oxford Playhouse.
Having grown up in Oxford and having worked there before, she knew the
place well, but now her brother Malcolm was the business manager, she
had even more reason to enjoy being at the theatre. When she returned
home to Thames Ditton she and Bill kept themselves busy during the day
with various projects: as well as their writing, they both liked the idea of
producing and directing. Bill had already organised shows during the war,
but at the beginning of 1954 the two of them mounted a production of
Ben Travers' *Rookery Nook* for the Elizabethan Players in aid of the
National Society for Cancer Relief. They became involved because Bill had
met Rodney Burmester, a leading light of the amateur company, in 1943

while doing a comedy turn for the navy. *Rookery Nook* took place in Sutton Public Hall and Ben Travers himself wrote a programme note wishing them every success. The production was reviewed in the local *Surrey Comet* under the headline 'Star produced amateur show – but could not see it', because Bill was of course on stage in *Seagulls.*

In 1954 Heather returned to do a few shows at Richmond Rep. In her spare time, she had completed a full-length play of her own called *Treble Trouble*, and the following year a production of it was mounted at Richmond Theatre by Alan Miles and Frederick Piffard. The play was a comedy about a working-class cockney family who think they have won the pools but discover in the end that it was all a mistake: not a very original storyline, and full of twists and turns, but *The Stage* said that 'taken by and large it is very amusing and the raciness of the dialogue more than makes up for any deficiency in the plot'. The *Surrey Comet* found it 'homely fun', but thought it was marred by overstatement of the plot facts. By now *Seagulls over Sorrento* had finished its tour and so Bill was able to play the father of the family, George Knowles, while June Ellis played the mother. Heather took the smallish role of the tart *without* a heart. It was twenty years since they had played opposite each other as juvenile leads in Arthur Rees' repertory seasons at Richmond, and Bill was quite nervous at appearing in his own wife's play. June Ellis remembers being apprehensive at the thought of doing a show with both the author and her husband in the cast, and because of his reputation thought Bill might be a bit touchy, but in fact he was charming and everyone was very happy working together on it.

Heather was thrilled to get something produced, but had no illusions about her writing. In an interview for the local paper she said she didn't really believe her 'little play' was going to happen until she saw the printed playbills for it. There was huge excitement backstage one evening when the cast heard that a West End management had been in to see the show. Despite the lukewarm reviews, it went down well with the audiences – so well in fact that the management decided to remount it a short while later and take it into the Garrick Theatre. The play was revised – a new character appeared – and was given a new title, *Home and Away*. By then only two of the original cast were free to go with it to the Garrick – Sheila Eves and Margaret St Barbe West. June Ellis was doing a television role and so Irene Handl played her part; Bill was busy on a film, and Heather thought it best not to do the West End run. Unfortunately, the show did not go down well this time and lasted a very short while. Nevertheless, the play was published and was later produced at Windsor Rep. Heather also sold the rights to a production company and it was made into a film by George Maynard for Conquest Productions. Directed by Vernon Sewell, it starred Jack Warner and Kathleen Harrison, Charles Victor and Thora Hird. It was subsequently even shown on television.

At the beginning of 1956 Bill took another role in the theatre, this time in the comedy *Ring for Catty*, which toured before going into the Lyric Theatre in Shaftesbury Avenue, at the heart of London's West End. He co-starred with Patrick McGoohan (who went on to become famous in the sixties in *Danger Man* and *The Prisoner*) in this play by Patrick Cargill and Jack Beale which was set in a TB sanatorium. Bill played a bad-tempered miner and McGoohan an ill-fated ex-bank manager. Terence Alexander, whom Bill had met up at Harrogate, also played a leading role, and he later remembered that there was not a great deal of love lost between the two stars, neither of whom were particularly easy-going. The show was the first production for Michael Codron, who for more than fifty years has been one of London's most successful producers.

*

Because of these theatre commitments, it was a year after *Tons of Trouble* before Bill's next film came out. *Yangtse Incident*, directed by Michael Anderson who had directed *The Dam Busters*, was the true story of the HMS *Amethyst*, which sailed up the Yangtse River during the Chinese civil war in 1949 to take supplies to the capital and relieve another British boat, the *Consort*. The Chinese government had given permission for the journey, but no one thought to consult the People's Liberation Army, and halfway up the river the *Amethyst* was fired upon from the bank. Several vital personnel, including the captain, were mortally wounded and the ship ran aground. The assistant naval attaché at the British Embassy in Nanking, Lieutenant-Commander John S. Kerans, who became naval advisor on the film, was sent to take command on the ship. After protracted negotiations with the People's Army failed, he decided to make a break for it and had to run the gauntlet of the communist batteries, while trying to navigate one of the most dangerous waterways in the world without a pilot. The production was made with almost documentary realism, using the HMS *Amethyst* herself, which was rescued from the scrapyard. This meant they were able to blow holes in her and dismantle parts to allow them to film vital scenes *in situ*. Cameras were still bulky then, and the problems of lighting the action sequences made for difficult shooting conditions; at one point a camera was mounted on a pair of roller skates to get a tracking shot, as no other equipment could be fitted into the available space.

Despite the problems everyone involved was filled with enthusiasm, although the actor Ian Bannen remembered Bill complaining bitterly at the time about the facilities for the actors, both on the shore and on the ship. They would spend long hours in the cold, rough sea. Bill's complaints did achieve some results, as Bannen remembered that the shore quarters were improved. But overall my grandfather certainly enjoyed making the picture: he kept a scrapbook of photos and details of the production, proud to have been involved in recreating such an heroic event. He always admired other people's bravery greatly.

Made in the tradition of the true British war picture (but more than ten years after the war had finished) the film was received, in general, very well, although a few of the critics, while praising the production values, wondered if we had had enough of the 'stiff upper lip' type of drama. Although Richard Todd was the star, once again Bill garnered much of the praise. Molly Hobman said in the *Evening Advertiser*:

> Where would British films be without the Royal Navy and Mr William Hartnell? The admirable film about the HMS *Amethyst*, *Yangtse Incident*, which opened in London last week, proved again that our producers can hardly go wrong with a sea story and that Mr Hartnell never goes wrong with a part. He is a great unsinkable of British pictures though for some reason no one ever seems to have thought of giving him the star part. In this film he is a leading seaman and gives one of those unforced, modest yet memorable performances such as one has seen in at least a score of pictures and often on stage.

In *Yangtse Incident* Bill, as Leading Seaman Frank, had a similar role as less than an officer but more than just one of the men: that in-between rank he played so often. Although his was essentially a straight part, Bill managed to provide light relief without ever overdoing it. Fred Majdalany, one of the few critics not over-thrilled with this type of film, wrote in *Time and Tide*: 'The humour is less forced than usual thanks largely to the pleasing domination of that department by William Hartnell.' There are some amusing scenes when Leading Seaman Frank is dressed in officers' uniform to accompany Lieutenant-Commander Kerans on his negotiating missions, which lays him open to much ribbing from fellow sailors. The reviewer Kathleen Rowland said of *Yangtse Incident*: 'We get glimpses of the Navy's sardonic humour (mainly exemplified without a word by the expressive eyebrows of William Hartnell, back on the lower deck).' There is perhaps no film which shows off his timing and the subtlety of his wry humour better than this one.

The picture opened with a grand premiere attended by His Royal Highness the Duke of Edinburgh, the Earl Mountbatten and many other important guests. It is the one premiere which I attended – although I was minus two months old at the time! Bill believed in the film so much that he made many personal appearances when it opened around the country. The family thought it was his best screen performance ever.

Chapter Ten
TELEVISION BEGINS TO TAKE OVER

IN THE EARLY FIFTIES Bill occasionally featured on the radio: Act 1 of *Seagulls over Sorrento* was broadcast live from the theatre one night, and in November 1953 he could be heard as Flight Sergeant Slingsby in *The Sea Shall Not Have Them*, a radio play by Gilbert Thomas. Television was still in its infancy and was not yet even broadcast throughout the day, but its popularity grew quickly. In November 1955 Bill appeared in his first TV programme, called *The Inward Eye*, playing a sympathetic role as a guide dog trainer. He was a natural for television with his contained, unstagey performances. Then, from January 1957, when he was asked to be a guest on a lunchtime programme, he was to be seen regularly on the small screen.

For several years his time was divided between filming at various film studios and recording his next television show. Bill was not able to fight his image as the tough sergeant figure which had begun with *The Way Ahead*. He had taken it on stage with *Seagulls over Sorrento* and now he was to take it into the new, popular medium in what was conceivably the first TV sitcom, *The Army Game*. Made by Granada, it was first shown on 19th June 1957, less than two years after the inception of commercial television. It concerned life in a forgotten army camp at Nether Hopping – not the most original idea, as the imported *Phil Silvers Show*, about a US army base, could be seen on the BBC, and *Private's Progress* and other films had already ridiculed the armed forces; but so many men had recently experienced life in the army there seemed to be an insatiable appetite for such material. Unlike the American *Phil Silvers Show*, this was

British through and through, with many old comedy stereotypes. Bill played Sergeant-Major Bullimore, Geoffrey Sumner the bumbling major who is more interested in his pigs, and well-known comics featured as privates, including Bernard Bresslaw as 'Popeye' Popplewell, Charles Hawtrey as 'Professor' Hatchett, and Alfie Bass as 'Excused Boots' Brisley. Michael Medwin played the 'wide boy' Corporal Springer, and Norman Rossington Private 'Cupcake' Cook. The show went out live at 8.30 p.m. on a Wednesday evening, initially once fortnightly. The actors rehearsed it in London and then went up to Manchester (where the regional television company was based) for the studio recording. Not everyone had televisions then, but *The Army Game* was screened in most pubs – even Heather used to watch the show at her local as my grandparents didn't buy a television set until the end of 1958.

Given how few television sets there were it was a huge success, and six months after its initial episode it was turned into a once-weekly programme, broadcast on a Friday night at 8.30 p.m. By the beginning of 1958 it had an estimated audience of six million. Recording was subsequently transferred to London, to the Chelsea Palace on the King's Road in Chelsea, an old music hall which has since been pulled down, with rehearsals for each episode starting on a Tuesday in a Presbyterian church hall. It was transmitted live. This meant that the director would have most of the shots pre-planned and would mix from one camera to another while the show was actually being recorded. Nowadays in television all editing takes place after filming and therefore the actors need to be word perfect and to say exactly the same lines in every take so that there is consistency when scenes are cut from one shot to another. Then, however, with largely static cameras, the director had a certain amount of freedom to ad-lib shots during the filming – if he was good enough, that is. Director Milo Lewis was brilliant at it. He could make the best of anything that happened spontaneously, and in the same way cover up a problem. The *Army Game* cast were experienced theatre actors, and were so skilled at comedy that at the read-through they had a tendency to rewrite the lines, which initially annoyed the scriptwriters. But because the show was such a hit, and the producers saw how well the actors worked together, they got away with their 'improvements'. And Milo Lewis could always make last-minute adjustments work.

JESSICA CARNEY

Bill was particularly brilliant at ad-libbing. One day in a producers' run-through (before the shoot) the men were all standing to attention on parade and Bill was inspecting them, walking down the line barking, 'Polish those buttons', 'Clean those shoes', when one of the men broke wind. Quick as a flash Bill retorted, 'And get that seen to!'

Norman Rossington, who recounted the story, remembered Bill as very wound up and tense, which was great for his performance but meant he could be a bit of a sergeant off-screen as well. As when doing *Seagulls over Sorrento*, he would pontificate about food – particularly on the train up to Manchester over a British Rail meal – and he was as fussy as ever about clothes. He noticed the way other people dressed, and couldn't understand that clothes simply weren't as important to some people as they were to him. In the early days of the show Rossington was broke and used to wear an old duffel coat. Bill kept saying to him, 'Why don't you get yourself a decent coat?' Rossington simply couldn't afford one at the time. Harry Fowler was another actor who joined the *Army Game* team as a regular; he and Bill had encountered each other several times in films over the years. He enjoyed having a drink with Bill and remembered that although he was chirpy and liked to tell a joke, he never had a devil-may-care attitude about his work and always seemed to be looking over his shoulder, worried about giving a good performance. They enjoyed a bet on the horses together, with Bill frequently having a 'hot' tip and always reminding Harry, 'Don't tell the wife' – rather pointless as Heather was certainly aware of his gambling, although I don't suppose she knew exactly how much he spent.

The producer, Peter Eton, claimed that they had a lot of help from the War Office who made no attempt to censure any of the silly antics and provided them with all sorts of equipment, which was just as well because the production team had to be accurate, otherwise they were flooded with letters from ex-servicemen. One episode in which Bill wore a belt while attending a court martial prompted letters complaining that all belts would have been removed at courts martial. The producer replied that they knew this, 'but Hartnell had to appear in the next scene wearing a belt and there was not time to change'. Such were the problems of live television.

Because the show was incredibly popular and regularly near the top of the ratings list, it featured frequently in the *Radio Times* and other magazines. When Bill got bitten by a horsefly less than six weeks after the start of *The Army Game*, and had to have a few weeks off because he developed blood poisoning, almost every paper carried the story. It was possibly the most highly publicised horsefly bite ever. The poisoning in some way aggravated an old problem he had with his eyes, which flared up several times over the next couple of years. It is possible that this problem was originally caused when his eyes were strained while making an early film: he had to keep looking at a large arc lamp, and although he asked for the scene to be lit in some other way, this was not an option. It was like looking at the sun and he suffered temporary blindness afterwards. It was not that his eyesight was bad – he only wore glasses for reading at quite a late stage – but it did seem to be a weak point and in 1960 he actually had an operation on his eye.

Bill stayed in the show for one year, though he was not in it every week. Then he recorded several episodes of *Dial 999*, a detective series starring Robert Beatty as a police inspector and Bill as a crook, for producer Harry Alan Towers. He also recorded *Take Your Pick* and a Christmas special called *Santa for Christmas*. Extremely busy during the late fifties, he went from film to television show to film, and there were also press calls and first nights, visits to doctors for film insurers, costume fittings, and always a few meetings with film directors about projects that didn't work out.

*

Heather and Bill moved from Thames Ditton to Brighton, on the Sussex coast, in the summer of 1955. They had enjoyed living on the island, but the bungalow was small, and they also liked the area around Brighton, where they had many friends, including the actress Anita Sharp-Bolster and the American writer Winifred Wolfe. Brighton was only an hour from London on the train, and the service ran until late so that actors could always get back after a show. This meant that Heather and Bill could still see plays in town; they always kept up with the latest productions, including the seminal *Look Back in Anger*, which marked the beginning of a new style in playwriting. Their flat in Chichester Terrace was on the first floor in a terrace of Regency houses, with large airy rooms overlooking the sea. Unfortunately, they discovered that a dipsomaniac lived on the ground floor, and when drunk she used to make a nuisance of herself trying to get into the flat to see Bill. Her husband sometimes used to phone up making terrible threats as well, and Bill became alarmed. They caused such terrible scenes that on one occasion Bill and Heather had to resort to calling the police. Eventually they couldn't stand it any more, and by the end of 1956 they were spending most of their time at a place in Cambridge Road.

Once in Brighton, Heather worked a few more times at the Richmond Theatre, but after this she took no more acting work. As Bill was so busy she was the one who ran around looking for somewhere else for them to live. Because of their bad experience in Brighton, they wanted a cottage in the country which would give them more privacy and also a garden (Chichester Terrace only had communal gardens) as they now had a new dog called Stumpy – a Staffordshire bull terrier with a broken tail which they adored. In March 1957 they moved to 'Greenacres' in Ditchling, a few miles north of Brighton.

They didn't own a car at this point and, no longer being in the centre of a town, Bill found it difficult to get to the local pub, where he liked to go on the evenings he wasn't working. So he purchased a motor scooter. Initially it seemed perfect for going up to the local, but he hadn't anticipated the effect of several whiskies on his navigation skills. After falling off the scooter into the ditch several times on his way home, he decided it wasn't such a good idea after all and the machine was sold just over a year later.

In the middle of all this Bill became a grandfather for the first time, and there were photos in all the papers of the 'flint-hearted' sergeant-major in 'civvies' holding me (looking podgy and uncertain) aloft. He liked to remind the public that he had a sense of humour and wasn't really the gruff, hard-nosed character of the series. In one double-page article with pictures of him relaxing at home he said how unlike the roles he played he was in real life – his hobbies were such gentle pursuits as fishing, gardening and bird watching. (Perhaps horse racing and pub crawling had slipped his mind.) The interviewer, Dick Francis, was taken for a walk round the garden and introduced to Mr and Mrs S, the pair of moorhens who lived on the pond, and shown where the field mice lived. But Bill did also mention that at times it could be hard not to bring the character he was playing into his private life, and that Heather had told him off for bringing Petty Officer Herbert (in *Seagulls*) and Sergeant-Major Bullimore home with him.

The lease on 'Greenacres' was a short one, so they were soon looking for somewhere else. About nine months later they moved not far away to Dymocks End, with Heather having to deal with all the clearing up and organising. Yet again this was only a temporary home, and in the next year they moved three more times. Heather must have spent her whole time packing and unpacking as Bill was often away filming. But they wanted somewhere they liked enough to buy. In spring 1959 Heather finally found a lovely cottage in Mayfield. It needed some renovation, but Bill saw it a few days later and liked it as well. They decided to purchase it and had some work carried out before they moved in. Old Mill Cottage is the place of which I have such vivid memories – the beamed interior and low ceilings, the wonderful landscaped garden with a stream running through it, all surrounded by woods and fields. They needed a car there as it was some way from the village, and about eight miles from Tunbridge Wells, the nearest town. They bought a blue Hillman, and Heather passed her driving test shortly after moving into the cottage. Every so often I stayed with my grandparents as my mother was by now busy with my new baby brother. Most of my time was spent with Heather, however, because Bill was working so hard and at this point I was too small to be of much interest to him. When he was at home he would often go off with a friend fishing, or take a trip to the races, in order to relax completely.

*

Of the films Bill made during the productive period just after *Yangtse Incident*, the best was probably *Hell Drivers* – one of three pictures released the month after I was born in which he played a leading role. For once he did not have to wear a uniform, but he did play another ruthless character: the manager of a haulage firm who is cooking the books with Patrick McGoohan, the company's top driver. McGoohan, as Red, does not like being challenged by Tom Yateley (Stanley Baker), the new employee; and the film depicts the rivalry between the two men, involving a great deal of stunt driving as they battle it out for supremacy in their vehicles. Bill meets a sticky end with Patrick McGoohan as the two of them are forced off the road. The critics likened the picture to *The Wages of Fear* and praised it for the 'gritty' excitement of the lorry chases.

The other two films which came out in July 1957 were very much second features. In *The Hypnotist* Bill played his familiar policeman role in a story about, not surprisingly, hypnotism and murder, while in *Date with Disaster* (initially called *The Vice*) he played a self-assured and experienced safe-breaker brought in to teach the ropes to a couple of novices. Ironically, while being questioned by the police at the end, he is the one who gives the game away by making a stupid mistake – trying to light a broken drill bit instead of a cigarette! Bill's next film, *On the Run*, came out nearly a year later. The story of a young boxer trying to avoid a gang who are after him for refusing to throw a fight, it was also a second feature. A review of the film began: 'It is a change to see William Hartnell as a big-hearted fellow rather than a crook, a sergeant-major or a policeman. Certainly he gets around with his parts, but it's not very often that we get the chance to see him domesticated.' My grandfather played a garage owner for whom the boxer goes to work, and whose daughter he falls in love with. I'm sure Bill enjoyed the change of image as well, even if the film wasn't top notch.

Perhaps the culmination of all Bill's roles as hard NCOs was Sergeant Grimshaw in the very first 'Carry On' movie, *Carry On Sergeant*, which was released in 1958. The idea was not terribly original, given that the story, about a tough sergeant with a useless bunch of recruits, was uncannily like the outline of *The Way Ahead*, with a bit of *The Army Game* thrown in. The film even managed to sign up some of those who had appeared in *The Army Game*, such as Bill, Norman Rossington and Charles Hawtrey – the latter sometimes used to spend the weekend with my grandparents since he and Bill had become quite friendly. Hawtrey was one of those in the hapless bunch of recruits who ended up as stalwarts of the 'Carry On' team – others were Kenneth Williams, Kenneth Connor and Hattie Jacques – but Bill's main adversary was played by Bob Monkhouse. Bob was at that time twenty-nine and one of television's new comedy stars – and very ambitious with it. He had been invited to play juvenile lead and he tried his hardest to get top billing. But of course that had been promised to my grandfather, who was by far the most experienced performer. Bob takes up the story himself:

> I argued and reasoned and blustered to get my name above the much more experienced and recognisable player but to no good effect. To some bad effect, however. Bill Hartnell had been informed of my demand and didn't like my uppishness one bit. From the first day of filming he made it quite clear that he had it in for me. During the rehearsal scenes together he

would pause after I spoke my lines, shake his head a little in mild disbelief, sigh, and look at director Gerald Thomas with a bleak air of expectation. Gerry would feel obliged to ask me to do something else with the words, to add more reality or speak faster or slower. I don't think Gerry knew what Bill was finding wrong with my efforts but he just had to respond somehow to the implicit disapproval from such a seasoned actor.

Monkhouse tried to get into Bill's good books by fetching him cups of tea (which were often refused or accepted with bad grace); he told anecdotes, and plagued Bill with questions about his film roles – all of which were rebuffed with comments such as, 'it was too long ago… it was a lousy picture… a rotten part,' or whatever. Bob earned Bill's further contempt by being unable to perform some of the basic exercises during training at the army camp, sequences shot in the paddock behind Pinewood Studios. His arms wouldn't support his weight when he had to swing on a rope over a mud hole. He fell into the mud three times in a row; each time he was hosed down and had to try again. This was the only thing he did which succeeded in making Bill laugh. He never managed the exercise and was the only member of the troop absent from that scene. Finally, he gave up trying to make friends with Bill.

Then, sadly, Bob's father died and he asked for a day off. The crew continued shooting scenes which didn't involve him, and he returned the following day, feeling mournful and not wanting to talk to anyone between shots. At lunchtime he sat on his own in a corner of the bar, staring into a whisky. He had just downed it when a hand placed another glass of Scotch on the table in front of him. He looked up to see Bill.

'Do you mind if I join you? I hear you lost your dad. Were you very close to him? No? What went wrong then?'

Bob found himself pouring out the story of his estrangement from his parents caused by his marriage eight years earlier. Bill encouraged him to tell him everything: how his mother had disowned him and how she influenced his father into doing the same, and his misery at never having achieved reconciliation before his father's death. This affected Bill and he put a comforting hand on Bob's arm a couple of times.

What Monkhouse didn't realise, of course, was just how much Bill understood the hurt of being estranged from a father – not that Bill even knew who his father was. By the time the story was finished, there was no time for lunch. Bob apologised:

'I'm so sorry, Bill. I couldn't eat anyway, but I've made you miss your meal.'

'No one makes me do anything, son. Listen to me for a moment. Your mum and dad were sadly mistaken when they cut you out of their lives. As a result, they've missed a lot of joy and pride in what you have achieved. Right now you're feeling sorry for yourself but you shouldn't. The sorrow you should be feeling is for your dad and what he lost, what he had to do without for the past eight years. Think fondly of him, poor chap, because he got it wrong. But think of this too – I'll bet that man's quietly followed every step of your career and silently cheered you on. Now… let's see if this bloody film is good enough to make your mum so thrilled with you she'll come round at last.'

Bob thanked him.

'No, don't do that. I don't want thanks. I don't do anything to be thanked. Tell you what I want. A letter from you one day, telling me you've made it up with your mum. I'd like that.'

Bob apparently wrote that letter to Bill in 1968. On a professional level, Bill was fiercely competitive, but on a personal level he could be warm and generous.

Peter Rogers, the producer of *Carry On Sergeant*, remembered that Bill needed 'handling with kid gloves' and was 'a man who appreciated a please and a thank you'; but, provided he was treated properly, he was always amiable and in no way obstructive. Rogers thought he viewed some of the comics on the team with a 'tolerant objectivity', but was utterly professional. They all had to be very professional because the film was shot extremely quickly. Gerry Thomas filmed it in six weeks; the actors simply rehearsed to camera and, according to Norman Rossington, they were lucky if they even got two takes. Anyway, the comedy was so successful that it spawned the whole succession of 'Carry On' films.

Bill did appreciate politeness, and usually returned it with equal consideration. He took a liking to his costume in *Carry On Sergeant*, and asked if he could keep it. The costume designer, Joan Ellacott, managed to persuade Bermans, the theatrical costumiers, to let him have it – apparently he said he could use it to garden in – and Bill sent her a charming letter of thanks saying that he thought actors on the whole could be a rude bunch, but he, on the other hand, never forgot a kindness. At times he was somewhat disparaging of other actors.

In his next film Bill was to work with an actor he did, however, admire hugely: James Cagney, to whom he had been occasionally likened by reviewers. Cagney was small and tough and had also started out as a comedy song-and-dance man (though Cagney was much more of a 'hoofer' than Bill was) and had ended up often playing crooks. In *Shake Hands with the Devil*, Cagney played an Irish professor who is involved in the country's armed struggle. The film had a big budget, American stars – Cagney, Don Murray, Dana Wynter – as well as big British names – Michael Redgrave, Dame Sybil Thorndike – and a wealth of Irish talent, including Cyril Cusack and others from the Abbey Theatre. Bill, as a sergeant, only had a small role, but ended up also helping Don Murray with his cockney accent. Directed by Michael Anderson, who made *Yangtse Incident*, it was the first major film to be made in the new Ardmore Studios at Bray, near Dublin. A contemporary article asked whether this was the start of a renaissance for Irish film making, though even with such a controversial subject as the IRA the movie doesn't seem to have been a huge success. The studios did, however, certainly become important for the Irish industry.

After working with his hero, Cagney, Bill next appeared with the comic genius Peter Sellers in *The Mouse that Roared*. Like many great comedians, Peter Sellers revelled in creating different characters, and having the lead play more than one role in a film is a familiar device, as in *The Goose Steps Out* (Will Hay), *Kind Hearts and Coronets* (Alec Guinness) and *Doctor Strangelove* (Peter Sellers again). In *The Mouse that Roared* Sellers played a role in drag, as Grand Duchess Gloriana, as well as the prime minister of the Duchy of Fenwick, which finds itself on the verge of bankruptcy. He decides to declare war on America, believing that the duchy will be given vast sums of money in reparations when they lose. Unfortunately, the man put in charge of the war effort (played by Sellers again) doesn't realise he is supposed to lose and, aided by Bill as the chain-mailed leader of the army, he brings the US to its knees. It is not one of Bill's best performances, and I cannot imagine Bill and Peter Sellers getting on particularly well; but there must have been some mutual respect, because he appeared again with Sellers a few years later in *Heavens Above!*, one of Bill's last films.

My grandfather's next film also involved the lead playing a double role. In *The Night We Dropped a Clanger* Bill worked with Brian Rix (later Sir Brian) who was known for his classic farces at the Whitehall Theatre as well as his comedy work on the screen. The storyline of *The Night We Dropped a Clanger* was remarkably like that of *The Goose Steps Out* (in which Bill had a small role in the forties): both films involved a lookalike being sent on a mission to Germany to track down information on the flying bomb, each succeeding despite his compete ineptitude. Bill as usual played the tough, barking company sergeant. A year or so later he appeared in another Brian Rix farce, *And the Same to You*, which featured other well-known comics such as Tommy Cooper and Sidney James. Brian Rix played Dickie Dreadnought, a vicar's nephew who becomes a prizefighter, trying to raise money for the church roof. Bill had fun playing his uncouth promoter, who dresses up in religious garb to fool the archdeacon.

Three other films which came out in 1959 and 1960 were very minor crime dramas. One, *Strictly Confidential*, from the same stable as *Date with Disaster*, with producer Guido Coen, writer Brock Williams and director Charles Saunders, was made at Twickenham Studios. In it Bill played the lead role as the manager of a factory which made indigestion tablets (Granny's Globules!). His roles in *The Desperate Man* and *Jackpot* were similar to others he had played: in the first he was a jewel thief and a murderer, the desperate man of the title, and the second yet another policeman. He was a victim of the typecasting resulting from the number of crime dramas churned out by the studios. Nothing seems to have changed. The industry is still obsessed with stories about policemen and detectives, with an unending stream of them on television even now. I'm sure Bill realised that many of these films weren't terribly good, but it was work and he knew many of the writers and directors of these films; they would phone him up, knowing they would get an instantly professional performance out of him. He did try, however, as in the following film, to inject a little something extra into the roles.

Piccadilly Third Stop, released in 1960, was made by Norman Williams, who knew Bill reasonably well. It was a quiet time at Pinewood Studios and the film was put together quickly as a follow-up to Williams' first picture, *The Shakedown*. When Bill got the script, which was about a playboy and his accomplice who hatch a plan to break into a safe in the office of an Eastern embassy, calling on the services of a retired safe-cracker (Bill's role) to help them, he went to the producer and asked if he could change the format of his character somewhat. He explained that he had heard a story about a gangster in the club business who, when he retired, disappeared completely from the scene and took up fishing. Apparently this character featured in the papers because he caught a particularly large fish, and the newspaper man sent to interview him asked what he used to do, to which he replied, 'I used to be a gangster.' Bill – so fond of fishing himself – fancied using the idea to give the 'role more depth', making the safe-cracker difficult to track down because he spends his time quietly fishing. He liked to give his characters a history.

*

On the first day of 1960 Bill appeared in an Australian/British television film called *The Flying Doctor*. Then in March he played the role of a merchant seaman in an episode of *Probation Officer* for ATV. He was in uniform again; but at least this was a sympathetic part, as a sailor who, fearing he is going blind, gets involved in a drunken brawl and ends up in court, hence the involvement with the probation officer. His next appearance on screen was in a Television Playhouse production called *No Home of Your Own*. This rehearsed from 2nd May and was recorded in Manchester on the 20th; eighteen days to rehearse and record a programme was a luxury after the tight schedule for *The Army Game*. It was a successful production and the following month he made another Television Playhouse, this time called *After the Party*. Bill seemed to be doing more television now than film, and in July he had discussions with Milo Lewis about going back into *The Army Game* for a season; he commenced work on this in September 1960 and carried on until its demise in the summer of 1961. Immediately that finished he started work at Beaconsfield on a TV film, *Ghost Squad*.

Bill then had a few quiet months. He spent a lot of time fishing at Newhaven and was probably feeling rather sorry for himself. In May 1961 he had been warned by his doctor that he really had to stop drinking so much. He wasn't an alcoholic, and no one I have spoken to who worked with him thought he drank any more than other actors, most of whom liked to unwind after a show, or a recording, in a bar. As someone who became intensely involved with his role, perhaps he needed the drink more than some to relax. But except for the odd nip he never drank while he was working and it never affected his performance. That he would have seen as completely unprofessional. But he did spend many of his evenings in the pub when he was 'resting'; and, although Heather would sometimes join him, she often took him up by car and left him there, and he would get a lift home. Bill didn't seem to know what to do with himself when he didn't have a job. If he was in London meeting his agent, Eric L'Epine Smith, for lunch, he would sometimes end up having several large gins and not eating. Occasionally he would try to drag Terry out for drinks in the evening, but with a young family my father was not keen to join him. Although Bill drank beer, he preferred gin and tonic or whisky, and it was beginning to affect his health. For a while after his doctor's warning, he took it easy, drinking only shandies and not coming back from the pub tight, but slowly he went back to his old habits.

He never became violent when drunk, though sometimes he would be bad tempered with Heather when he got home. Terry Carroll accompanied him on some of his regular drinking sessions, and they might drive for miles on a pub crawl, trying to find the 'right' pub, sometimes when they were both way over the limit. This was long before breath tests, however; the roads were quieter and the intensive publicity campaigns of later years hadn't yet drummed into everyone how unacceptable this behaviour was. Terry recalls:

> Bill would go into a pub half wanting to be recognised, but then when he was there he would say 'Oh God, I can't stay in this bar.' It is in fact possible to walk into somewhere and see flickers of recognition. If you ignore it, though, it doesn't impinge on your personal space. But Bill didn't deal with it like this – for him it was a real love-hate situation. He might go into a pub and the barman would say, 'Evenin', Sergeant!' and Bill would mutter profanities under his breath about *The Army Game*, and then say out loud, 'Oh, you've seen it, then?' Another habit of his was drinking after hours. He liked to go into a pub and drink half-pints, making them last a long time, often standing around being critical of everything. Towards the end of the evening he would get fidgety and start asking the landlord, 'Are you going to call time, then?', even before it was time to do so. Finally when the pub was closed and perhaps only the landlord, myself and Bill were left, he would say, 'Right now, we'll have double Scotches all round', and he would start the serious drinking, always being very generous.

Why he liked to drink this way I can only surmise. Perhaps it was partly the attraction of doing something slightly wicked, and partly because a pub after hours is more intimate and Bill liked to feel he had a personal relationship with the landlord. Of course, to begin with the landlord was usually thrilled to have someone famous in his bar, but after a time he would begin to feel tired while Bill, oblivious, would be getting rapidly more and more inebriated; he would often eventually have to be persuaded to leave. On the way home he would sometimes urge Terry to drive faster and faster, screaming with delight like a little boy, asking, 'How fast are we going now?' all the time. Terry didn't seem to put up much resistance to Bill in these situations. Luckily they never had an accident. Bill rarely drove himself to the pub as he knew he was unlikely to leave it in a fit state to drive.

As things were quiet workwise, Eric L'Epine Smith and my father were trying to find a stage play for him to do. There were several scripts he was sent which he didn't like, and then an abortive production for which he started rehearsing, but which didn't come to fruition. Then in late October 1961 he decided to do *The Cupboard* at the Arts Theatre, near Leicester Square. It opened on 15th November for a limited run until 9th December.

*   ⟿

For some reason television work for Bill dried up, and in 1962 he worked comparatively little, though by most actors' standards he had always worked pretty consistently. Perhaps he was simply too typecast from his *Army Game* role, or perhaps younger directors were shy of using him because of his reputation of being such a stickler. Only some people saw him in this way, as others I have spoken to say his attitude was never anything other than punctiliousness.

Things were not going too well on the domestic front, either. Because he had been so busy over the last few years, Heather had spent most of her time looking after him in the traditional sense, cooking his meals, running the home and taking him to and from the station at all hours. She had abandoned her own career, although she had continued writing a little and had directed a couple of shows for the local amateur dramatics society. If Bill had been having affairs during this time, he had kept quiet about it, and Heather seemed to be able to jog along, spending a considerable amount of time with her grandchildren. However, while she was in hospital in August, having an operation on her foot, Bill found himself a girlfriend in the village. He spent very little time at home over the next few months and Heather found proof of his infidelity. She was deeply hurt, as he had been lying about where he had been and now he could scarcely be bothered to hide his indiscretion. It also seemed worse because it was so close to home. She wrote in her diary that she would neither forgive nor forget about this, but somehow they managed to keep a semblance of home life.

Heather decided, however, that rather than run around after Bill all the time, she would try to resuscitate her career. She made several visits to London to meet directors, and eventually she was asked to do a TV role, starting rehearsals at the end of December. Unfortunately, the winter of 1962/63 was the worst for years, and Old Mill Cottage was off the beaten track. The first big freeze came at the beginning of December; and, by the time Heather had been asked to do the television show, they were cut off because of deep snow. They had no electricity for a while and transport came to a standstill because of snowdrifts. My grandparents could get to the shops only when the local farmer took Heather over the fields on a tractor. She gave up all hope of doing her TV role, and even the film Bill was due to start work on at the end of the year was postponed because travel was simply impossible. Snow lay that winter for two whole months.

Although he did no television in 1962, Bill did make three films during the year. The first was *This Sporting Life* for Karel Reisz and Lindsay Anderson, about an ex-miner who becomes a rugby star, and his relationship with the owner of the house in which he boards. Bill worked on this from the end of March right through till the end of May, though he was only required sporadically. For once he had a really good character part to play: Johnson, the rather pathetic old man who lives in a hostel, hangs about the rugby crowd and likes to think of himself as a bit of a talent scout. He was working with two stars, Richard Harris and Rachel Roberts, who were neither easy nor predictable, so there was no room for anyone else to be difficult. Karel Reisz wrote to Bill after shooting to say how much he had appreciated his patience 'under what must have been sometimes almost impossible circumstances. Many thanks indeed. We have now seen all the location material, and both Lindsay and I are delighted with Johnson, I hope you will be proud of him when you see the picture.' Lindsay Anderson said that Bill must have been aware that it was an ambitious film and also that his work in it was never exhibitionist. Bill 'understood very well the character of Johnson... so directing him was never difficult or complicated... there was eccentricity in his role in our film which was quite different from the sort of parts I had been used to seeing him play. To be honest, to me he was always a very good, very professional actor and a pleasure to work with.' Bill must have appreciated the producer and the director's faith in him, and the chance to play such a different role.

The film was a great success. It explored issues not usually dealt with by British movies. Penelope Gilliat's review for the *Observer* summed it up:

> Lindsay Anderson's *This Sporting Life* is a stupendous film. It has a blow like a fist. I've never seen an English picture that gives such expression to the violence and capacity for pain that there is in the English character. It is there in Shakespeare, in Marlowe, in Lawrence and in Orwell and Hogarth, but not in our cinema like this before.

It was also an important film for Bill.

Chapter Eleven

A TRUE ORIGINAL:
DOCTOR WHO TAKES OFF

BILL WAS VERY PROUD to have been cast in *This Sporting Life*, but after finishing it he had little work in the following months, apart from a few days filming on a mediocre thriller, *Tomorrow at Ten*. Then in the autumn of 1962 he made his second picture with Peter Sellers, *Heavens Above!*, for the Boulting Brothers; in it he played a bigoted major shocked by Sellers' unlikely liberal-minded vicar.

This Sporting Life was released in January 1963, and even though he gave a wonderful performance the offers did not exactly come pouring in. However, he did make two films in the early part of the year. *The World Ten Times Over* starred Sylvia Syms and June Ritchie. Syms plays an embittered nightclub hostess who is pregnant. Bill plays her father, a country teacher unaware of her lifestyle. When he comes to visit, she tries to shock him, taking him to the club where she works. He is an upright man who does not know how to reach his estranged daughter, and sadly they part unable to understand each other in any way. Sylvia Syms found Bill a very considerate actor to work with, which she appreciated because it was an emotional film to make. She was feeling fragile as she'd just had a baby, and was under a lot of stress with the film company pressuring her to lose weight quickly. She liked his direct and 'unprecious' style of acting and remembers that, although he was reserved, he did like to have a joke.

The next film, *To Have and to Hold*, in which Bill played a police inspector, was a story not unlike *Double Indemnity* with a police sergeant, played by Ray Barrett, falling in love with a woman who involves him in a plot to murder her husband. Unexceptional and undemanding in terms of acting, the picture was based on yet another thriller by Edgar Wallace. It was to be Bill's last film appearance.

My grandfather knew that his performance in *This Sporting Life* was good and he had hoped it would finally prove that he wasn't just 'the nasty little sergeant' in *The Army Game*. He hoped it had shown him as an actor of great depth and therefore worthy of parts other than endless NCOs and policemen. But he was not the only actor to be frustrated by the lack of good roles. His ambitions to play Shylock and Polonius would forever remain unfulfilled. However, he would get the chance to create a character for which people would remember him in the years to come. Someone at least had taken note of his performance as Johnson.

Verity Lambert was a young BBC producer brought in to assist Sydney Newman in the creation of a new science fiction series, aimed largely at children but made by the drama department. She thought that the quality of eccentricity evinced in *This Sporting Life*, together with the authority and toughness he had shown in other films, would be right for their enigmatic central character, a man who travelled through time and space. Much has been written about the genesis of *Doctor Who*: from Bill's point of view it was a huge departure from anything he had done before and was a big risk.

On 20th May 1963 Bill appeared in the *The Planemakers* for ATV; from then till the beginning of July, apart from meeting with an American director for a film which didn't work out, things were very quiet. Then on 11th July my father telephoned Bill about coming up to London to meet some people from the BBC regarding a new TV series. He travelled up the following day and met Verity Lambert and Waris Hussein, the director, for lunch. Bill could be bigoted and was not known for his tolerance, so what he thought when he met the two people responsible for the programme, one a very young Indian director, the other a female producer who had no experience of either producing or directing, is anybody's guess. They were both only in their mid twenties; Verity said that it must have looked as if they were the kindergarten asking him to work with them. Anyway, they told him the premise of *Doctor Who*: a bizarre old man whose origins are shrouded in mystery, accompanied by his granddaughter, Susan, travels through time and space in a machine called the TARDIS, which is disguised as a police telephone box. They take with them two of Susan's teachers, Ian and Barbara, who stumble upon their secret. Their journeys backwards and forwards through time involve them in exciting adventures and visits to many strange worlds.

The central character could almost have been written for Bill: someone frail-looking who was cantankerous, but capable of being warm and considerate. Verity felt that the character should have a childlike quality, sometimes completely adorable and sometimes aggressive and unpredictable. Bill was won over by their enthusiasm, and when he read the script he saw that this was an opportunity for him to create a real 'character' – something with a little magic and completely different from the soldiers, policemen and crooks of his past.

Negotiations continued for a short while and finally everything was confirmed. On 7th August Bill went up to town to try on the wig which was to become such a characteristic feature of his tenure of the role (even now, if it comes up in conversation that my grandfather was the first Doctor Who, everyone says, 'Oh, the one with the long white hair'). Many people assumed it was his own hair, but it helped to age him – he was fifty-five but looked older in the role. Whatever Bill thought of Verity and Waris initially, they quickly gained his confidence. This was typical of Bill – he liked and respected those who were professional about their work. Verity remembered that Bill was very inventive with his character and had lots of suggestions about his costume; he loved the slightly Edwardian feel which helped the sense of 'other-worldliness'.

The first rehearsal for the series took place on Saturday 21st September 1963, and the pilot episode was recorded the following Friday. But as most *Doctor Who* fans know, that initial programme was reshot because, among other things, it was decided that the Doctor's character was too aggressive. In the second version Bill was able to soften it and bring in a little more humour, his comedy experience being precisely one of the reasons he was cast.

Bill trusted Verity implicitly and they had an amicable working relationship. She said, 'He absolutely loved the part – he was endearingly proprietorial about it, and he simply became the Doctor. Some actors do envelop themselves with the part and when they are not acting there's this person waiting to be invaded, rather like a workaholic who is rather lost outside their work.' Bill said in various interviews that he allowed the character to 'hypnotise' him. The stories were so fantastical that it was the only way he could believe in them, and that, he thought, was vital to the success of the programme. It was his absolute commitment to the role which made him sometimes 'difficult'. He could always sense if someone didn't take it as seriously as he did and his hackles rose immediately if a new director came on to the series with the attitude, 'I'm worthy of better than this – a mere children's show.' However unspoken that attitude was, it would convey itself to Bill instantly. He hated condescension and would be crotchety with these people, especially if a highly educated director deigned to correct his pronunciation (of a strange place or a historical figure say); this brought out all his insecurity concerning his upbringing and schooling. There were those, however, who knew just how to handle him: Dennis Spooner, one of the script editors, who possessed enormous tact, was always able to iron out any problems.

The actors and production team certainly had many difficulties to contend with. Here was a programme with wildly adventurous stories, and yet they were initially given the oldest studio, with ancient cameras and perhaps the worst facilities in the BBC – Lime Grove Studio D. It was amazing they didn't trip over cables all the time they were so cramped. Sometimes the fire sprinklers went off because it got so hot. They did move to various other studios at a later stage, but the space was never ideal.

Although the programme didn't go out live, it was shot almost as if it did. The crew didn't have the editing technology available now, and so were only allowed about four or five breaks in the tape, and these only if absolutely necessary, such as when the TARDIS dematerialised, or when there was a costume change which it was impossible to cover with an alternative shot. If something went wrong it meant having to go back to the point at which the tape was last stopped, and there simply wasn't the studio time to do this. That is why so many fluffs stayed in. There were no total disasters, because they couldn't afford them, but there were some hairy moments. One Verity remembered occurred in the Marco Polo story when Waris Hussein had a real monkey on the shoulder of the actor Tutte Lemkow. The problem arose when the monkey was frightened, with predictable results… In a small studio the smell of monkey became rather overpowering.

Actors laugh when the media depict acting as a glamorous job. Rehearsals for the programme took place Monday to Thursday in one of the several old drill halls or Territorial Army centres. But the facilities were poor, and later on the venue was changed to the London Transport Assembly Rooms, used for London Transport trainees, near Television Centre in Shepherd's Bush. Bill sometimes complained that the young men playing snooker in an adjacent room disturbed him. In fact he liked nothing better than a game of snooker himself. There would be a producer's run-through on the Thursday morning in the rehearsal room, in time for any last-minute adjustments; on the Friday they would move into the studio to get used to the set; then there would be a rehearsal to camera. Recording took place in the evening, with everyone retiring to the BBC club, or a nearby pub, to unwind afterwards, although it was often nearly closing time.

Inevitably, with such an ambitious concept, there were problems with the sets. There never seemed to be enough time or storage space; the BBC design team was overloaded dealing with all the weird and wonderful creations for the series, so outside contractors had to be used in addition – and even they became stretched to the limit. Nevertheless, Raymond Cusick (responsible for much of the design work, including the Daleks) remembered being complimented by Bill on various occasions. The actors, however, had to remember not to lean against the flats (scenery), because they were often insecure and might either have shaken or toppled over completely. The console – the technical heart of the TARDIS – used to get very hot when the lights in it were left on for some time, and they had to be careful not to touch it.

Bill would get annoyed when technicalities got in the way of acting, or when they had to wait around for special effects to be tried out. He loved devising bits of 'business', though. He and Carole Ann Ford, who played Susan, his granddaughter, had worked out a whole sequence of button pressing and lever pulling to work the TARDIS, to make it seem real to them. Bill would be furious if the directors tried to get him to do something inconsistent, or if he couldn't do the sequence properly because of the camera angle. He knew that children are the most observant audience and they would pick up on anything illogical. In one later story involving the Daleks, Bill and his companions ended up outside the locked TARDIS without the key. According to the script they got in by means of the Doctor's 'magic' ring. As far as Bill was concerned he didn't have a magic ring. He had never had one before, and he knew that the importance of the key to the TARDIS, which had a complicated locking system, had been stressed in earlier episodes. He was furious that the Doctor was now relying on 'magic', which he thought was completely unfaithful to the concept of the programme; even though the producer argued that it was acceptable in science fiction terms, Bill believed it made nonsense of the show. But eventually there proved to be no other way into the TARDIS. Probably the only reason Bill finally agreed to go ahead was because the director was Douglas Camfield, whom he liked and normally enjoyed working with.

Bill was right, of course. The fan magazines were filled with articles about the technical details he knew were so important. William Russell (later known as Russell Enoch), who played Ian, one of Susan's teachers, remembers that Bill used the rehearsals to work out the minutiae, and in the camera rehearsal he would always be taking note of which camera was on him. In contrast, Russell would often be fooling about, not taking it so seriously. Bill would get cross with him on these occasions, and was not above bossing the other actors around either. According to Verity, some of them could take it and some couldn't: 'He could be quite intimidating if you didn't know that under this spiky exterior he was very sweet – marshmallow in fact. He could be cutting – but I think it was a defensive thing. He was rather like the character – sometimes he was nice, sometimes he wasn't…' Bill did love to giggle, though, and like everyone he enjoyed breaking the mood with a joke. Russell remembers that he especially liked to make Carole Ann Ford laugh. She, for her part, adored working with him.

Carole Ann remembers the first time they all met; the room seemed a little like a doctor's waiting room as they sat there eyeing each other. She, Bill and the other two companions, William Russell and Jacqueline Hill, all became close, but she and Bill had a special rapport. He was very grandfatherly towards her – she was young and he took it upon himself to be responsible for her. Carole Ann was affectionate and tactile with everyone on set and Bill would get protective, warning her that people might get the wrong idea. *Doctor Who* was her first experience of having a regular pay cheque and she loved the clothes. Carole admits she was a bit of a spendthrift. It was the heyday of Mary Quant, the King's Road and

Carnaby Street, and she would often turn up in a new outfit, hoping to persuade the designers to let her wear more exciting costumes in the programme. Bill was a bit shocked by her extravagance, saying she would regret it and should be saving (not that he was good at that himself) as an actor never knew when the next job would come along. She got fed up of his nagging and eventually retaliated, telling him to back off: 'It's my money; I'll spend it how I like.' Bill apologised profusely and made it up to her by sending her flowers.

Another extravagance of Carole's was champagne; she often used it to treat herself to a champagne cocktail after the show. Bill thought it a little decadent and one day had a moan at her about this as well. She exploded again. The following lunchtime he turned up with a jeroboam of champagne and said, 'Have some on me.' He was very particular about apologising if he felt he had gone too far.

He might have told Carole Ann not to be extravagant, but he wasn't setting a very good example himself. The other regulars couldn't help but notice his gambling; in fact they all started to put little bets on the horses, influenced by him. William Russell remembers Bill telling the story of the hot tip for the Grand National, which because it was an outsider was going to be the greatest killing of all time. Bill was obviously fond of telling how he nearly made such a huge sum of money because of the enormous odds – if it had won, he would have made perhaps a quarter of a million he claimed; as already recounted, the horse led the field all the way and then ran off near the end. Bill's remonstrations, every time he lost money, that he would never bet on a horse again never lasted long of course.

The only time Bill had a serious altercation with Verity Lambert he apologised in his usual demonstrative way. One recording day he was angry about something the *Radio Times* had or hadn't done – probably with good reason, Verity felt – but he couldn't get it out of his head and consequently it affected his performance to the extent that he dried (forgot his lines) badly. Verity was annoyed because he was normally so professional and in the pub afterwards she knew she had to say something because it had been so unfair on everyone else: 'I understand that you were cross, but you should never have allowed it to affect your work. I'm shocked and I think it was terribly unprofessional of you.' Bill was completely taken aback and the next day she received a huge bunch of flowers by way of apology. It was their only real confrontation. For Bill the programme was never quite the same once Verity moved on in July 1965.

When shooting moved to Riverside Studios the food at the canteen was so awful that the regulars – Verity, her secretary Val Speyer, the production secretary, the current script editor and the four main actors – got into the routine of bringing in contributions for lunch on recording day. Sometimes they took it in turns to provide meals, becoming quite competitive. Bill once brought in a huge hamper from Fortnum and Mason, with game pie, paté and other goodies. The ritual was, however, fairly exclusive, and William Russell doesn't remember any of the guest cast members being asked to join them. At other times they went to pubs along the river, and occasionally they would go out for a meal in the evening. It was a somewhat lonely existence for Bill because he stayed in digs in Ealing as it proved impossible to get up to London and back to Mayfield every day. He could have stayed in a hotel, but preferred to be somewhere more homely. He travelled up by the 8.20 train on a Monday morning – it was not a straightforward journey and rehearsals had to start at 11 a.m. to allow him to get to west London – and then he travelled back to Sussex late on Friday or on a Saturday morning, Heather collecting him at the station.

*

Heather made many concessions to Bill during *Doctor Who*. When he got home he would spend the weekend relaxing or learning lines for the following week's show if they had a script, and Heather would tiptoe around so as not to disturb him. Often he was too tired on the Saturday to do much, but – despite the warning from the doctor about the early stages of hardening of the arteries – he often went to the pub on a Sunday. He doesn't seem to have reduced his consumption a great deal. He had various drinking companions, and occasionally Terry Carroll would come over and stay for the weekend. One evening Terry was driving Bill home to Mayfield from a pub in Blackboys, rather the worse for wear, when he spied a roadblock and began to slow down.

Bill asked, 'Why are you slowing up?'

'The police,' said Terry.

'**** the police,' said Bill. They were duly flagged down, Bill insisting, 'Leave this to me.' Dressed in well-tailored trousers and shirt, he swept out of the car as if he was wearing his *Doctor Who* cloak and wig, shouting, 'Don't you know who I am? I'm Doctor Who, Doctor BLOODY WHO! Now get all this rubbish out of the way, my friend. I need to get home and we are very busy people!'

No doubt now they would both be arrested, but somehow they managed to get away with it then; either the police were so bemused by this crazed actor behaving as if he were in full costume that they laughed, or perhaps they were looking for stolen cars rather than lunatic drunken drivers.

Whenever Terry arrived home with Bill after one of these drinking sessions, Bill always wanted something to eat. Heather knew this and would always leave food out for them, having retired to bed. But as with most people when they are drunk, Bill would get giggly and make a great deal of noise, going 'shhh…' and bumping into things. Typically he would then get out a 'special' (everything he had was always 'special') bottle of whisky, despite already having had plenty to drink. He and Terry would start on their midnight feast when he might suddenly notice there was something missing – say a jar of pickles – and he would then shout and swear, and was not above getting Heather out of bed to get them for him.

It was very important to Bill that everything was 'just right' with his food. The only thing he didn't profess to know anything about was wine, because he didn't particularly like it. Terry Carroll remembers that when they sat down for Sunday lunch, 'He would cross-examine Heather on where the meat came from if he hadn't personally purchased it and he would look around the table to check everything was there. He might suddenly complain bitterly: "There's no mint sauce!" and then insist on going and making it himself… He'd disappear, go out to the garden and pick some mint, chop it, and all this would take half an hour. So the food would be cold. The finesse was tremendous, the way the table was laid, the quality of the napkins, everything had to be perfect, then when the meal began he would just dive in. His manners left a lot to be desired, which must have been irksome to Heather who was so refined.'

Eating a meal with Bill, Terry reported, would run something like this: 'He would make a fuss about the carving, be generous with the meat, and then the conversation would go:

'Bill: "Sprouts?"

'Terry: "No thanks."

'Bill: "Why ever not?"'

'Terry: "Not terribly fond of them."'

'Bill: "Of course you're fond of them… they're good for you… here you are."'

'And so he would bully you through a meal, which is understandable if you are a recalcitrant child, but not when old enough to know your own like and dislikes!'

Food was simply one of Bill's hobby horses and he would pontificate about it at home much as he did to actors with whom he was working. He took himself very seriously on these occasions and everyone had to be serious with him – although he could tell a funny story, he couldn't laugh at himself. One of his convictions was that the quality of food had deteriorated during his lifetime due to over-mechanisation and the use of agricultural chemicals. The trouble was, at this stage of life he'd sometimes become confused over the long words, and Heather (and any other guests) would have to try desperately not to laugh.

*

This trait of tripping over words with several syllables caused much hilarity on the *Doctor Who* set. Carole Ann Ford remembers that they had a fault locator in the TARDIS, and when things went wrong the Doctor had to shout at her to go and check the 'fault locator'. Once when Bill got a bit flustered he shouted, 'Susan, the fornicator, the fornicator!' Another time they had 'a brassiere' instead of 'a brazier'. Sometimes she would see a twinkle in his eye, indicating that perhaps the first time he had said it, it was a genuine mistake, but then because he realised it made people laugh he would repeat it. Maureen O'Brien, who replaced Carole Ann Ford after the first season as the young female companion figure, soon realised that Bill had problems with long words. In her very first episode he had to say to her, 'This will be your first exploration, my dear.' But what he came out with was, 'This will be your first exploitation, my dear.' The whole studio burst out laughing, and he glanced around with a confused look on his face, unaware of what he had said, but eventually joining in. He often made people laugh without realising it.

Val Speyer (Verity's assistant) remembers an incident during the recording of the story 'The Aztecs':

We were all 'up in the box' during recording and Bill was supposed to say 'The Aztecs are coming.' What came out was 'The Anzacs are coming'! Donald Wilson, who was head of the script department, was with us that day, and he just about fell off his chair laughing.

Bill wasn't the only one who got things wrong, though, as in that same story one of the actors playing an Aztec had to say 'The contest is begun.' At the Wednesday run-through in front of the producer, he banged his sticks together and announced loudly, 'The contest is ended.' Everyone glanced at Bill, expecting him to explode. He was very red in the face, but it became apparent that it was with suppressed laughter – just the same as everyone else.

Bill tried to cover up his little fluffs by making absent-mindedness one of the Doctor's idiosyncrasies. It was his own idea to keep getting the name of William Russell's character wrong: instead of 'Chesterton' he called him Chesserman, Chessington or whatever. He probably really did get it wrong the first time, and then decided it could become a familiar trait, and it helped get a bit of comedy into his characterisation. Perhaps partially because of this tendency he believed that the programme shouldn't have long technical words in it anyway, as they would, he claimed, confuse children who were watching. The producers told the writers to avoid words or names which were complicated, to reduce the risk of mistakes. Waris Hussein says that the pressure on Bill, doing a new programme every week, shooting up to forty-eight weeks of the year with such a small core cast, was very great and it's not surprising that Bill fluffed occasionally, given that there wasn't the opportunity to do lots of takes as is possible nowadays. But it is conceivable that this problem was one of the early signs of arteriosclerosis, as he never tripped over his lines when he was younger. It is an insidious disease of which the sufferer is often initially unaware.

*

Bill valued his audience, and was particularly aware of children's reactions to the programme because of his own grandchildren. He was thrilled that the show became so popular, and always had time for the fans. His loyalty to them was unswerving, even though it added to his already heavy workload: the amount of fan mail was staggering. Because the programme was such a full-time commitment, with only a few weeks off a year,

Heather answered most of the letters, although Bill signed countless photographs, opened fêtes and attended many other events. One such occasion was the crowning of the carnival queen at Brasted, a village in Kent. The request for him to do this came from the carnival committee but their letter was accompanied by a petition signed by over five hundred children, headed, 'Please, oh please, Doctor Who, all the children of Brasted and the surrounding villages would like you to come to Brasted on August Bank holiday to crown our Gala Queen. Please say you will come.' It was just addressed to 'William Hartnell, Mayfield, Kent' (which was the wrong county) but it still got to him. The Post Office became used to strangely addressed envelopes, though most of course went via the BBC.

Other requests Bill received were not as easy to fulfil. In June 1966 he received the following letter from the Physical Society at the University of Nottingham:

Dear Mr Hartnell,

I am at the moment involved in arranging a programme of lectures for the society during the coming academic year, and I wondered if you could spare a little of your valuable time to visit Nottingham and address the society on a subject of your own choice (preferably connected with your 'Time Travels'). The academic staff up here informs me that you are indeed a bona fide scientist, so perhaps this common bond will persuade you to consider this invitation quite seriously.

The society normally meets at 4.30 p.m. on a Friday afternoon and at the present time there are a few dates available in the Autumn term and most dates in the Spring term are available. However should these dates be at all inconvenient, I am sure that we could arrange a special meeting to suit you. Of course, all travelling expenses would be reimbursed. I look forward to receiving your reply and hope that you will be able to accommodate us.

It was signed by the president of the Physical Society, and sent on proper university paper, so I assume it was not a hoax. Perhaps they were muddling up my grandfather with Dr Kit Pedler, a genuine doctor who became the programme's unofficial scientific adviser!

Although unfortunately not a real scientist, Bill was always very concerned about the content of the programmes. He understood that children liked to be scared – that they found it exciting to peep from behind the sofa – but he never wanted them to be seriously frightened, and made comments in the later stages of the programme if he thought it was getting too violent. He appeared on *Junior Points of View* (the programme which viewers could write into with comments and criticisms) twice, in the January and September of 1964, to talk about *Doctor Who* and defend it against criticisms of being too horrific. He was also responsible for removing the hint of an incestuous relationship between Richard the Lionheart and his sister in the story set during the Crusades, which he thought unsuitable for the show.

Bill always had faith that *Doctor Who* would be a success because he knew that if you suspended your own disbelief when acting in something, you could make the audience do the same. So although many of the cast in the first story, set in the Stone Age, were extremely sceptical as they ran around wearing animal skins yet miraculously speaking modern English, Bill was sure it would work. The actors all preferred the historical settings, because they were well researched and had some basis in fact. Stories such as those set during the French Revolution, 'The Reign of Terror', or in twelfth-century Palestine, 'The Crusade', involved dressing up in wonderful costumes, and re-enacting exciting events. Bill particularly liked them because he was interested in history anyway, and he believed in Sydney Newman's original proposition that the programme should have some educational value.

But it was the science fiction stories which the children actually enjoyed the most; and the arrival of the Daleks in the second storyline, and their reappearance every so often, helped ensure the popularity of the programme. The Daleks often featured in children's letters to Bill. They were easy for kids to draw, and school teachers seemed to have cottoned on to this. An endless stream of pictures of Doctor Who, the TARDIS and the Daleks dropped through his letterbox. Sometimes he'd receive a huge envelope with a letter from every child in a class, together with a note from their teacher confessing to being a fan as well. One such beautifully illustrated letter, from Whitgrave Infants School in Wolverhampton, reads:

Dear Dr Who,
   I like your programme very much and I would like to know how your time machine works your programme is very thrilling and especially your adventure with the daleks bye bye for now
   Love Dennis

On 18th September 1965 Bill flew up to RAF Finningley in Yorkshire to help them celebrate the Battle of Britain Day. He thoroughly enjoyed his visit and was given a signed photo with a note of thanks from the Wing Commander for all his hard work in making it such a memorable day. The following year, on Saturday 23rd July, he was flown to another air station, this time to open the Royal Naval Air Service Air Day at Culdrose, in north Cornwall. Although not in a Doctor Who costume, he emerged on the specially built stage from the TARDIS to the cheers of hundreds of children, and there was a mock battle with the Daleks complete with smoke bombs, the models apparently made by the sailors themselves. Great fun was had by all, despite the fact that, according to a local paper, the Daleks' 'destructive force became evident from the first when some mysterious anti-magnetic device blotted out Doctor Who's opening remarks'. There was an air display and even a Dalek train for the children to ride on. Bill 'created a sensation… not only was he besieged for hours by autograph hunters, but children by the score kept coming up and expressing their admiration. He was like a modern version of Father Christmas.' Bill annotated the photograph album he was presented with to commemorate the day with these lines:

My Boy Scout act paid its way, I think.
    Brave, gritty men, and with a Captain I liked very much. The Almighty be with them now, and forever more.

Several of the 'companions' remember how proud Bill was when he came into rehearsals on the Monday after one of these events, his hard work often having contributed to larger collections than ever before for whatever charity the organisers were supporting. He never asked for an appearance fee and was always pleased to help raise money for a good cause, though the one he championed personally was Guide Dogs for the Blind. (This was because he had been so impressed by the guide dog training centre he had visited while researching his role for *The Inward Eye*, his first TV play.) He also enjoyed these trips because of the adoration of the fans. Maureen O'Brien remembers one evening when she and her husband Michael decided to take Bill out for a meal, to a special Chinese restaurant they knew in the East End of London. Bill suggested a drink beforehand, so they went into a pub. He was surrounded and completely lionised at the bar; people bought him drinks and wouldn't leave him alone, and Maureen said, 'You could see they adored him, and he adored being adored, and I had never realised that. As he sat there and held court he was in seventh heaven… it was very touching to see how happy he was.' They didn't get to the restaurant until 11.30 p.m. by which time Bill had lost interest in eating.

Bill had been very upset when Carole Ann Ford left, and initially Maureen was a little frightened of him. However, he soon warmed to his new companion, and she to him, taking on the role of laughing him out of his tempers. This was hard work sometimes, but she liked the fact he was so direct and honest and, although protective of her, never patronising. She was amused by the almost childlike way he would get overexcited about things. I'm sure one of the reasons Bill liked her so much was she took *Doctor Who* seriously as well. At the weekly script conference she would be outraged if the story was inconsistent, perhaps leaving her crying at the end of one episode with tears streaming down her face and then having a jolly mood at the beginning of the next. The writers were flattered to have their work taken seriously, but the rest of the team would raise their eyes to heaven when she complained – apart from Bill, who understood completely.

One day Bill and Maureen O'Brien hatched a plan. They decided they liked Peter Purves when he did a one-off character role in an early episode of a Dalek story, 'The Chase'; so they went to the producer and suggested him for the role of Stephen Taylor, the new companion, to be introduced at the end of the story as the successor to Jackie Hill and William Russell, who were leaving. And so began a very happy partnership.

Bill and Peter Purves got on wonderfully. Peter recalls several amusing incidents. Sometimes Bill used to visit the flat Peter shared with his wife. One evening after rehearsal they were sitting in the living room having a drink and just chatting generally when Peter said, 'What about Ken Tynan, then?' It happened to be the Monday after the weekend when Tynan had been the first to utter the word 'fuck' on television. Bill flew off the handle and shouted, 'What a disgrace, I've never heard anything like it – I mean televisions are in people's living rooms – you wouldn't fucking go into someone's living room and say things like that, would you?' Peter and his wife collapsed with laughter and Bill sat there looking cross for a while, completely unaware of what he had said. It was funny because Bill was such a gentleman, always charming to Peter's wife; he wouldn't normally have dreamt of using that sort of language in front of her. But when he got cross he got carried away.

They used to have lunch together, one of Bill's favourite places being Bertorelli's, which had a branch in Shepherds Bush. They knew him there and always gave him the best table, and the waitresses, dressed in their trademark little white aprons, used to spoil him. Peter, who says he was certainly no gourmet at the time, remembers:

> About the second or third time we ate together, I can't remember what I was having, but Bill had a steak and when it arrived it was absolutely blood red. I had never seen anyone eat a 'blue' steak. Bill tore into this thing like a lion tearing into a joint which had been thrown into the cage. He was obviously thoroughly enjoying it but I said, 'Good God, Bill, that's raw!' and he muttered, 'Bloody great...' 'But don't you have to have it cooked more than that?' and so he said, 'Try it...', called the waiter over and ordered me a steak. I said I had them well done and in his usual way of assuming everyone would have what he liked, he said, 'You'll have it rare...' A huge blood red fillet steak was put in front of me and much to my amazement it was delicious, the best thing I'd ever eaten. He also got me to try steak tartare later on, which was one of his favourite dishes.

Bill encouraged Peter to be more experimental about food, and they often had a curry in the evening. He could be very generous and often treated Peter, who reciprocated when he could.

Although they often talked, Peter said it was usually about inconsequential stuff. Bill's conversation was anecdotal – he would talk about movies, but rarely about himself. According to Peter, 'You had to observe him to learn about him, rather than rely on what he said: he played his cards close to his chest and revealed little of his history.'

Peter was one of those to whom Bill imparted his ideas about the art of television acting. He believed on TV there was no point in doing big gestures, that everything should be very tight and close to the face. So all his gesticulations were designed specifically for the small screen: he waggled his finger, grasped his chin and frequently brought his hands up to his lapels. This somewhat bizarre theory is certainly not the secret of television acting, but it was what made his character so eccentric; it helped him create something quirky and entirely unique.

Chapter Twelve
DOCTOR WHO BOWS OUT

UNAWARE THAT IT WAS due to the onset of arteriosclerosis, Bill found it frustratingly harder and harder to remember his lines. I'm certain much of his bad temper was caused by his anger at himself for making slips of the tongue. It was all the more disconcerting for him because he had always been such a quick studier. He'd had to be, given all those years in weekly rep. Earlier in his career he would sit in a dressing room going through the racing form while the other actors were cramming lines. He was always intolerant of those who couldn't learn easily and would say mockingly, 'I've only had the script the same number of days…' Peter Purves remembers Bill being cross at his own failings. He would shout and swear if he got something wrong; everyone would have to wait till he calmed down and then they would go on as if nothing had happened. But inevitably, if you are having memory problems, you end up blaming any little thing that distracts you, which is why Bill got cross with people playing table tennis or snooker in the next room.

Val Speyer, who was Verity Lambert's secretary during *Doctor Who*, remembers that: 'Sometimes he drove us to the point when we would stand in the middle of the office and shout, but if anyone outside said anything against him, they were faced by the regulars formed almost into a lynch mob!' Bill liked the security of a familiar production team and acting with performers he knew well, which was why he was resistant to changes in personnel. He believed in the original concept of a regular group travelling together. He got on well with the first three companions,

William Russell, Jackie Hill and Carole Ann Ford, and came to be very fond of the next two, Maureen O'Brien and Peter Purves.

But when John Wiles took over as producer from Verity Lambert, the companions started to come and go rapidly. Bill found this destabilising, and didn't like the methods employed, either: it seems actors are often the last to know what is to happen to the character they have breathed life into. Maureen O'Brien was told on her return from the holiday period that she was to be written out at the end of that story. To discover that you will have no job in four weeks' time is not the most pleasant experience. Bill believed the audiences enjoyed building a rapport with familiar faces. John Wiles, who was never entirely happy producing the show, also suggested writing Bill out of the series; this was, however, vetoed higher up.

Whatever problems he was having himself, if Bill was particularly pig-headed with John Wiles it was probably because he thought that Wiles did not have the best interest of the series at heart. He had become so absorbed in the part that he even once suggested to the writers that it would be better if they merely outlined what they wanted him to say, leaving it up to him to supply the dialogue, because after all he knew best what the Doctor would say under the circumstances. His feeling of superiority was only natural when you consider how many years he had been appearing in films and on television. Unfortunately, inexperienced directors were often given the task of directing *Doctor Who*, and nothing annoyed Bill more than the feeling that he had to teach other people their jobs.

On one occasion, when a new crew was working on the programme for the first time, the director called them to work on the console. There was a pause, and someone admitted that none of them knew how to make it function. Hearing this, Bill shouted, 'For Christ's sake, doesn't anyone know how to do anything?' He had to show them the switch for the hydraulic pump which made the console go up and down. That sort of incompetence made him nervous and irascible, because he didn't want to have to worry about the technical aspects of the show.

Generally the actors enjoyed themselves, but there were notorious incidents when Bill was difficult with guest leading actors. I believe some of this was simply professional jealousy. Julian Glover, an extremely well-respected actor, who played Richard the Lionheart in 'The Crusade' (considered to be one of the best of the stories in terms of writing, performing and directing) remembers only 'this grumpy old bloke sitting in the corner [apparently] scowling in disapproval at all I did! But as I'd been told that this was par for the course I didn't let it get to me...'; but there were others upset by Bill. 'The Myth Makers' was a story set in ancient Greece around the fall of Troy, with Max Adrian as King Priam and Francis de Wolff as Agamemnon. Adrian, whom Bill had actually worked with in films many years before, was distressed by the fact that Bill was cold-shouldering him. What mystified him was that Bill had been perfectly pleasant when they had worked together previously. He confided in Peter Purves and, knowing that Bill could be very bigoted, wondered if it was perhaps his Jewishness which had turned Bill against him. Bill often came out with xenophobic comments, whether about the London Transport trainees at the rehearsal space (who annoyed him by trying to peep through doors during rehearsals) or about a 'foreign' director. His so-called dislike of Jews was based on the fact that he believed the film industry had been taken over by them and that they were money men rather than artists – exactly the same view expressed about accountants now when people complain that 'accountants have taken over the BBC'. But all those loudly expressed opinions were contradicted by his behaviour at a personal level. Bill adored Carole Ann Ford and Verity Lambert who were both Jewish, and had great respect for Waris Hussein, who was Indian; and according to Val Speyer, although Bill claimed not to like foreigners, 'as one of his greatest friends on the show was half Greek and half Maltese, I didn't see how this could figure. However, if he liked someone, they weren't a foreigner, they were a friend!'

Although most people seemed to think that Bill's attitude towards Max Adrian was to do with bigotry, there were other reasons for his bad temper during the four 'Myth Makers' episodes. It was the first story to be shot after the seasonal break, which had lasted six weeks that year. When he turned up for the first rehearsal of the new show, not feeling his best (having just spent a week in bed with a bad cold), he was greeted with the news that Maureen O'Brien was to be written out of the series at the end of the story. Being very fond of her, he was upset both by the fact she was leaving and by the way it was handled. Not only did he have to cope with a new producer (this was John Wiles' first credited story) and the fact his cherished companion was leaving, but he also had to compete with two other larger-than-life actors with strong roles in these particular episodes:

both Max Adrian and Francis de Wolff had big personalities. Maureen looked up to Max Adrian as a wise and wonderful old man of the theatre, and had long conversations with him, hanging onto his every word. She remembers noticing that Bill was jealous. Bill liked to think that he was the one she looked up to; after all, they had worked together for some time and he had given her the benefit of his advice on everything from acting to marriage. ('Don't get married,' he said, 'it'll tie you down.') I think he felt usurped, and that was why he cut Max Adrian dead. Because he was upset, he had more trouble with the script than usual, which led to an incident with Francis de Wolff. Bill kept getting angry because he was struggling with his lines in the scene involving Agamemnon's feast and this was holding everything up. Francis was supposed to say, 'Come in Doctor, sit down and have a ham bone,' but he turned to Bill and said, 'Come in Doctor, sit down ham and have a bone.' Everyone collapsed but Bill went puce.

This is not to excuse his temper tantrums, but just to explain that there were sometimes issues involved of which the others were not aware. On top of all this, during the shooting of 'Myth Makers', Bill's aunt Bessie died. I'm sure this affected him too, as she was the only family member who had seemed to care about him when he was young, and he had taken trips down to Devon over the years to see her, though latterly she made it clear she didn't approve of his drinking. Bill was not even able to go to the funeral; but Heather went, and, as Bessie had no children, dealt with all the necessary family matters.

Not all of John Wiles' time on the programme as producer was characterised by ill humour. Both Peter Purves and Jean Marsh recalled an incident when they all laughed so much they simply couldn't go on with the scene. It took place during a technical run-through in the studio, with John Wiles present in the producer's box. Jean Marsh was playing a short-lived companion, Sara Kingdom; at one point she was supposed to activate the TARDIS by pulling a lever, but the knob came off in her hand. She started to giggle, and when they tried to do the scene again she set everyone else off. The producer was livid and came rushing out of the control room telling them to behave as they were holding everything up. But he was so manic and furious that it just made things worse, and when they tried to do the scene again everyone was laughing so uncontrollably that they couldn't continue.

In the end a grim voice sounded over the tannoy ordering Jean Marsh off the set. 'And don't come back till you've stopped laughing,' it boomed.

Jean muttered through her giggles, 'That may be never.'

Bill was standing slightly apart, but he heard her and added with a grin, 'Just make sure it's after lunch.'

None of those working on *Doctor Who* thought Bill drank any more than the rest of them. But he had drunk spirits consistently over the years and the damage had been done. He also smoked heavily; and, although he had been wiry when young, he had never been a particularly healthy person – after his thirties his only real exercise (apart from anything energetic at work) was taking the dog for a walk. It was obvious to all that over the three years of *Doctor Who* the strain was beginning to affect him. He certainly had several bad colds and bouts of 'flu during the series, and he always found any fight scenes difficult. He would become breathless but, because the programme was shot as if live, he would have to carry on with the scene. It is very evident in a sequence from 'The Romans' that he is finding it hard to catch his breath after a tussle – all the more realistic, but not the happiest situation for an actor. There was an occasion (in October 1964) when he was injured during a camera rehearsal; he was being carried in a stretcher down a ramp from the Dalek spaceship when the supports of the ramp gave way. Bill fell awkwardly on his spine and was temporarily paralysed, but he recovered enough to do the recording that evening. Heather's diary shows that he really did feel rotten on his return to Mayfield and he spent several days in bed; however, X-rays revealed no permanent damage, and after a week of rest he returned to work. In these situations some very quick rewriting had to take place; in this case he was made to fall unconscious at the beginning of the episode and so played no part in the action – the shots of the Doctor are of a stand-in with his face hidden.

However, Martin Jarvis, who played the Prince of the Menoptra, the butterfly creatures in 'The Web Planet', recalls, 'I particularly remember during the rehearsals of one of the episodes he was ill and could only rehearse for one day before we recorded – yet he was word perfect and a great example to a young actor.' This was in February 1965, and in fact Bill went up to London only for the Friday, rehearsed that day and recorded in the evening – proof that he wasn't always bad with lines, although inevitably people remember the fluffs and the mistakes more than the times everything went smoothly.

Certainly there were directors with whom Bill got on brilliantly: he liked Douglas Camfield, Paddy Russell, Christopher Barry and others. John Gorrie, who directed 'The Keys of Marinus', was inexperienced and fresh from the director's course. He remembers Bill coming up to him with comments and suggestions. Innocently John turned to him and said, 'I don't think you should have to concern yourself with those issues – after all, you have enough to worry about with the words and the moves.' The whole room froze, expecting Bill to explode, but he didn't. He looked at John and said, 'Hhhmm, er, yes, of course, thank you...' They had a very good working relationship after that because John had inspired confidence in my grandfather.

Julia Smith directed the last but one story of Bill's era as the Doctor, 'The Smugglers', which was the first story to entail location shooting away from London. They went down to Penzance for a couple of days, and although there was apparently some trouble between Bill and the management of the hotel where he was staying, Julia Smith said that whatever he did away from the set never worried her. She found him a very professional actor; anyway, she was used to temperamental theatre actor-manager types. Bill loved Cornwall and I'm sure he relished filming down there.

When they came back to London to do the studio shots, Julia Smith was amused, though at the time frustrated, by his pedantry when she asked him to move and press a button on the console. 'Rehearsals were held up for ages because he had to tell me exactly what happened to the TARDIS if he pressed that particular button. I couldn't do anything about it... he was away in never-never land!' But she realised that total belief in this fantasy was his way of making it come alive.

By this time, however, Bill was obviously tired and finding the routine more and more taxing. He was becoming increasing difficult to work with (according to internal BBC documentation), and it was decided for all concerned that it would be better if he bowed out of the series. On Saturday 16th July 1966 Bill came home after the recording day and told Heather he had agreed to relinquish the role, and that his final appearance would be that October. In August 1966 the news that he was to quit appeared in all the papers.

*

On hearing that he was to leave the show hundreds of fans wrote to him. This is a typical letter:

> What a shock! First thing in the morning to read that you are going to desert us in October. What are we going to do without you, even if someone else took your place it just won't be the same. When Susan, and then Barbara and Ian left, it was bad enough, but not you, Oh please don't do it – please don't!!! We have never missed an episode since it started and we have models of the Daleks and your Tardis here at our house just because we are so mad about your programme. Even the baby stopped everything and just sat staring at our TV when the old familiar Dr Who music began.
>
> My family are heartbroken. Please Dr Who think again. Be an exception to the rule and stay by your guns. Stick to your programme – you made it, and without you it would be nothing, NOTHING. Even the Doctor Who films aren't the same because we are thinking 'That's not really Doctor Who just someone who is taking the part.'
>
> If you leave us you won't only break our hearts, but a million others as well. We need you and most of all we want you to stay.
>
> This is a plea from only a small part of a very large audience I know.
>
> Your most ardent admirers,
> The Pointing Family of Bristol

The *Doctor Who* films the family mention were spin-offs from the series and had starred Peter Cushing. They were the idea of two businessmen: Walter Tuckwell, who had seen the potential for the licensing of Dalek merchandise, and Milton Subotsky, a film maker specialising in horror movies. The budget was obviously huge compared with the TV programme, and the films had the advantage of being shot in colour. As they were made during the time Bill was working for the BBC, we'll never know whether he would have been cast if he could have been released from his contract. Perhaps Peter Cushing was considered a bigger draw. In any event, he commented:

> I had played Winston Smith in *1984* on TV and it was probably the highlight of my TV career. I'd like to have done the film version but they gave it to Edmund O'Brien. I still don't know why. The next thing is, I'm playing Doctor Who while Bill Hartnell is doing it on TV. That's the way it goes, down one minute and up the next. After a time you get used to it.

Following the end of the third season, Bill was to make one final story which would finish with him 'regenerating' into a second 'reincarnation' with Patrick Troughton taking over as the Doctor. Bill had a great deal of respect for Patrick and certainly approved of the choice. In order to have a complete rest, Heather and Bill spent four of the six weeks' break on holiday in Cornwall; but obviously Bill found it hard to adjust to the idea of giving up the role, as Heather's diary reveals that he spent a lot of time in pubs drinking too much. The stress of it all made him vulnerable to infection again, and after the first two episodes of his last story, 'The Tenth Planet', he developed bronchitis and had to have penicillin injections. He was forbidden by his doctor even to attempt the recording that week, so had to be written out of the second to last episode. The concept that the Doctor's body had simply worn out and that was why he had to 'regenerate' into another, younger self, was not so far from the truth. My grandfather really was exhausted.

The costume designer on the final four episodes was Sandra Reid (now Alexandra Tynan). She took over from Daphne Dare who had worked on the programme from the beginning, but was familiar with the set-up as she had shared an office with Daphne for some time. Sandra was used to hearing the saga of what it was like to work on *Doctor Who*, and so she was a little apprehensive at first. She asked Daphne how to handle Bill.

Daphne said, 'He'll probably test you a bit just to see what you are made of, but don't lose your cool – just stay calm and he'll realise that it's all right.'

And sure enough, on her first day Sandra went along and introduced herself to him – just to make contact as he was already costumed.

> He seemed a little absent-minded, and then a bit later one of the dressers came along and said that Mr Hartnell wanted to see me. I thought, oh dear, here we go… I went to find him and he complained that he couldn't find his hat. I looked around and luckily I spotted it under a script and he said, 'Oh, I'd forgotten where I left it.' Perhaps he had misplaced it, but I couldn't help feeling that he was seeing how I would react to him being grumpy – but he always made a joke about it and was always charming after that.

Sandra remembers the day the 'transformation' to Patrick Troughton was recorded, 8th October 1966. Patrick was very sympathetic about the whole issue – he didn't want to make Bill feel as if it was 'the end'. Patrick came in to the studio and said, 'OK, who's who?' and made everyone laugh; but he was aware that for my grandfather it was a sad day, and he treated Bill with a great deal of sensitivity. Bill was being very professional, but was extremely quiet. Daphne Dare was impressed that Bill went out with such grace.

*

Bill found it difficult to cope with the change, and he spent many days going to the races – and to the pub – with his friend Bob Pither, often coming back inebriated. Heather was obviously under stress because of the way he was behaving. She had stomach problems, and shortly after the last *Doctor Who* was filmed she had to go into hospital for an operation. Bill visited her most days, but he had already been booked to appear in pantomime that Christmas, so had to make various trips to London for wig and costume fittings. The pantomime was *Puss in Boots*, and although Bill's character was called Buskin the Cobbler, to the audience he was always going to be the Doctor. I have a vague memory of my father saying that the management had to change the original wig somewhat so it wasn't quite so like the Doctor Who one. They rehearsed in London before opening in Ipswich; the production then moved to Southend, Cheltenham and Taunton. It was a spectacular affair, with elaborate scenery, an orchestra and a cast of twenty-one, so not an easy show to tour. It was this production I remember visiting as a child, and although I found it exciting, my parents knew that Bill was not up to scratch in his role. Like many actors who have been doing television for a while, he had forgotten how much vocal projection was needed in a theatre, and perhaps because of his illness he simply could not project enough. My family were not the only ones to realise that the pantomime was not a good production, though I'm sure most of the children loved it. John Kennedy Melling reviewed *Puss in Boots* for *The Stage*, saying:

> … production lapses at Southend's giant Odeon were mainly acoustical, the orchestra being too loud, and some principals too quiet. The costumes, dancing and décor were all good, especially a dissolve from a gauze to a tableau vivant. William Hartnell, as Doctor Who transformed into a cobbler and apparently left there, was little heard and little used…

The show was playing huge venues normally used for film, which obviously cannot have helped the situation, as acoustics in a cinema are very different from those in a theatre. Now the actors would certainly be miked, but without amplification Bill obviously found it a struggle.

During the production Bill acquired a new girlfriend from among the cast, and Heather found out about it. My grandmother was by now so fed up with this behaviour that she apparently let it be known that the girl could have him if she wanted. That decided it. Bill didn't want to leave Heather; that was what was so ridiculous – he was outwardly very proud of her. During *Doctor Who* Maureen O'Brien remembers that he frequently boasted about his wife and how wonderfully she looked after him. But that didn't stop him causing Heather unhappiness. Folded between the pages of a book I found a letter from Bill to Heather with a heartfelt apology for his behaviour, saying that he knew he hadn't been a good husband. I don't know what date it was written, whether it was after this or a previous indiscretion. Their relationship was complicated: although he seemed to make Heather miserable, she admired his talent, and enjoyed his success, but was driven to distraction by his heavy drinking and womanising. And he admired and needed her so much yet still chased after other women.

One of the highlights of Bill's time in *Doctor Who* was an invitation to appear on *Desert Island Discs*, the radio programme created by Roy Plomley, in which a celebrity is supposedly marooned on a desert island. While chatting to Plomley about their careers, guests had the chance to play their favourite records and explain why they would take these particular pieces to relieve the solitude. Bill was very proud to have been picked to do the show: he saw it as a sign of recognition of his status within the industry. He commented to Maureen O'Brien that 'everyone will be surprised by my choices – a lot of classical stuff'. Even at this stage of his life he was still insecure about being thought uneducated and uncultured. Music was not in fact very important to Bill, and his selection included many 'popular' pieces, such as Beethoven's Sonata No. 4 in A (Kreutzer) played by Yehudi Menuhin, Jack Payne playing the El Alamein Concerto, and Rachmaninov's Piano Concerto No. 2 in C minor. His love of musical comedy is reflected in the choice of his old heroes, Flanagan and Allen, singing 'Underneath the Arches', and Charlie Chaplin's own composition, 'The Spring Song'. He also chose Paul Robeson singing

'Trees' and Louis Armstrong's 'Lawd, You Made the Night Too Long', both of which he found profoundly moving. If Bill revealed his unsophistication at all, it was in his choice of luxury (every 'castaway' is allowed a luxury, and a book in addition to the Bible and Shakespeare). His luxury was a waterproof box of cigarettes. His book was in keeping with his interest in history: G. M. Trevelyan's *English Social History*. My grandfather went up to London to record the show on Monday 2nd August 1965, and it went out on air on 23rd August.

*

After the pantomime, Bill needed to discard the image of *Doctor Who* if his career was to survive. In February 1967 he rehearsed and recorded an episode of *No Hiding Place* called 'The Game'. In it he played an ex-Indian army sergeant turned rent collector. He had to speak a few words of Hindustani, which were taught to him by a couple of the Indian actors in the programme. But it was hard to shake off the image of the Doctor, as James Hastie commented in the *Scottish Daily Express*:

> *No Hiding Place* has made a powerful return to the screen. Lockhart had been 'defrosted' to a certain extent and the stories are much more clear cut and interesting. But I could not believe in William Hartnell last night as an irritable retired army sergeant. He is Dr Who. I could not help hoping that Lockhart would suddenly turn into a Dalek.

Over the next few months Bill seemed to be very unsettled. He went to the pub nearly every night, frequently returning drunk, much to Heather's understandable consternation. He needed something to occupy himself. Always interested in the production side of the industry, Bill and Heather decided that year to set up a company called Theatrical Holdings Ltd with the objective of assisting in the promotion of theatrical productions, but providing a percentage of the required backing. Eric L'Epine Smith was to administer the company, and he and Peter Rogers, Gerald Thomas (both of 'Carry On' fame) and S. G. Bannister (an accountant) would each put in £1,000 capital. They would have a reading committee and would make a maximum investment of £2,500 in any one play. A letter setting all this out was sent by Eric to Heather in May 1967, but it also stated that they needed three others to join the scheme. Perhaps they never found these three others, because for whatever reason the project does not seem to have got off the ground.

Then in December Bill secured a guest role as Harry Swift in the popular police series *Softly Softly*, which he rehearsed and then recorded in January. By the beginning of 1968 he seems to have got over his period of turmoil, during which he had spent a lot of time drinking, and though obviously still lost without much work, he was more content to potter at home. He played with the dog (a young Staffordshire bull terrier called Honeybunch, who replaced their beloved Stumpy) and more regularly visited his grandchildren with Heather. In one letter to a fan he claimed that he suffered 'a breakdown' after giving up *Doctor Who*, and he certainly doesn't seem to have been happy for over a year. Perhaps he was becoming aware of his failing memory.

On 25th April 1968 Bill went up to London to meet director Val May to talk about doing a new Robert Bolt play at the Bristol Old Vic. The Bristol Old Vic had a very good reputation, and was one of the foremost theatres outside London at the time. Negotiations were concluded and he went off to stay in Bristol. Val May's assistant on the production was a young director called John David. John David was thrilled to be working there, but a little in awe when Val May asked him to assist on *Brother and Sister* because he had been used to working at the Little Theatre, the studio space, with people who were easy to handle. Now he was faced with the prospect of two elderly actors with 'reputations'. Sonia Dresdel, who played the sister of the title – Bill played the brother – was known as a 'grande dame' of the theatre. According to John, 'She was a very good actress who didn't suffer fools gladly, rather too bright to have been traipsing round the provinces, and she should have been at the National or the RSC. She was very demanding and also knew that she could intimidate people by giving them her "look"'. Some of this description was equally true of Bill, but Sonia was very theatrical and Bill couldn't compete with her. By this time he was slightly stooped and he had difficulty concentrating on the words in the read-through. Sonia immediately marked him out as a rival. Basil Henson, also in the cast, was a consummate professional, and the other actors were very good as well, so Bill was to bear the brunt of her anger, and she tended to be very unreasonable with him, making a huge fuss even if he was only slightly late with a cue.

John David felt that Bill didn't totally understand his part. He remembers that during the first read-through of a speech about a boy his character disliked, it became clear that Bill didn't fully realise its meaning because he added 'poor boy' to the end. He said to Val May, 'I hope you didn't mind, Val, I thought I'd put in "poor boy" as it seemed a nice sort of sentimental echo.'

The whole company froze, but Val May handled it beautifully, replying, 'What an interesting idea. Let me think about that for a while and perhaps we will have a chat about it later.' Bill had seen an opportunity to get some sympathy, but 'poor boy' was completely at odds with the piece, and he was of course talked out of using it.

Bill's character was in a wheelchair, so he didn't have to worry about moves, but he did have problems learning the lines. John David was often deputed to help him go through the words. Bill seemed grateful that there was someone there to help, and he was never difficult with John. On one occasion, when they were together with another couple of actors in the theatre bar, going through the lines, someone mentioned *Doctor Who*. According to John David, it was as if a switch had been thrown. Bill grabbed John's arm and said, 'Do you remember that overcoat I wore, the Edwardian overcoat – do you know it was mine and they never paid me a penny for it.' He was deeply intense about this slight – it was as if it had been one of those grievances that had been going round and round in his head for two years. He was still fastidious about his clothes and was very fussy about the costume for his role in *Brother and Sister*.

Bill played an old man who was losing his grip and Sonia Dresdel, as his dominant sister, was often in charge of where he was on stage, though thankfully she wasn't always the one to control the wheelchair. She did, however, sometimes take advantage and place him in a position that was not very helpful. He would say to her in the wings, 'I really think the chair should be a little further away when we do that bit.'

'Oh really?' she would say, not changing the location at all when they went on. John David said it was fascinating to watch this awful duel going on between them, with Bill pretending not to notice the way she was behaving, because it mirrored the situation in the play. After a rehearsal, or a show, when Sonia had left, John remembers Bill relaxing over a drink and being charming and telling funny stories – there were flashes of his old wit and flirtatiousness, though he was obviously feeling his age by this point.

Bill saw *Brother and Sister* as his return to legitimate theatre, and hoped that the production would transfer; the fact it didn't wasn't anything to do with the performances, according to John David. It was not one of Robert Bolt's most successful pieces of writing and didn't really come together as a play.

*

In August Bill went up to town to start rehearsing for a play in Croydon. There were obviously problems during the first week as long discussions went on between Bill and Eric L'Epine Smith over the phone on the Saturday night. Bill stated that he would not go back to the production, but nevertheless he walked out of the house on Sunday and went up to town. Heather was worried sick about him, and her diary entry for the Monday reads:

> Worried about Bill all day. Got Terry to ring theatre – he is at rehearsal after saying he wouldn't go. But I fear the worst. His self-confidence has been shattered – I don't think he'll ever know it now.

The rehearsal period was reasonably short, only two weeks (now it would be more likely to be three or four weeks); and although Bill opened in the play, he was out of it after a week – whether because he was asked to leave or whether he walked out I don't know, because the family never kept any record of the production. I presume he simply couldn't remember the lines. The diary entry shows that for all their troubled relationship Bill and Heather were still very protective towards each other.

The rest of the year was quiet, but in January 1969 Bill did one more television production, called *The Prodigal Son*, some of which entailed travelling to Newcastle. I have been unable to find out any further details of this as the project was either abandoned or changed its name before being broadcast. In 1969 Bill had a couple more interviews for film or television jobs, but Eric and my father at the agency knew that he was restricted by his health, which was beginning to seriously worry him. Although he was only sixty-one the arteriosclerosis was profoundly affecting him, and he made several visits to the doctor that autumn. It was hard to find parts he was right for, but in February 1970 he went up to

London to rehearse for 'Alain', an episode of *Crimes of Passion*, for ATV. One of the two main guest stars for that week, he played a character called Henri Lindon. He stayed in London for the duration of the job, because the cottage was snowed up. The programme was broadcast on Heather's birthday, 27th April. His last acting work was on 27th November 1970, a day's filming at Elstree studios for a film called *Dr Phebus* according to Heather's diary, a film which might well have been *The Abominable Doctor Phibes*.

His last, that is, apart from a reprise of his role as the first Doctor in *Doctor Who* for a special episode made to celebrate the tenth anniversary of the programme in 1973. The series, as popular as ever, had thrived, and the Doctor had gone through a second 'regeneration' and was now played by Jon Pertwee. The idea of a project involving more than one Doctor had been kicking around for some time. Patrick Troughton had been approached and had agreed to do a one-off; and so Barry Letts, the producer, phoned Bill at home, getting directly through to him as Heather was out. Bill readily agreed, and so Terrance Dicks, who was script editor at the time, proceeded to commission scripts from Bob Baker and Dave Martin in which all three Doctors dashed about fighting monsters.

At around the time the director was due to join the show, Barry Letts received a frantic telephone call from my grandmother saying, 'I hear that you've asked Bill if he would appear in a show – well I'm afraid he can't possibly do it. He doesn't realise how ill he is – I know he'd love to do it and he would try, but there is no way he could cope with a recording day...'

Barry said he would get back to Heather and went rushing in to the rest of the production team to give them the bad news. The whole concept was to include all three Doctors and they desperately wanted Bill in it, so Barry phoned Heather with a new plan, asking if Bill could possibly manage to do one day's filming. He would be sitting down with his lines on prompt boards held up in front of him. Heather felt that he might just be able to do that. The writing team worked out a way of changing the scripts so that Doctors two and three took part in all the action, and every so often Doctor number one would comment on what was happening, or give them a few cogent words of advice by means of a monitor.

In October 1972 the wig and costume supervisors travelled to Bill's home, and then he was taken to Battersea for a photo session with the other two Doctors. On 6th November he was driven by car to Ealing where he was filmed for the inserts. This enabled the producers to have him 'present' throughout the four episodes of the story. Terrance Dicks was thrilled that everything worked out well in the end and felt that it was a fitting tribute:

> Bill had this absolutely classic Doctor line. There was the feeling that he could see through the screen in some way and so he looks at Troughton and Pertwee and says, 'So this is what I've come to – a dandy and a clown!'

When the episode was shown, it was very apparent how ill Bill was.

*

Old Mill Cottage was quite isolated, and nearly every winter my grandparents were cut off by snow. There seem to have been frequent power cuts (quite apart from any caused by the miners' strike) and sometime a telephone wire would go down and then they would be without a phone. All in all it became obvious that as Bill's condition worsened it was impractical for them to live there. They were also short of money, because although the wage for *Doctor Who* had been good, he had always been generous to other people, as well as spending a great deal on drinking and gambling. He had been too proud to sign on to the dole and had earned very little since leaving the programme in 1966. So in early 1972 Heather put their beloved cottage on the market.

In June they moved temporarily to a rented cottage a few miles away between Horam and Hellingly. Heather had to organise everything, and it soon became clear that Bill could not be left on his own. Sometimes she would return from a trip to the shops to find someone had called at the door and Bill had given away a precious item, such as his ring. Therefore, a few months later, it was decided that they should move in with my parents near Marden, Kent as we had enough space to create an annexe. A small kitchen and bathroom were built into the garage area at the end of the house, which together with a living room and bedroom gave Bill and Heather some independence. She looked after him with great patience. Over the years he must have been very challenging to live with, but I'm sure she was not the only wife to have put up with his kind of behaviour, and in many ways they admired each other. Bill became vague and affable as he got worse, shuffling around gently or just sitting in a chair quietly, hardly recognising anyone. He spent some time in hospital in August 1974, and then was moved in permanently at the end of December. Heather visited the hospital every day. Bill died quietly in his sleep on 23rd April 1975.

But *Doctor Who* lives on – surviving a long hiatus – and since then many different actors have played the role on television (plus Richard Hurndall recreating Bill's performance for the twentieth-anniversary production). Fan clubs sprang up round the world as the programme was sold to more and more countries, and fans continued to write to my grandmother even after Bill's death. She was invited to attend the twentieth-anniversary celebration at Longleat House, the *Doctor Who* retrospective at the National Film Theatre, and various conventions. She was always thrilled by the loyalty of the fans. Heather died in December 1984. People still write to me, some having discovered the early stories for the first time, telling me what pleasure his performance gave them.

*

Bill would have been so thrilled to know that the character he had brought to life in 1963 had become a kind of folk hero. The Doctor must be one of the most familiar screen characters ever. Of course, the writers and production team are in part responsible for creating *Doctor Who*, but I am certain that Bill's varied acting background enabled him to bring such depth to his characterisation that he helped ensure the success of the programme. His comedy training gave him good timing, and his years in films and then TV gave him technique, on top of which he had what Maureen O'Brien described as an 'inner compulsion'. Just as people believed he really must have been a sergeant in the army to play one so convincingly in films and TV, so he really was the eccentric Doctor.

Bill may not have become a great classical actor, or a huge movie star like Robert Donat or James Cagney, but he was 'immortalised' in books and cartoons, and in various other merchandise, which was something to be proud of. And yet several of those who worked with him felt that he always seemed to be a little bitter at the way his career had progressed. If only he had known that fifty years later it would still be possible to buy a six-inch figurine of him in costume. Many theatre reviewers, from his early days in rep to his leading role in *Seagulls over Sorrento*, singled him out for praise. He pasted up the following cutting from the *Thames Valley Times* in April 1937:

> We laughed ourselves silly at some of Billy Hartnell's antics. The lines were genuinely witty and the flippant Ronnie made the most of them. To see him wrestle with what he described as 'vulcanised steak' very nearly produced a condition bordering on hysteria in the lady next to me.

Beside this he wrote, 'I can't be such a bad actor? The time will come I hope when notices like this will appear in the London papers – so help me God!' He longed to be thought a great actor, and exuded a mixture of insecurity and ambition.

Bill wasn't brilliant in every picture he made. A few of his film performances are misjudged (usually when the director has not been sensitive enough to stop him doing too much), but most are good and some – such as those in *The Way Ahead*, *Yangtse Incident*, *This Sporting Life* and *Brighton Rock* – are, I believe, definitive. Given a strong director, a Carol Reed or a Lindsay Anderson, his work was exemplary. He frequently received glowing reviews. For example the *Daily Telegraph* said of him in *Yangtse Incident*:

> William Hartnell, never known to give a bad performance, plays Leading Seaman Frank with such inner conviction that the very set of his shoulders as he follows the Chinese officers says more than most men's faces.

Often the best thing in some very mediocre films, he was frustrated by the lower-quality ones, but he hated being out of work and never really had sufficient offers to be able to pick and choose; and in any event, maybe he sometimes made the wrong decisions, as with *The Third Man*.

Not possessing the tall, dark good looks associated with so many leading men of the forties and fifties – when Bill headlined it was always as a slightly offbeat character – perhaps it was inevitable that he was not able to maintain the 'star' status of his British National films. But the feeling that he didn't have the right background to be given leads seemed to keep nagging at him, though this was just as likely to be down to his looks. One critic said of them:

> He has the sort of face that might come with the milk in the morning, or which might grin broadly at you as he gives you your bus ticket. He looks

as if he'd be happy growing 'spuds' on an allotment and having a few with the boys at the local.

He so wanted to be privileged. Once he could afford it, he always had the best hand-made clothes. During the war, when money and food were short, he made sure his family never went without. He would do everything he could in order to impress and was often extravagant and generous. He was ashamed of his background and yearned to be cultured, urbane and clever, and yet was disparaging of the 'old school tie set'. All his best work was in roles that were true to his background, rather than anything to which he aspired. That gritty, tough quality with a dash of sensitivity was his best asset.

Once he had achieved some success Bill could be very bloody-minded. One of the symbols of status in films is the chair in the studio with your name on the back, so that you have somewhere to sit if not featuring in a particular shot. Leslie Phillips recalls that Bill was very possessive towards his chair on one film, and was always angry if he came on set to find someone sitting in it. He made such a fuss that one night various members of the crew found some steps and a platform to put his seat on, making it look like a throne. When he came in the next day he took one look at this construction, quietly walked up the steps and regally sat in his chair. Everyone applauded.

Bill could be intolerant, bigoted, irascible and very tense while working, but many people say how different he was when he let his hair down. Director of photography Eric Cross, BSC, who worked with him on an early 'quickie', filmed him in *The Dark Man* and then also a few years later in *Private's Progress*, got to know him quite well. He felt that Bill's public face could be very different from his more relaxed persona. He found him very witty and generous, and always enjoyed working with him – but maybe that was partly because Eric was a cinematographer, and so there could never be any sense of competition between them.

But if Bill did like you he was loyal. If he thought actors were not being well represented he would introduce them to Eric L'Epine Smith and my father, in whom he had every confidence, in an attempt to help their careers: he did this for both Maureen O'Brien and Nicholas Courtney from *Doctor Who*. When Peter Purves was at one point uncertain whether or not the producer was going to renew his contract, Bill apparently said to him, 'If they don't, I'll threaten to leave.'

*

There are many reasons why actors have a compulsion to act: because they would rather be someone other than themselves, because they like showing off, because they need to entertain – and if this means to give people enjoyment, then my grandfather surely succeeded, because the character of Doctor Who was beloved and remembered by so many.

Perhaps a comment from Martin Jarvis, who appeared with him in one of the earlier *Doctor Who* episodes, sums up the view expressed by many people I spoke to:

> Thinking about his career I am suddenly struck by how very different a character, in his dotty amiability and eccentricity, William was able to convey from the sharp crooks he often played in movies. Perhaps his versatility has been a little unrecognised.

Appendix 1
FILMOGRAPHY

THE DATES GIVEN ARE for the release of the film, rather than when it was made.

Bill had walk-on or small roles, all uncredited, in the following films:

1929

June   ***The Unwritten Law*** (30 mins)
dir: Sinclair Hill; scr: Leslie Howard Gordon, from play by Violet Hackstall Smith
An early short in which a girl shelters an escaped convict but then discovers he killed her husband.

1930

August   ***School for Scandal*** (76 mins)
prod/dir: Maurice Elvey; scr: Jean Jay, from play *The School for Scandal* by R. B. Sheridan
Early filmed version of a play with Basil Gill, Madeleine Carroll and Ian Fleming in the cast. Others with small unnamed roles included Anna Neagle and Rex Harrison.

1931

December   ***Man of Mayfair*** (83 mins)
prod: Walter Morosco; dir: Louis Mercanton;
scr: Eliot Crawshay Williams, Hugh Percival, from novel *A Child in Their Midst* by May Edginton

A film starring Jack Buchanan and Joan Barry with Lilian Braithwaite, in which Buchanan plays a lord who poses as a workman to win the love of a revue star, whose mother believes her to be merely a dresser.

1932

September   **Diamond Cut Diamond** (70 mins)
prod: Eric Halum; dir: Fred Niblo, Maurice Elvey;
scr: Viscount Castlerosse
Adolphe Menjou, Claude Allister and Benita Hume star in a crime drama where two international jewel thieves are outwitted by a lady crook.

From this point Bill's parts were speaking roles except where mentioned.

November   **Say It With Music** (British & Dominion, 69 mins)
prod: Herbert Wilcox; dir: Jack Raymond;
scr: William Pollock

Himself	Jack Payne
Mrs Weston	Joyce Kennedy
Betty Weston	Sybil Summerfield
Philip Weston	Percy Marmont
Dr Longfellow	Evelyn Robert

Freddy Schweitzer, Anna Lee, **Billy Hartnell**
BBC Dance Band
A musical piece where a bandleader befriends a composer who has lost his memory after a near-fatal plane crash: the music helps him to recover.

November   **That Night in London** (78 mins)
prod: Alexander Korda; dir: Rowland V. Lee
(BH not credited)

Dick Warren	Robert Donat
Eve	Pearl Argyle
Harry Tresham	Miles Mander
Capt. Paulson	Roy Emerton
Bert	Graham Soutten
Ribbles	Lawrence Hanray

Insp. Brody	James Knight
Max Rivers Girls	

A crime drama in which Warren embezzles money from a bank and heads for the bright lights of London. BH not mentioned, but he does say in an article that his first film break came in one of similar title, starring Donat.

1933

February   ***Follow the Lady*** (Fox, 49 mins)
prod: George Smith; dir/scr : Adrian Brunel

Mike Martindale	**Billy Hartnell**
Suzette	Marguerite Allen
Lady Saffron	Marie Hemingway
Paul Barlow	Basil Moss
Flash Bob	D. A. Clarke-Smith
Parsons	Vincent Holman

A comedy involving a mix-up between two bachelors and a French girl with a baby who tries to blackmail them after a night out.

March   ***I'm an Explosive*** (Fox, 50 mins)
prod: Harry Cohen; dir/scr: Adrian Brunel, from novel by Gordon Phillips

Edward Whimperley	**Billy Hartnell**
Professor Whimperley	Elliot Makeham
Anne Pannel	Gladys Jennings
Lord Ferndale	D. A. Clarke-Smith
Miss Harriman	Sybil Grove
Mould	Harry Terry
Shilling	George Dillon
French Girl	Blanche Adele

A comedy in which a professor believes his younger brother Edward (mistaking it for whisky) has swallowed a liquid he's invented which makes the body into an explosive. In fact no such thing has happened, but the Chemical Warfare Dept. is induced to settle a claim for a large sum of money with which he marries his girlfriend.

September   ***The Lure*** (Paramount, 65 mins)

prod/dir: Arthur Maude; scr: uncredited from novel by
J. Sabben-Clare

Julia Waring	Anne Grey
Paul Dane	Cyril Raymond
John Baxter	Alec Fraser
Billy	**Billy Hartnell**
Peter Waring	Philip Clarke
Merritt	P. G. Clarke
Dorothy	Doris Long

A rather feeble thriller in which Dane and Baxter are guests at
a house party and both fall in love with a young widow who is
there. The situation is tense because Baxter has stolen a
valuable gem from Dane's brother. Baxter is murdered, but
an ingenious plan, involving fake suicide, unmasks the killer.

1934

February   ***Seeing is Believing*** (British & Dominion, 70 mins)

dir: Redd Davis; scr: Donovan Pedelty

Ronald Gibson	**Billy Hartnell**
Geoffrey Cooper	Gus McNaughton
Marion Harvey	Faith Bennett
Nita Leonard	Vera Boggetti
Sir Robert Gibson	Fewlass Llewellyn
Mme Bellini	Joan Periera
Lady Mander	Elsie Irving

A comedy about an aspiring detective, Gibson, who mistakes
two detectives for jewel thieves, accuses a girl of stealing a
bracelet – but then falls in love with her. His father intervenes
and clears everyone's name.

June   ***The Perfect Flaw*** (British Fox, 50 mins)

prod/dir: Manning Haynes; scr: Michael Barringer

Phyllis Kearnes	Naomi Waters
Louis Maddox	D. A. Clarke-Smith
Richard Drexel	Ralph Truman
Bert	Wally Patch
Henry Kearnes	Charles Carson

Jack Robbins	Romilly Lunge
Vickers	**Billy Hartnell**
Jennings	Hal Walters

Junior partner Drexel gets involved with ambitious clerk Maddox whose get-rich-quick scheme goes awry and leads to a plot to kill a rich stockbroker, but he is thwarted. Typical 'quickie' drama.

1935

January   *Swinging the Lead* (Universal, 63 mins)
prod: Paul Weiner; dir: David MacKane; scr: George Rogers

Freddie Fordum	**Billy Hartnell**
Joan Swid	Moira Lynd
Inigo Larsen	Gibb McLaughlin
Mrs Swid	Maire Ault
Benjamin Brown	George Rogers
Peggy	Nita Harvey

Comedy about an inept gang of crooks who get their hands on a personality-changing drug. A rival gang and the police are also after it, which leads to a crazy chase.

September   *While Parents Sleep*
(Transatlantic/British & Dominion, 72 mins; reissued 1941)
prod: Paul Soskin; dir: Adrian Brunel; scr: Anthony Kimmins

Bubbles Thompson	Jean Gillie
Mrs Hammond	Ellis Jeffries
Lady Cattering	Enid Stamp-Taylor
Jerry Hammond	McKenzie Ward
Col. Hammond	Athole Stewart
Lord Cattering	Davy Burnaby
Bedworth	Albert Rebla
Neville Hammond	Romilly Lunge
George	**Billy Hartnell**
Taxi Driver	Wally Patch
Garage Man	Ronald Shiner
Coffee Stall Man	Edgar Driver

Frothy, but not brilliant, comedy of manners about a shop girl who declines to expose an affair between her boyfriend's brother and Lady Cattering. In so doing she teaches a snobbish family a lesson in civility.

September **Old Faithful** (Radio Pictures, 67 mins)
prod: George Smith; dir: MacLean Rogers;
scr: Kathleen Butler
(BH not credited)

Horace Hodges	Bill Brunning
Lucy Brown	Glennis Hodges
Alf Harris	Bruce Lister
Joe Riley	Wally Patch
Lily	Isobel Scaife
Martha Brown	Muriel George
Edwards	Edward Ashley Cooper

A romance where old Hodges refuses to give up his hansom cab in favour of a new-fangled taxi, but finds that his daughter has fallen in love with a taxi driver, who posed as a plumber to woo her.

October **The Guv'nor** (Gaumont, 88 mins)
prod: Michael Balcon; dir: Milton Rosmer;
scr: Maude Howell & Michael Balcon

Francois Rothschild	George Arliss
Madelaine	Viola Keats
Barsac	Frank Cellier
Mme Barsac	Mary Clare
Flit	Gene Gerrard
Paul	Patric Knowles
Dubois	George Hayes
Mrs Granville	Henrietta Watson
Car Salesman	**Billy Hartnell**

A comedy of mistaken identity where a tramp, Rothschild, is made director of a bank because of his name. He's used in a complicated plot to swindle a girl out of a valuable mine, but he thwarts this and goes back to a life on the road. BH enthusiastically tries to sell Rothschild a car in a comedy cameo.

November	**The Shadow of Mike Emerald** (Radio Pictures, 61 mins)

prod: George Smith; dir: MacLean Rogers;
scr: Kathleen Butler & Anthony Richardson
(BH not credited)

Mike Emerald	Leslie Perrins
Lucie Emerald	Marjorie Mars
Lee Cooper	Martin Lewis
John Ellman	Vincent Holman
Clive Warner	Atholl Fleming
Ryder March	Neville Brook
Rollo Graham	Basil Langton

Emerald is a crooked financier. One associate commits suicide, the other three vow vengeance when their prison terms are up. Emerald escapes from jail, but is traced through his wife.

1935/36

La Vie Parisienne (Paris Nero Films)
dir: Robert Siodmak from an Offenbach operetta
(BH not credited)
Max Dearly, Conchita Montenegro, Neil Hamilton
The English version of a French film, which would have been made simultaneously, with a slightly different cast.

1936

March	**The Crimson Circle** (Universal, 76 mins)

prod: Richard Wainwright; dir: Reginald Denham;
scr: Howard Irving Young
(BH not credited)

Derrick Yale	Hugh Wakefield
Felix Marle	Noah Beery
Jack Beardmore	Niall McGinnis
James Beardmore	Basil Gill
Insp. Brabazon	Gordon McLeod
Insp. Parr	Alfred Drayton
Sylvia Howard	June Duprez
Millie MacRoy	Renee Gadd
Sgt. Webster	Paul Blake

Lawrence Fuller   Ralph Truman

Thriller about a crime inspector unmasking the mysterious leader of a blackmail gang, involving the murder of three prominent businessmen. Not particularly good.

September   ***Nothing Like Publicity*** (Radio Pictures, 65 mins)
prod: George Smith; dir: MacLean Rogers;
scr: Kathleen Butler & H. F. Maltby, from story by
Arthur Cooper

Pat Spencer	**Billy Hartnell**
Denise Delorme	Marjorie Taylor
Miss Bradley	Moira Lynd
Bob Wharncliffe	Max Adrian
Sir Arthur Wharncliffe	Gordon McLeod
Lady Wharncliffe	Dorothy Hammond
Sadie Sunshine	Ruby Miller
Mr Dines	Aubrey Mallalieu
Butler	Vincent Holman
Maid	Isobel Scaife

Spencer is a freelance press agent who befriends a young actress and takes her with him to interview a publicity-shy American heiress, Bradley. Mistaken for the heiress and her solicitor, they end up being given the Wharncliffe family diamonds she had come to purchase. They are exposed as imposters, but before the jewels are handed over, the real American lady turns up and her impersonator is shown to be a jewel thief. Spencer turns this to his advantage, and gets his exclusive story.

December   ***Midnight at Madame Tussauds***
(Premier Sound Films/Paramount, 66 mins)
prod: J. Steven Edwards; dir: George Pearson;
scr: Roger McDougall, Kim Peacock

Carol Cheyne	Lucille Lisle
Sir Clive Cheyne	James Carew
Harry Newton	Charles Oliver
Nick Frome	Kim Peacock
Gerry Melville	Patrick Barr

Stubbs	**Billy Hartnell**
Brenda	Lydia Sherwood
Modeller	Bernard Miles

Thriller in which a financier bets he can spend the night in the Chamber of Horrors. He finds himself the intended murder victim of the man who wants to marry his ward. They fight and the adventurer falls into the torture pit. The film, one of the last to be shot by Pearson, who rated as one of England's top directors of silent films 1915-25, shows the silent-movie influence. BH does a Chaplinesque comedy turns as a reporter with Melville as his partner.

US title: *Midnight at the Wax Museum*

1937

May   ***Farewell Again***
(Pendennis/London Films/United Artists, 85 mins)
prod: Erick Pommer; dir: Tim Whelan;
scr: Clemence Dane, Patrick Kirwan
A well-made film starring Flora Robson and Leslie Banks showing life aboard a troopship when the troops learn that leave has been cut to six hours ashore before they return to active service in the Far East. BH simply appears in a crowd scene.

US title: *Troopship*

1938

December   ***They Drive by Night*** (Warner Bros/First National, 84 mins)
prod: Jerome Jackson; dir: Arthur Woods; scr: Derek Twist

Shorty Matthews	Emlyn Williams
Walter Hoover	Ernest Thesiger
Molly O'Neill	Anna Konstam
Wally Mason	Allan Jeayes
Murray	Anthony Holles
Charlie	Ronald Shiner
Marge	Yolande Terrell
Pauline	Julie Barrie
Mrs Mason	Kitty de Leish
Landlady	Jennie Hartley

| Bus Conductor | **Billy Hartnell** |
| Det. Pryor | Joe Cunningham |

A good atmospheric thriller. Matthews is fresh out of prison and finds his old flame strangled. Fearing he will be accused of murder, he hitches a lift to London. BH plays a small part as a sympathetic bus conductor.

1939

March *Too Dangerous to Live* (Warner Bros/First National, 74 mins)
prod: Jerome Jackson; dir: Anthony Hankey, Leslie Norman; scr: Paul Gangelin, Connery Chapman, Leslie Arliss, from novel *Crime Unlimited*

Jacques Leclerq	Sebastian Shaw
Marjorie	Greta Gynt
Collins	Reginald Tate
Lou	Anna Konstam
Murbridge/Wells	Ronald Adam
Insp. Cardby	Edward Lexy
Saunders	Ian MacLean
Selford	Henry Caine
Manners	George Relph
Mrs Herbert	Tonie Edgar-Bruce

Billy Hartnell

A detective poses as a jewel thief to gain a gang's confidence. He falls in love with the niece of his victim and is trapped in a blazing garage but manages to get out by using Morse Code.

September *Murder Will Out* (Warner Bros, 65 mins)
prod: Sam Sax; dir: Roy William Neill; scr: R. W. Neill, Austin Melford, Brock Williams, Derek Twist

Dr Paul Raymond	John Loder
Pamela Raymond	Jane Baxter
Stamp	Jack Hawkins
Campbell	Hartley Power
Nigel	Peter Croft
Morgan	Fred Burtwell
Dick	**Billy Hartnell**
Inspector	Ian Maclean

Richard George, Aubrey Mallalieu, Peter Miles, Roddy McDowall

A confusingly plotted thriller where threats are made to the Raymonds over some jade. Bodies disappear, as do the people they think are helping: they turn out to be the crooks, who are killed when their plane crashes.

1942

March
Flying Fortress (Warner Bros/First National, 109 mins)
prod: Max Milner; dir: Walter Forde; scr: Gordon Wellesley, Edward Dryhurst, Brock Williams

Jim Spence	Richard Greene
Sidney Kelly	Carla Lehmann
Lady Deborah Ottershaw	Betty Stockfeld
Shy Kelly	Donald Stewart
Harrington	Charles Heslop
Lord Ottershaw	Sidney King
Collinson	Basil Radford
Sheepshead	Joss Ambler
Dan Billings	Edward Rigby
Taxi Driver	**Billy Hartnell**

John Boxer, Peter Croft, Tommy Duggan, Hubert Gregg, Robert Beatty

A war adventure picture about an irresponsible US millionaire who has caused the death of a passenger. He reforms and joins the RAF. Spence becomes the hero of a bombing raid over Berlin by climbing out on to a wing in mid-air. The action scenes are good, but it starts slowly.

March
They Flew Alone (RKO/Radio Pictures, 103 mins)
prod/dir: Herbert Wilcox; scr: Miles Malleson, from story by Lord Castlerosse

Amy Johnson	Anna Neagle
Jim Mollinson	Robert Newton
Mr Johnson	Edward Chapman
Pauline Glover	Nora Swinburne
Mr Johnson	Joan Kemp-Welch
Mac	Brefni O'Rorke

Lord Wakefield	Charles Carson
School Mistress	Martita Hunt
Official	Anthony Shaw
Mayor	Eliot Makeham
Solicitor	David Horne
Barber	Aubrey Mallalieu
Salesman	Miles Malleson
Postmaster	Charles Victor
Governor General	Hay Petrie
Recruiting Officer	John Slater
Operator	Percy Parsons
Operator	Cyril Smith
Editor	George Merritt
Housekeeper	Muriel George
Collie	**Billy Hartnell**
Officer	Peter Gawthorne
Mechanic	Ronald Shiner
BBC Commentator	Charles Maxwell
Commentator	Gerry Wilmott

A wartime biopic about the famous flying pioneers of the Air Transport Auxiliary. The film depicts their aerial feats and their marital problems, ending with Johnson going down in the English Channel in 1941. Excitingly made, but the leads were possibly miscast.

US title: *Wings and the Woman*

June
Suspected Person (Associated British, 78 mins)
prod: Warwick Ward; dir/scr: Lawrence Huntington

Jim Raynor	Clifford Evans
Joan Raynor	Patricia Roc
Insp. Thompson	David Farrar
Carol	Anne Firth
Franklin	Robert Beatty
Dolan	Eric Clavering
Tony Garrett	Leslie Perrins
Detective Saunders	**Billy Hartnell**
Davis	Eliot Makeham

Jones	John Salew
Simmons	Stan Paskin

Raynor ends up with the proceeds from a bank robbery in which two Americans, Franklin and Dolan, have killed their partner. They trace their money through Raynor's girlfriend, but Scotland Yard are also on to it. Raynor's sister tries to persuade him to give the money back. BH plays Insp. Thompson's right-hand man.

July

Sabotage at Sea (British National, 74 mins)
prod: Elizabeth Hiscott; dir: Leslie Hiscott;
scr: Michael Barringer

Diane	Jane Carr
Capt. Tracey	David Hutcheson
Jane Dighton	Margaretta Scott
Steward	Wally Patch
Cook	Ronald Shiner
John Dighton	Felix Aylmer
Daphne Faber	Martita Hunt
Chandler	Ralph Truman
Digby	**Billy Hartnell**
Engineer	Arthur Maude

Not very convincing story about a captain who finds he has a saboteur on board ship. A rigger is murdered and the captain traces the guilty party to discover he is also the saboteur.

August

The Peterville Diamond (Warner Bros, 85 mins)
prod: Max Milner; dir: Walter Forde; scr: Gordon Wellesley, Brock Williams

Teri	Anne Crawford
Charles	Donald Stewart
Lady Margaret	Renee Houston
The Robber	Oliver Wakefield
Dilfallow	Charles Heslop
Joseph	**Billy Hartnell**
President	Felix Aylmer
Dan	Charles Victor
Police Chief	Joss Ambler

Luis   Paul Sheridan

While on holiday with her husband in Mexico, neglected wife Teri is bought a huge diamond by her business-obsessed husband. A jewel thief tries to gain the diamond by wooing her, but doesn't succeed. With witty dialogue, it is an enjoyable light comedy.

August **The Goose Steps Out** (Ealing, 79 mins; reissued 1946, 1955)
prod: Michael Balcon; assoc. prod: S. C. Balcon;
dir: Will Hay, Basil Dearden; scr: Angus McPhail,
John Dighton

William Potts/Muller	Will Hay
Max	Charles Hawtrey
Hans	Peter Croft
Kurt	Barry Morse
Krauss	Peter Ustinov
Lena	Anne Firth
Prof. Hoffman	Frank Pettingell
Vogel	Leslie Harcourt
Gen. Von Goltz	Julien Mitchell
ADC	Jeremy Hawk
Schmidt	Raymond Lovell
Rector	Aubrey Mallalieu
Maj. Bishop	John Williams
Col. Truscott	Laurence O'Madden
Soldier	Leslie Dwyer
Pilot	Richard George
German Officer	**Billy Hartnell**
Adolf Hitler	Billy Russell

Potts is a teacher who is the double of a German spy. Sent to Germany, he finds himself teaching trainee spies while trying to find out about a secret bomb the Germans are developing. BH plays a small role as a German officer.

1943

April **The Bells Go Down** (ABFD Ealing, 90 mins)
prod: Michael Balcon; assoc. prod: S. C. Balcon;
dir: Basil Dearden; scr: Roger MacDougall, Stephen Buck

Tommy Turk	Tommy Trinder
Ted Robbins	James Mason
Sam	Mervyn Johns
Nan	Philippa Hiatt
McFarlene	Finlay Currie
Bob	Philip Friend
Susie	Meriel Forbes
Ma Turk	Beatrice Varley
Brooks	**Billy Hartnell**
Pa Robbins	Norman Pierce
Ma Robbins	Muriel George
Lou Freeman	Julian Vedey
June	Leslie Brook
Pte Bill	Charles Victor
Sergeant	Frederick Piper
Soldier	Ralph Michael
Varetta	Andreas Malandrinos

A film set in the East End of London during 1939 which glorifies the community spirit during the Blitz. Turk is one of several who volunteer for the Auxiliary Fire Service. BH plays an authoritative recruit who has been in the International Brigade.

June   ***The Dark Tower*** (Warner Bros, 93 mins)
prod: Max Milner; dir: John Harlow;
scr: Brock Williams, Reginald Purdell, from play by
Alexander Woollcott/G. S. Kaufman

Phil Danton	Ben Lyon
Mary	Anne Crawford
Tom Danton	David Farrar
Torg	Herbert Lom
Towers	**Billy Hartnell**
Willie	Frederick Burtwell
Mme Shogun	Josephine Wilson
Eve	Elsie Wagstaff
Dr Wilson	J. H. Roberts

Torg is a hypnotist hired by circus-owner Danton, whose brother does a trapeze act with Mary. Torg falls in love with her and tries to hypnotise her into dropping her partner. Friends kill Torg to end his influence over her. Lom's first film.

November   ***Headline*** (Ealing, 76 mins)
prod: John Corfield; dir: John Harlow; scr: Ralph Gilbert Bettinson, Masie Sharman, from novel by Ken Attiwell

Anne	Anne Crawford
Brookie	David Farrar
L. B. Ellington	John Stuart
Mrs Ellington	Antoinette Cellier
Dell	**Billy Hartnell**
Paul Grayson	Anthony Hawtry
Betty	Nancy O'Neil
Mrs Deans	Merle Tottenham
Sub Editor	Joss Ambler
Jones	Richard Goolden

Rather implausible story about a crime reporter finding that his boss's wife is the missing witness to a murder. He tries to solve the crime without letting his boss know.

December   ***San Demetrio London*** (Ealing, 104 mins)
prod: Robert Hamer; dir: Charles Frend; scr: Robert Hamer, Charles Frend, from story by F. Tennyson Jesse
A war film starring Walter Fitzgerald, Mervyn Johns and Robert Beatty, based on a true story. A tanker is crippled at sea and abandoned. However, some of the crew who fail to be picked up manage to bring her back home. BH only in a crowd scene.

1944

June   ***The Way Ahead*** (Two Cities Films, 115 mins)
prod: Norman Walker, John Sutro; dir: Carol Reed; scr: Eric Ambler, Peter Ustinov, from original story by Eric Ambler

Lt Jim Perry	David Niven

Ted Brewer	Stanley Holloway
Lloyd	James Donald
Luke	John Laurie
Sid Beck	Leslie Dwyer
Bill Parsons	Hugh Burdon
Stainer	Jimmie Hanley
Sgt Ned Fletcher	**Billy Hartnell**
C. O.	Reginald Tate
Commander	Leo Genn
Marjorie Gillingham	Renee Ascherson
Mrs Gillingham	Mary Jerrold
Proprietor	Raymond Lovell
Col Walmsley	A. E. Matthews
Buster	Jack Watling
Rispoli	Peter Ustinov
Herbert Davenport	Raymond Huntley
Officer	Trevor Howard
Sam	John Salew
Mrs Perry	Penelope Ward

Esma Cannon, Eileen Erskine, Grace Arnold, John Ruddock, Bromley Davenport, Tessie O'Shea, Lloyd Pearson

A film intended to do for the army what *In Which We Serve* did for the Navy. A bunch of new and rather unwilling recruits, who come from a wide variety of backgrounds, are put through their paces by a tough sergeant, played by BH. The men finally become a dependable and close-knit unit under the command of Lt Perry and go off to face the enemy in North Africa. Some wonderful characters and performances raised it far above other propaganda films.

1945

January   *The Agitator* (British National/Anglo American, 104 mins)
prod: Louis H. Jackson; dir: John Harlow;
scr: Edward Dryhurst; from novel by William Riley

Peter Pettinger	**Billy Hartnell**
Lettie Shackleton	Mary Morris
Tom Tetley	John Laurie

Ben Duckett	Moore Mariot
Charlie Bromfield	Edward Rigby
Mark Overand	Frederick Leister
Mrs Montrose	Cathleen Nesbitt
Joan Shackleton	Moira Lister

George Carney, Eliot Mason, J. H. Roberts

Pettinger is a young mechanic at Overands who feels angry because his father was cheated out of the money for an invention. Old Overand hears this and leaves the works to him, even though he is a social agitator. After six turbulent months as managing director, he learns to be more tolerant. A thought-provoking film which becomes too lightweight.

January   ***Strawberry Roan*** (British National/Anglo American, 84 mins)
prod: Louis H. Jackson; dir: Maurice Elvey;
scr: Elizabeth Baron

Chris Lowe	**Billy Hartnell**
Molly Lowe	Carole Raye
Morley	Walter Fitzgerald
Mrs Morley	Sophie Stewart
Dibben	John Ruddock
Bill Gurd	Wylie Watson
Emily	Petula Clark
Gladys Moon	Joan Maude
Mrs Dibben	Joan Young
Dealer	Kynaston Reeves
Dr Lambert	Norman Shelley
Auctioneer	Ellis Irving
Emily	Pat Geary
Silas	Charles Doe
Shepherd	Gordon Begg
Fred	Percy Coyte
Auctioneer's assistant	Charles Paton
Vicar	Patric Curwen
Preacher	Richard Turner
Chris's Maid	Janet Morrison
Nurse	Josie Huntley Wright

1st Bridesmaid   Rosemary Riggs
2nd Bridesmaid   Patricia Stainer

Farmer Chris Lowe marries a showgirl. He neglects the farm and her extravagant tastes help ruin him; after an argument she rides off and is thrown from her horse. When she dies, he is overcome with grief and sells the farm, going to work as foreman for the new owner.

October   ***Murder in Reverse***
(British National/Anglo American, 88 mins)
prod: Louis H. Jackson; dir/scr: Montgomery Tully, from story by 'Seamark'
WH headlined above title

Tom Masterick	**William Hartnell**
Peter Rogers	Jimmy Hanley
Doris Masterick	Chili Bouchier
Fred Smith	John Slater
Sullivan	Brefni O'Rorke
Jill Masterick	Dinah Sheridan
Jill Masterick (child)	Petula Clark
Crossley KC	Kynaston Reeves
Blake KC	John Salew
Spike	Edward Rigby
Docker	Ben Williams
Mrs Green	Ethel Coleridge
Mrs Moore	Maire O'Neill
The Tailor	Wylie Watson
Landlord of the North Star	Scot Sanders
Woman Customer	Maudie Edwards
Man Customer	Cyril Smith
Sam Wung See	K. Lung
Interpreter	Paul Ley
Mrs Peterson	Mary Norton
Detective Sergeant Howell	Ellis Irving
Clerk of Court	Hendry White
Judge	Aubrey Mallalieu
Foreman of the Jury	Alfred Harris

American Soldiers	Sonny Muller,
	Johnny Catcher
Woody	Ivor Barnard
Police Sergeants	Dick Francis
Crossley's Guests	Peter Gawthorne,
	Geoffrey Dennis,
	Cyril Luckham

Tom Masterick is a stevedore, content with his lot working at Limehouse Docks, until fellow worker Smith runs away with his wife. They fight, and although Tom swears he has seen Smith alive afterwards, the latter has disappeared and Tom is found guilty of murder. A reporter takes up his case so he is reprieved from the death sentence. On release for good conduct fifteen years later his only thought is to find Smith. He is helped by the journalist, now an editor, and his daughter. Also released in France as *Meurtre à Crédit*.

1946

May

Appointment with Crime

(British National/Anglo American, 97 mins)

prod: Louise H. Jackson; dir/scr: John Harlow

Leo Martin	**William Hartnell**
Insp. Rogers	Robert Beatty
Carol Dane	Joyce Howard
Gus Loman	Raymond Lovell
Gregory Lang	Herbert Lom
Noel Penn	Alan Wheatley
Sgt Charlie Weeks	Cyril Smith
Jonah Crackle	Ivor Bernard
Joe Fisher	Wally Patch
Casson	John Rorke
John Brown	Ernest Butcher
Winkle	Kenneth Warrington
Cleaner	Wilfred Hyde-White
Spearman	Albert Chevalier
Mrs Wilkins	Elsie Wagstaff
Detective Mason	Ian McLean

Prison Governor	Ian Fleming
Harry Millerton	Frederick Morant
Dusty	Paul Croft
Doctor	Alfred A. Harris
Chief Prison Officer	Joe Cunningham
Hatchett	Victor Weske
Mick	Harry Terry
Smokey	James Knight

Howard Douglas, Anders Timberg, John Clifford, Jimmy Rhodes, Andre Belhomme, Ivor Barnard, Iris Hunter-Symon, A. G. Guinle.

Martin is a ruthless crook who is caught by the wrist at the beginning of the film and ends up the same way, trapped by a train window. He takes revenge on his accomplices for leaving him to get caught during a smash-and-grab raid, killing one of them and framing the other on his release from prison. He talks his way into Lang's gang and uses blackmail to raise money for a new life; eventually he is caught when the dance-hall girl he has been protected by realises the truth. A tough, uncompromising film supposedly made as a deterrent to crime, but which ran into problems with the censors.

1947

February   ***Temptation Harbour*** (ABPC, 104 mins)
prod: Victor Skutezky; dir: Lance Comfort;
scr: Victor Skutezky, Frederick Gotfurt, Rodney Ackland
from novel by Georges Simenon

Bert Mallinson	Robert Newton
Camelia	Simone Simon
Jim Brown	**William Hartnell**
Insp. Dupre	Marcel Dalio
Betty Mallinson	Margaret Barton
Tatem	Edward Rigby
Beryl Brown	Joan Hopkins
Mabel	Kathleen Harrison
Mrs Gonshall	Irene Handl

Fred	Wylie Watson
Reg	Leslie Dwyer
Porter	W. G. Fay
Station Master	Edward Lexy
Frost	George Woodbridge
Mrs Frost	Kathleen Bontall
Teddy	Dave Crowley
Mrs Titmuss	Gladys Henson
CID Inspector	John Salew

Mallinson, an honest railway signalman, witnesses two men fighting on a quayside; one of them, together with a suitcase, falls in the water. Bert is unable to save the man, but finds that the suitcase is full of money. He decides not to hand in the cash for the sake of his daughter, and he leaves town with her and golddigger Camelia. WH plays the original crook who pursues Bert, and who Bert then accidentally kills in a fight. He gives himself up and returns the money to the police.

February **Odd Man Out** (Two Cities Films, 116 mins)
prod/dir: Carol Reed; scr: F. L. Green, R. C. Sherriff

Johnny	James Mason
Lukey	Robert Newton
Kathleen	Kathleen Ryan
Dennis	Robert Beatty
Pat	Cyril Cusack
Shell	F. J. McCormick
Fencie	**William Hartnell**
Rosie	Fay Compton
Constable	Denis O'Dea
Father Tom	W. G. Fay
Theresa	Maureen Delany
Tober	Elwyn Brook-Jones
Nolan	Dan O'Herlihy
Granny	Kitty Kirwan
Maudie	Beryl Measor
Cabbie	Joseph Tomelty

An atmospheric and well-made film in which IRA man Johnny escapes from prison. He is wounded and, while pursued by the police, is painted by mad artist, hidden by fiery publican Fencie, and operated on by a doctor. He meets up with his girl on the way to the docks. She shoots as the police move in, so that they will be killed together.

December **Brighton Rock** (ABPC/Pathe, 91 mins)
prod: Roy Boulting; dir: John Boulting; scr: Graham Greene, Terence Rattigan, from novel by Graham Greene

Pinkie Brown	Richard Attenborough
Ida Arnold	Hermione Baddeley
Dallow	**William Hartnell**
Rose	Carol Marsh
Cubbitt	Nigel Stock
Spicer	Wylie Watson
Prewitt	Harcourt Williams
Fred hale	Alan Wheatley
Phil Corkery	George Carney
Colleoni	Charles Goldner
Judy	Virginia Winter
Frank	Reginald Purdell
Publican	Basil Cunard
Brewer	Harry Ross
Police Inspector	Campbell Copelin
A Singer	Constance Smith

Norman Griffiths & his Orchestra

A brutal and realistic look at gang warfare in Brighton. Pinkie's gang kill a reporter in revenge, but Pinkie worries that a young waitress, Rose, will betray him. To validate her evidence he decides to marry her. Ida, a friend of the reporter, sets out to solve the crime, discussing it with her friend, Corkery. Still afraid that Rose will betray him, Pinkie tries to kill her, but she is saved at the last moment and falls to his death from the pier. Even his right-hand man, Dallow, has been shocked by his ruthlessness.

1948

March   ***Escape*** (20th Century, 79 mins)
prod: William Perlberg; dir: Joseph L. Mankiewicz;
scr: Philip Dunne, from play by John Galsworthy

Matt Denant	Rex Harrison
Dora Winton	Peggy Cummins
Insp. Harris	**William Hartnell**
Girl	Betty Ann Davies
Parson	Norman Wooland
Grace Winton	Jill Esmond
Convict	Frederick Piper
Rogers	Cyril Cusack
Miss Pinkem	Marjorie Rhodes
Salesman	John Slater
P. C.	Frank Pettingell
Judge	Frederick Leister
Defence	Walter Hudd
Crown	Maurice Denham
Farmer Browning	George Woodbridge
Sir James	Stuart Lindsell
Plain Clothes Man	Michael Golden
Phyllis	Jacqueline Clarke
Mr Pinkem	Frank Tickle
Titch	Peter Croft
Car Driver	Ian Russell
Shepherd	Patrick Troughton
Policeman	Cyril Smith

A good, taut remake of the 1930 thriller, in which Denant is an ex-RAF officer escaped from Dartmoor. He had been serving a sentence for accidentally killing a policeman, who was manhandling a prostitute. Dora takes him in and gives him food; when surrounded by police, she persuades him to give himself up, but he knows she will wait for him.

1949

June   ***Now Barabbas Was a Robber*** (Warner Bros, 87 mins)
prod: Anatole de Grunwald; dir/scr: Gordon Parry, from play
by William Douglas Home

Tufnell	Richard Greene
Governor	Cedric Hardwicke
Mrs Brown	Kathleen Harrison
Roberts	Ronald Howard
Chaplin	Stephen Murray
Warder Jackson	**William Hartnell**
Kitty	Beatrice Campbell
Paddy	Richard Burton
Rosie	Betty Ann Davis
Brown	Leslie Dwyer
Gale	Alec Clunes
Smith	Harry Fowler
Spencer	Kenneth More
Winnie	Dora Bryan
Jean	Constance Smith
Woman	Lilly Kahn
'Erb Brown	David Hannaford
Medworth	Julian d'Albie
Richards	Peter Doughty
Jones	Percy Walsh
Anderson	Glyn Lawson
King	Gerald Case

Victor Fairly, Dandy Nichols

A good drama about a group of criminals in prison, with
well-drawn characters. It tells their stories: the murderer,
Tufnell, under sentence of death; a meek bank clerk led astray
by a girl; an Irish nationalist, Paddy; a bigamist and a
smuggler. Some of them are released by the end.

June   ***The Lost People*** (Gainsborough, 88 mins)
prod: Gordon Wellesley; dir: Bernard Knowles, Muriel Box;
scr: Bridget Boland, Muriel Box, from play *Cockpit* by
Bridget Boland

Capt. Ridley	Dennis Price
Lili	Mai Zetterling
Jan	Richard Attenborough
Marie	Siobhan McKenna
Peter	Maxwell Reed
Sgt Barnes	**William Hartnell**
Professor	Gerard Heinz
Anna	Zena Marshall
Milosh	Olaf Pooley
Priest	Harcourt Williams
Droja	Philo Hauser
Rebecca	Jill Balcon
Capt. Saunders	Grey Blake
Duval	Marcel Poncin
Wolf	Peter Bull
Prisoner	Charles Hawtrey

Tutte Lemkow, Paul Hardtmuth, Nelly Arno

An inexperienced captain takes control of an old theatre used as a dispersal centre for displaced persons. Barnes, the more streetwise sergeant under him, tries to warn him how difficult it will be to keep the peace between the different political and national groups. A suspected case of the plague makes them all pull together, but they learn about tolerance only when an innocent young girl in love is killed.

1950

March   ***Double Confession*** (85 mins)
prod: Harry Reynolds; dir: Ken Annakin;
scr: William Templeton, Ralph Keene, from novel *All on a Summer's Day* by John Garden

Jim Medway	Derek Farr
Ann Medway	Joan Hopkins
Paynter	Peter Lorre
Charles Durham	**William Hartnell**
Kate	Kathleen Harrison
Insp. Tenby	Naunton Wayne
Hilary Boscombe	Ronald Howard

Leonard	Leslie Dwyer
Church	Edward Rigby
Sgt Sawnton	George Woodbridge
Man in Shelter	Henry Edwards
Mme Zilia	Vida Hope
Mme Cleo	Esma Cannon
Collector	Roy Plomley

Mona Washbourne, Jennifer Cross, Andrew Leigh, Fred Griffiths, Diane Connell, Jane Griffiths, Hal Osmond, Norman Astridge, Betty Nelson

Medway finds his estranged wife and another man at the bottom of a cliff. He confronts his wife's lover, Durham, saying he is going to frame him for it. Durham sends his henchman, Paynter after him but fails to kill him. It is revealed that the wife committed suicide, but the man had been pushed. Paynter tries to confess, then flees onto a roof. Durham, instead of trying to talk him down, encourages him to jump. The police sort out the tortuous plot, but most of the audience found it totally confusing.

1951

February ***The Dark Man*** (Independent Artists, 91 mins)
prod: Julian Wintle; dir/scr: Jeffrey Dell

Insp. Jack Viner	Edward Underdown
The Dark Man	Maxwell Reed
Molly Lester	Natasha Parry
Superintendent	**William Hartnell**
Carol Burns	Barbara Murray
Samuel Denny	Cyril Smith
Detective Evans	Leonard White
Adjutant	John Singer
Major	Geoffrey Sumner
Sergeant-Major	Sam Kidd
Walsham Police Sergeant	Geoffrey Bond
Walsham Police Inspector	Gerald Anderson
Carol's Mother	Betty Cooper
Charles Burns	Robert Long

Hotel Proprietress	Grace Denbigh Russell
Doctor	Norman Claridge
Taxi Driver	John Hewer

The Dark Man kills someone during a robbery, then kills a cab driver. Seen by a girl cyclist, he pursues her, and tries to murder her twice, but fails. He is finally cornered by the police, and meets his end on an army practice firing range.

August   **The Magic Box** (Festival Film Productions, 118 mins)
Made for the Festival of Britain
prod: Ronald Neame; dir: John Boulting; scr: Eric Ambler, from book by Ray Allister

William Friese-Greene	Robert Donat
Edith Harrison	Margaret Johnston
Helena Friese-Greene	Maria Schell
Maurice Friese-Greene	John Howard Davies
Claude Friese-Greene	David Oake
Kenneth Friese-Greene	James Kenney
Miss Tagg	Renee Asherson
Jack Carter	Richard Attenborough
Lord Beaverbrook	Robert Beatty
Father	Edward Chapman
Reporter	Michael Denison
Maid	Joan Dowling
Butler	Henry Edwards
Dacres	Leo Genn
House Agent	Marius Goring
Mrs Clare	Joyce Grenfell
Sitter	Robertson Hare
Mother	Kathleen Harrison
Sergeant	**William Hartnell**
Mrs Stukeley	Joan Hickson
Broker's Man	Stanley Holloway
PC Charlie	Jack Hulbert
Sergeant	Sidney James
Mary Jones	Glynis Johns
Gotz	Mervyn Johns

Doctor	Barry Jones
Industry Man	Peter Jones
Industry Man	John Longden
Conductor	Miles Malleson
Sir Arthur Sullivan	Muir Matheson
Colonel	A. E. Matthews
Sitter	John McCullum
Alfred	Bernard Miles
Man	Richard Murdoch
PC 94B	Laurence Olivier
Platform Man	Cecil Parker
Father	Frank Pettingell
Arthur Collings	Eric Portman
Harold	Dennis Price
Ledley	Michael Redgrave
Lady Pond	Margaret Rutherford
Fairground Barker	Ronald Shiner
Nurse	Sheila Sim
William Fox-Talbot	Basil Sydney
Man	Ernest Thesiger
Sitter	Sybil Thorndike
Bob	David Tomlinson
John Rudge	Cecil Trouncer
Industry Man	Peter Ustinov
Guttenberg	Frederick Valk
Industry Man	Charles Victor
Receptionist	Kay Walsh
Bank Manager	Emlyn Williams
Tom	Harcourt Williams
Sitter	Googie Withers
Cashier	Joan Young

This biographical history of William Friese-Greene was the industry's contribution to the Festival of Britain. Friese-Greene was the portrait photographer responsible for inventing the movie camera (patented two years before by Edison). The story traces his financial hardships – his first wife dies, his second leaves him in the face of bankruptcy. He ends up broke, dying at a film industry meeting. Filled with cameos by famous actors all agreeing to alphabetical billing.

1952

December   ***The Ringer*** (London Films, 78 mins)
prod: Hugh Percival; dir: Guy Hamilton; scr: Val Valentine, Leslie Storm, from play *The Gaunt Stranger* by Edgar Wallace

Maurice Meister	Herbert Lom
Dr Leonard	Donald Wolfit
Lisa	Mai Zetterling
Cora Ann Milton	Greta Gynt
Sam Hackett	**William Hartnell**
Insp. Bliss	Norman Wooland
John Lenley	Denholm Elliott
Mrs Hackett	Dora Bryan
Insp. Wembury	Charlie Victor
Commissioner	Walter Fitzgerald
Gardener	John Stuart
Bell	John Slater
Strangler	Edward Chapman

A master of disguise, 'The Ringer', is after a crooked lawyer, Meister, whom he holds responsible for the suicide of his sister. Meister employs ex-con Hackett as a bodyguard, and the police try to protect him, but the police doctor turns out to be the Ringer. He strangles Meister with a wire from a burglar alarm and then escapes.

August   ***The Holly and the Ivy*** (British Lion, 83 mins)
prod: Anatole de Grunwald, Hugh Percival;
dir: George More O'Ferrall; scr: Anatole de Grunwald, from play by Wynyard Browne

Rev. Martin Gregory	Ralph Richardson
Jenny Gregory	Celia Johnson
Margaret Gregory	Margaret Leighton
Michael 'Mick' Gregory	Denholm Elliott
David Patterson	John Gregson
Richard Wyndham	Hugh Williams
Aunt Lydia	Margaret Halstan

Aunt Bridget	Maureen Delany
Company Sergeant-Major	**William Hartnell**
Major	Robert Flemyng
Lord B	Roland Culver
Clubman	John Barry
Neighbour	Dandy Nichols

A beautifully cast film about a widowed reverend who gathers his family round him for Christmas at the vicarage, among them the two children who have left home – Michael, a soldier, and Margaret, a hard-drinking journalist. Margaret turned to drink on the death of the child she'd had out of wedlock by a man who died in the war. She confides this to Michael and her elder sister, Jenny, who has remained at home to look after their father. The film ends with Margaret taking Jenny's place at home, so the latter can marry her long-time fiancé.

November ***The Pickwick Papers*** (Renown Pictures 115/109 mins)
prod: George Mintley, Noel Langley; dir/scr: Noel Langley, from novel by Charles Dickens

Samuel Pickwick	James Hayter
Mr Jingle	Nigel Patrick
Mr Winkle	James Donald
Rachel Wardle	Kathleen Harrison
Martha Bardell	Hermione Baddeley
Mrs Leo Hunter	Joyce Grenfell
Mrs Tomkins	Hermione Gingold
Sgt Buzfuz	Donald Wolfit
Sam Weller	Harry Fowler
Job Trotter	Sam Costa
Tony Weller	George Robey
Grandma Wardle	Mary Merrall
Miss Witherfield	Athene Seyler
Tracy Tupman	Alexander Gauge
Augustus Snodgrass	Lionel Murton
Cabman	**William Hartnell**
Roker	Noel Purcell

Mr Wardle	Walter Fitzgerald
Dr Payne	Raymond Lovell
Mr Justice Stareleigh	Cecil Trouncer
Perker	Noel Willman
Isabel	Joan Heal
Emily Wardle	Diane Hart
Aide	Max Adrian
Dr Slammer	Felix Felto
Fogg	Alan Wheatley
Dodson	D. A. Clarke-Smith
Mrs Nupkins	Hattie Jacques
Nupkins	Jack McNaughton
Boy	David Hannaford
Fat Boy	Gerald Campion
Arabella	June Thorburn
Snubbins	Barry Mackay
Foreman	Gibb McLaughlin

A jolly adaptation of the Dickens classic set in 1830. The Pickwick Club is composed of a group of middle-aged, middle-class men who set out on a tour to study English life. Meeting up with Jingle they get into all sorts of scrapes including a duel, a spell in debtors' prison, etc. All turns out well in the end, of course. Full of wonderful performances by our best light comedians and comediennes – WH is almost unrecognisable in full character make-up.

1953

May

Will Any Gentleman? (Associated British, 84 mins)
prod: Hamilton G. Inglis; dir: Michael Anderson;
scr: Vernon Sylvaine from his own play

Henry	George Cole
Florence	Veronica Hurst
Charley	Jon Pertwee
Mrs Whittle	Heather Thatcher
Dr Smith	James Hayter
Insp. Martin	**William Hartnell**
Angel	Diane Decker

Beryl	Joan Sims
The Great Mendoza	Alan Badel
Hobson	Sidney James
Mr Jackson	Brian Oulton
Mr Billing	Alexander Gauge
Receptionist	Josephine Douglas
Stage Manager	Peter Butterworth
Bookmaker	Wally Patch
Mr Frobisher	Lionel Jeffries
Stout Man	Richard Massingham

Wilfred Boyle, Jill Melford, Diana Hope, Martyn Wyldeck, Frank Birch, Arthur Howard, Brian Wilde, Nan Brainton, Lucy Griffiths, Harry Herbert, Russ Allen, Sylvia Russell, Jackie Joyner, Eleanor Fazan, Lillian Knudsen.

Henry is a meek bank clerk unwillingly persuaded to take part in a hypnotist stage show. He does not snap out of the trance and starts living riotously, spending the bank's cash and making advances to other women. Finally the Great Mendoza returns him to normal. Amusing and well produced.

1955

July   ***Footsteps in the Fog*** (90 mins)
prod: M. J. Frankovich, Maxwell Setton; dir: Arthur Lubin; scr: Lenore Coffee, Dorothy Reid, Arthur Pearson, from novel by W. W. Jacobs

Stephen Lowry	Stewart Granger
Lily Watkins	Jean Simmons
David McDonald	Bill Travers
Alfred Travers	Ronald Squire
Insp. Peters	Finlay Currie
Elizabeth Travers	Belinda Lee
Herbert Moresby	**William Hartnell**
Matthew Burke	Barry Keegan
Mrs Park	Marjorie Rhodes
Rose Moresby	Sheila Manahan
Brasher	Peter Bull

Dr Simpson	Frederick Leister
Jones	Victor Maddern
Magistrate	Percy Marmont
Cons. Farrow	Peter Williams
Vicar	Arthur Howard
Grimes	Norman Macowen
Corcoran	Cameron Hall

Set in 1905 when maid Lily discovers Lowry, her employer whom she secretly loves, has killed his wife. She blackmails him into making her housekeeper. He tries to kill her, but in the fog gets the wrong girl. Put on trial, he is saved by Lily's testimony. Lowry gives himself small doses of poison so Lily can be arrested for attempted murder, but he overdoes it and dies. She is accused of his murder. Well performed, but slow.

December   ***Josephine and Men*** (Charter/British Lion, 98 mins)
prod: John Boulting; dir: Roy Boulting; scr: Roy Boulting, Frank Harvey, Nigel Balchin

Josephine Luton	Glynis Johns
Charles Luton	Jack Buchanan
Alan Hartley	Donald Sinden
Donald Hewer	Peter Finch
Insp. Parsons	**William Hartnell**
Frederick Luton	Ronald Squire
Henry	Victor Maddern
May Luton	Heather Thatcher
Salesman	Thorley Walters
Inspector	Hugh Moxley
Porter	Laurence Naismith
Registrar	John Le Mesurier
Girl	Lisa Gastoni

Leo Ciceri, Pauline David, Sam Kydd

Josephine always falls for the underdog – she abandons wealthy fiancé Hartley for struggling playwright Hewer. When he becomes successful, she goes back to Hartley when he turns up after a massive swindle. When he's cleared, she returns to Hewer. Not a very successful comedy.

1956

February   ***Doublecross*** (Beaconsfield, 71 mins)
prod: Donald Taylor; dir: Anthony Squire;
scr: Anthony Squire, Ken Bennett, from Ken Bennett's novel
Queer Fish

Albert Pascoe	Donald Houston
Whiteway	**William Hartnell**
Alice Pascoe	Fay Compton
Anna Krassin	Delphi Lawrence
Dmitri Krassin	Anton Diffring
Chief Constable	Frank Lawton
Fred Trewin	John Blythe
Clifford	Allan Cuthbertson
Harry Simms	Bruce Gordon
Insp. Harris	Raymond Francis
Rose	Ann Stephens

Robert Shaw, Helena Pickford, Toby Perkins, Harry Towb, Gene Anderson

Fisherman-cum-salmon poacher Pascoe accepts money to ferry two men and a woman across the Channel – the woman reveals they are Soviet spies. He strands the men in a cove and returns with the girl to a hero's welcome, though narrowly escaping prosecution for poaching. Not very successful either as a thriller or a comedy.

March   ***Private's Progress*** (Charter/British Lion, 102 mins)
prod: Roy Boulting; dir: John Boulting; scr: John Boulting, Frank Harvey

Pte Percy Cox	Richard Attenborough
Bertram Tracepurcel	Dennis Price
Maj. Hitchcock	Terry-Thomas
Stanley Windrush	Ian Carmichael
Egan	Peter Jones
Sgt Sutton	**William Hartnell**
Capt. Bootle	Thorley Walters
Prudence Greenslade	Jill Adams
Pte Horrocks	Ian Bannen

Pte George Blake	Victor Maddern
Pte Dai Jones	Kenneth Griffith
Sgt-Maj. Gradwick	John Warren
Padre	George Coulouris
Pat	Derek de Marney
Mr Windrush	Miles Malleson
Col. Panshawe	Michael Trubshawe
Psychiatrist	John Le Mesurier
Expert	Henry Oscar
German	Christopher Lee

Brian Oulton, Nicholas Bruce, David Lodge, David
King-Wood, Frank Hawkins, Basil Dignam, Henry
Longhurst, Theodore Zichy, Michael Ward, Robert Bruce,
Ludwig Lawinski, Sally Miles, Irlyn Hall, Marianne Stone,
Lockwood West, Jack McNaughton, Eynon Evans, Glyn
Houston, Ronald Adam, Lloyd Lamble

A popular farcical comedy in which bumbling upper-class
undergraduate Windrush is called up for the army in World
War II. He is soon taught various dodges by scroungers such
as Cox. Through his uncle he gets involved in stealing art
treasures from behind enemy lines. He brings this off more
through luck than judgement, but gets his comeuppance.
WH as usual plays the straight sergeant who gets him in the
end.

March   **Tons of Trouble** (Shaftesbury, 77 mins)
prod: Elizabeth Hiscott, Richard Hearne; dir: Leslie Hiscott;
scr: Leslie Hiscott, Richard Hearne

Mr Pastry	Richard Hearne
Bert	**William Hartnell**
Sir Hervey Shaw	Austin Trevor
Angela Shaw	Joan Marion
Jevons	Robert Moreton
Insp. Bridger	Ralph Tryman
Psychiatrist	Ronald Adam
Diana Little	Junia Crawford
Cracknell	Tony Quinn

Doctor	John Stuart
Yvonne Hearne	

An amusing farce in which eccentric caretaker Mr Pastry looks after two apartment boilers, Mavis and Ethel. Because of his devotion to these he gets mixed up with a big business deal and the police. He gets sacked but reinstated just in time to save one of the boilers from blowing its top.

1957

April   ***Yangtse Incident: The Story of HMS Amethyst***
(Wilcox-Neagle/Associated British, 112 mins)
prod: Herbert Wilcox; dir: Michael Anderson;
scr: Eric Ambler, from book by Lawrence Earl and idea by
Frank Gollings and Official Admiralty Records
Technical Adviser: Commander J. S. Kerans

Lt-Cdr Kerans	Richard Todd
Leading Seaman Frank	**William Hartnell**
Col. Peng	Akim Tamiroff
Lt Weston	Donald Houston
Capt. Kuo Tai	Keye Luke
Charlotte Dunlap	Sophie Stewart
Flight Lt Fearnley	Robert Urquhart
Lt Hett	James Kenney
Lt Strain	Richard Leech
Lt Berger	Michael Brill
PO McCarthy	Barry Forster
Mr Monaghan	Thomas Heathcott
Walker	Sam Kydd
Williams	Ewan Solon
Martin	Brian Smith
Roberts	John Charlesworth
Mr McNamara	Kenneth Cope
Petty Officer	Alfred Burke
Crocker	Keith Rawlings
Bannister	Ian Bannen

Bernard Cribbins, Cyril Luckham, Gene Anderson, Ray Jackson, John A. Tinn, Karl Rawlings, Andy Ho, Cesar

Da'Rocha, Ya Ming, Dennis Clinton, Anthony Chinn, Murray Kash, Peter Hutton, A. Chong Choy, Gordon Whiting, Basil Dignam, Garcia Tay, Ralph Truman, Richard Coleman, Allan Cuthbertson

A well-made film telling the true story of HMS Amethyst, trapped on the communist-dominated Yangtse River in 1949. During a rousing battle scene the captain is killed. Endless negotiations take place between the Chinese and Lt-Cdr Kerans, accompanied by Leading Seaman Frank dressed up as an officer, before they make a break for freedom.

US title: *Battle Hell*

July

Hell Drivers (Rank, 108 mins)

prod: Benny Fisz; dir: Cy Endfield; scr: Cy Endfield, John Kruse, from John Kruse's book

Tom Yately	Stanley Baker
Red	Patrick McGoohan
Gino	Herbert Lom
Lucy	Peggy Cummins
Cartley	**William Hartnell**
Ed	Wilfred Lawson
Dusty	Sidney James
Jill	Jill Ireland
Tinker	Alfie Bass
Scotty	Gordon Jackson
Jimmy Yately	David McCallum
Johnny	Sean Connery
Ma West	Marjorie Rhodes
Blonde	Vera Day
Assistant Manager	Robin Bailey
Mrs Yately	Beatrice Varley
Pop	Wensley Pithey
Tub	George Murcell
Spinster	Jean St Clair
Chick	Jerry Stavin
Doctor	John Horsley
Nurse	Marianne Stone

Barber Joe	Ronald Clarke

Yately is an ex-convict who gets a job driving trucks along dangerous roads. Top driver Red and manager Cartley are running a racket with drivers having to make extra runs with the two of them splitting their pay. During a terrific lorry race Red tries to push Yately's lorry over a cliff but it is he himself who hurtles to his death.

July **The Hypnotist** (Anglo Amalgamated, 74 mins)
prod: Alec Snowden; dir/scr: Montgomery Tully, from play by Falkland Cary

Dr Francis Pelham	Roland Culver
Mary Foster	Patricia Roc
Val Neal	Paul Carpenter
Insp. Ross	**William Hartnell**
Susie	Kay Callard
Barbara Barton	Ellen Pollock
Sgt Davies	Gordon Needham
Dr Bradford	Martin Wyldeck
Dr Kenyon	Oliver Johnson
Mrs Neal	Mary Jones
Psychiatrist	John Serret
Nurses	Helene Gilmer, Patricia Wellum
Atkins	Edgar Driver
Chief Designer	Robert Sansom
Mechanic	Douglas Hayes
Engineer	Salvin Stuart
Control Officer	Gordon Harris
Nurse	Jill Nicholls
Secretary	Jessica Cairns
Mrs Briggs	Hilda Barry
Val as a lad	Tim Fitzgerald
Manservant	Tom Tann
Police Constable Green	Dennis McCarthy
Constable	Richard Stewart

An unlikely story in which Neal, a test pilot, suffers from blackouts and goes to see Pelham, a psychiatrist who uses hypnotism to treat patients. Pelham tries to mesmerise the pilot into killing his wife, but when he fails to do so, he kills her himself and frames Neal. Eventually Neal's fiancée uncovers the truth and saves him.

US title: *Scotland Yard Dragnet*

July

Date with Disaster (Fortress Productions, 61 mins)
prod: Guido Coen; dir: Charles Saunders; scr: Brock Williams

Miles	Tom Drake
Tracy	**William Hartnell**
Sue	Shirley Eaton
Don	Maurice Kaufmann
Insp. Matthews	Michael Golden
Ken	Richard Shaw
Charles	Charles Brodie
Judy	Deirdre Mayne
Sgt Brace	Peter Fontaine
Young Man	Robert Robinson
Constable	John Drake
Sergeant	Robert Mooney

With the help of a professional criminal, Tracy, two out of three partners in a garage business plan to relieve it of £20,000. Things go wrong for the crooks, who kidnap Miles's girl. But Miles saves her himself. Very much a second feature.

1958

June

On the Run (United Artists, 70 mins)
prod: Edward J. & Harry Lee Danziger; dir: Ernest Morris; scr: Brian Clemens, Eldon Howard

Wesley	Neil McCallum
Kitty Casey	Susan Beaumont
Tom Casey	**William Hartnell**
Bart Taylor	Gordon Tanner
Driscoll	Philip Saville
Joe	Gilbert Winfield

Wesley is a boxer who has refused to throw a fight. He is on the run from a gang and takes a job in a country garage, falling in love with the owner, Casey's, daughter. She urges him to stand up to the gang and he beats them – predictable, but good fight sequences.

August   ***Carry On Sergeant*** (Anglo Amalgamated, 83 mins)
presented by: Nat Cohen & Stuart Levy; prod: Peter Rogers; dir: Gerald Thomas; scr: Norman Huddis, from *The Bull Boys* by R. F. Delderfield; additional material: John Antrobus

Sgt Grimshaw	**William Hartnell**
Charlie Sage	Bob Monkhouse
Mary Sage	Shirley Eaton
Capt. Potts	Eric Barker
Nora	Dora Bryan
Cpl Copping	Bill Owen
Horace Strong	Kenneth Connor
Peter Golightly	Charles Hawtrey
James Bailey	Kenneth Williams
Miles Heywood	Terence Longdon
Herbert Brown	Norman Rossington
Capt. Clark	Hattie Jacques
Andy Galloway	Gerald Campion
Gun Sergeant	Cyril Chamberlain
1st Specialist	Gordon Tanner
2nd Specialist	Frank Forsyth
3rd Specialist	Basil Dignam
4th Specialist	John Gatrell
5th Specialist	Arnold Diamond
6th Specialist	Martin Boddey
Medical Corporal	Ian Whittaker
Stores Sergeant	Anthony Sager

Joanne Stewart, Edward Judd, Helen Gross

The first of the 'Carry On' films. Grimshaw is a tough drill sergeant about to retire, who is desperate to win the Best Squad Award with his last intake of National Service recruits. Unfortunately they are a completely useless bunch. A talented cast run the gamut of old army jokes and, despite Grimshaw's shouting, they find he has a heart of gold, so with a supreme effort they win the award for him.

1959

June

Shake Hands with the Devil (Troy Films/ Pennebaker Productions/United Artists, 111 mins)
prod: George Glass, Walter Seltzer; dir: Michael Anderson; scr: Ivan Goff, Ben Roberts, Marion Thompson, from novel by Reardon Connor

Sean Lenihan	James Cagney
Kerry O'Shea	Don Murray
Jennifer Curtis	Dana Wynter
Kitty O'Brady	Glynis Johns
Chris Noonan	Cyril Cusack
The General	Michael Redgrave
Lady Fitzhugh	Sybil Thorndike
Mary Madigan	Marianne Benet
McGrath	John Brelin
Cassidy	Harry Brogan
Judge	Lewis Casson
Mike O'Callaghan	John Cairney
Clancy	Harry H. Corbett
Terence O'Brien	Richard Harris
Sgt Jenkins	**William Hartnell**
Michael O'Leary	Niall MacGinnis
Paddy Nolan	Ray McAnally
Liam O'Sullivan	Noel Purcell
Mrs Madigan	Eileen Gowe
Captain	Allan Cuthbertson
Captain	Peter Reynolds
Capt Flemming	Alan White
Sir Arnold Fielding	Clive Morton
Donovan	Patrick McAlinney
British General	John Le Mesurier
Doyle	Paul Farrell
Eileen O'Leary	Eithne Dunne

Tommy Connor	Wilfred Downing
Willie Caffery	Donal Donnelly
Sergeant, Black and Tans	Ronald Walsh
Col. Smithson	Christopher Rhodes

A strong thriller set in Dublin in 1921. Lenihan, a medical professor, is also a militant member of the IRA. He tries to influence some of his students to take up arms, including O'Shea, who takes refuge with the IRA after his friend is killed by the Black and Tans. Jennifer, the daughter of a top British official, is kidnapped. O'Shea sees that Lenihan's devotion to violence has gone beyond idealism and is forced to shoot him to stop him killing Jennifer, with whom he has fallen in love and whose death would have jeopardised a peace treaty.

June **The Mouse that Roared** (Columbia, 90 mins)
prod: Walter Shenson, Jon Penington; dir: Jack Arnold;
scr: Roger MacDougall, Stanley Mann, from novel *The Wrath of Grapes* by Leonard Wibberley
Tully Bascombe/Gloriana/

Count Mountjoy	Peter Sellers
Helen Kokintz	Jean Seberg
Will	**William Hartnell**
Prof. Kokintz	David Kossoff
Benter	Leo McKern
Snippet	MacDonald Parke
Secretary of Defence	Austin Willis
Roger	Timothy Bateson
Cobbley	Monty Landis
Mulligan	Robin Gatehouse
Announcer	Colin Gordon
O'Hara	George Margo
Chester Beston	Larry Cross
Pedro	Harold Kasket
Ticket Collector	Jacques Cey
Cunard Captain	Stuart Sanders
Cunard 2nd Officer	Ken Stanley

US Policeman	Bill Nagy
Telephone Operator	Mavis Villiers
British Ambassador	Charles Clay
French Ambassador	Harry de Bray
Army Captain	Bill Edwards
Soviet Ambassador	Guy Deghy
Reporter	Robert O'Neill

The European Duchy of Fenwick is on the verge of bankruptcy and declares war on America, hoping to be well reimbursed in defeat. Tully Bascombe doesn't know he's supposed to lose and, assisted by Will, he captures the American Q Bomb. He ousts Fenwick's premier Count Mountjoy and negotiates a treaty between the US and Queen Gloriana.

September **The Night We Dropped a Clanger**
(Sydney Box Associates/Four Star/Rank, 86 mins)
prod: David Henley; dir: Darcy Conyers; scr: John Chapman

Wing Commander Blenkinsop/	
Arthur Atwood	Brian Rix
Sir Bertram Buckpasser	Cecil Parker
Sgt Bright	**William Hartnell**
Second Lieutenant Thomas	Leslie Phillips
Belling	Leo Franklin
Lulu Billingsgate	Liz Fraser
Ada	Hattie Jacques
Mme Grilby	Vera Pearce
Second Lieutenant Grant	John Welsh
Mrs Billingsgate	Irene Handl
Farmer	Larry Noble
Dancer	Julie Mendez
WAAF Hawkins	Sarah Branch
Air Cdr Turner	Oliver Johnson
Wing Commander	John Chapman
Corporal	Gilbert Harrison
Wing Cdr Jones	Arnold Bell
Wing Cdr Priestly	David Jones

Monty's Double	Geoffrey Denys
Gen. Grimble	Charles Cameron
Hammerstein	Denis Shaw
Pilot	Peter Burton

Blenkinsop is a top British secret service man and his double, Atwood, is a latrine orderly. Orders get mixed up and Blenkinsop gets sent to Africa, while Atwood goes to France to investigate the buzz bombs. He becomes a hero when he captures a flying bomb by accidentally defusing it. The secret service man tries in vain to prove who he is, and it is only in post-war years when they meet up that they resume their normal identities.

November **Strictly Confidential** (Rank, 62 mins)

prod: Guido Coen; dir: Charles Saunders; scr: Brock Williams

Cdr Bissham-Ryley	Richard Murdoch
Maj. Rory McQuarry	William Kendall
Maxine Millard	Maya Koumani
Grimshaw	**William Hartnell**
Warder	Colin Rix
Capt. Sharples	Ellis Irving
Barman	Larry Burns
Insp. Shearing	Bruce Seton
Rizzi	Paul Bogdan
Mellinger	Normal Rees
Hot Dog Man	Harry Ross
O'Connor	Beresford Egan
Dennis Wood	

Not very successful comedy in which the two main characters have just been released from jail and get hired by a rich young widow to run her factory. She doesn't know about their past and they don't know she's using them to play around with shareholders.

December **The Desperate Man** (Anglo Amalgamated, 57 mins)

prod: Jack Greenwood; dir: Peter Maxwell;

scr: James Eastwood, from Paul Somer's novel *Beginners Luck*

| Carol Bourne | Jill Ireland |

Curtis	Conrad Philips
Smith	**William Hartnell**
Lawson	Charles Grey
Hoad	Peter Swanick
Landlord	Arthur Gomes
Insp. Cobley	John Warwick
Miss Prew	Patricia Burke
Grocer	Ernest Butcher

Doris Yorke, Jean Aubrey, Brian Weske, Marian Collins
Not a particularly good thriller in which reporter Curtis and girlfriend Bourne stumble across a murder while they are taking a break in Sussex. They track down the man responsible, jewel thief Smith, but he holds Bourne hostage in a castle to force Curtis to help him. Eventually the thief falls to his own death from the battlements.

1960

February *And the Same to You* (Eros, 70 mins)
prod: William Gell; dir: George Pollack;
scr: John Paddy Carstairs, John Junkin, Terry Nation, from the play *Chigwell Chicken* by A. P. Dearsley

Dickie Dreadnought	Brian Rix
Wally Burton	**William Hartnell**
Horace	Tommy Cooper
Cynthia	Vera Day
Sammy Gatt	Sidney James
Rev. Sydney Mullett	Leo Franklin
Percy Gibbons	Tony Wright
Mildred	Renee Houston
George Nibbs	Dick Bentley
Pomphret	John Robinson
Bishop	Miles Malleson
Trout	Ronald Adam
Iris	Shirley Ann Field
Tubby	Arthur Mullard
Police Constable	Terry Scott
Manicurist	Jean Clarke

Mike	Tommy Duggan
Butch	Rupert Evans
Jake	George Lee
Bert Bender	Lindsay Hopper
Secretary	Jennifer Phipps
Master of Ceremonies	Jack Taylor

The vicar's nephew becomes a boxer after knocking out a prizefighter, but outwardly maintains his religious appearance, while his crude promoter poses as a church official to fool the archdeacon. The vicar sees it as a way of raising money for the church roof. The Archdeacon finds out and threatens to stop the fights but is blackmailed over his wife's gambling.

March   ***Jackpot*** (Eternal Films, 71 mins)
prod: Maurice J. Wilson; dir: Montgomery Tully;
scr: Montgomery Tully, Maurice Wilson, from story by
John Sherma

Supt Frawley	**William Hartnell**
Kay Stock	Betty McDowell
Sam Hare	Eddie Byrne
Carl Stock	George Mikell
Lenny Lane	Victor Brooks
Peter	Tim Turner

Minor crime drama in which a convict wants to go straight. His wife is unwilling to share his new life so he gets involved with an old friend, a safe-cracker, in a robbery on a nightclub.

September ***Piccadilly Third Stop*** (Rank, 90 mins)
prod: Norman Williams; dir: Wolf Rilla; scr: Leigh Vance

Dominic Colpoys-Owen	Terence Morgan
Serephina Yokami	Yoko Tani
Joe Pready	John Crawford
Christine Pready	Mai Zetterling
Colonel	**William Hartnell**
Edward	Dennis Price
Mouse	Ann Lynn
Toddy	Charles Kay

Albert	Douglas Robinson
Bride's Mother	Gillian Maude
Father	Trevor Reid
Police Sergeant	Ronald Leigh Hunt
Private Detective	Alan Rolfe
Fop	Tony Hawes
Bride	Judy Huxtable
Groom	Michael Behr
Police Superintendent	Reginald Hearne
Chemmy Dealer	Clement Freud

Toby Perkins, Ann Doonan, Sonia Fox, Anthony Doonan
A playboy, Colpoys-Owen, and accomplice, Pready, hatch a
plan to break into an Eastern embassy when they get friendly
with the daughter of a foreign ambassador. She accidentally
let slip that her father left $280,000 in a safe. She becomes so
involved with Colpoys-Owen that she even helps plan the
heist which entails breaking in through an old underground
tunnel.

1962

September **Tomorrow at Ten**
(Blakeley's Productions/Mancunian Film, 80 mins)
prod: Tom Blakeley; dir: Lance Comfort; scr: Peter Millar,
James Kelly

Insp Parnell	John Gregson
Marlow	Robert Shaw
Anthony Chester	Alec Clunes
Bewley	Alan Wheatley
Sgt Grey	Kenneth Cope
Robbie	Helen Cherry
Freddy	**William Hartnell**
Mrs Parnell	Betty McDowell
Dr Towers	Ernest Clark
Mrs Maddock	Renee Houston
Specialist	Noel Howlett
Nurses	Bernadette Woodman,
	Marguerite McCourt

Briggs	Ray Smith
Henry	John Dunbar
Jonathan	Piers Bishop

Marlow kidnaps the son of millionaire Chester and demands a ransom. He has hidden the boy in a remote house with a time-bomb hidden in a doll. A fight breaks out and Marlow is killed before revealing where the boy is hidden. The police rush to find him by the deadline – but the child has deactivated the bomb by immersing the doll in water.

1963

January   ***This Sporting Life*** (Independent Artists/Rank, 134 mins)
prod: Albert Fennell, Karel Reisz; dir: Lindsay Anderson;
scr: David Storey

Frank Machin	Richard Harris
Margaret Hammond	Rachel Roberts
Gerald Weaver	Alan Badel
Johnson	**William Hartnell**
Maurice Braithwaite	Colin Blakely
Anne Weaver	Vanda Godsell
Judith	Anne Cunningham
Len Miller	Jack Watson
Charles Slomer	Arthur Lowe
Wade	Harry Markham
Jeff	George Sewell
Phillips	Leonard Rossiter
Dentist	Frank Windsor
Doctor	Peter Duguid
Waiter	Wallis Eaton
Head Waiter	Anthony Woodruff
Mrs Farrer	Katherine Parr
Lynda	Bernadette Benson
Ian	Andrew Nolan
Riley	Michael Logan
Hooker	Murray Evans
Gower	Tom Clegg
Cameron	John Gull

Trainer	Ken Traill

A bleak and powerful film in which Machin, an ex-miner, wants to play professional rugger. Johnson, a lonely old man who does some talent spotting, helps introduce him to the right people. Machin rents a room in the house of lonely widow Hammond and tries to impress her, but she remains aloof, even after they start a physical relationship. He becomes rich and famous but is so uncouth he causes trouble. Machin and Hammond fight and he leaves but soon realises he cannot live without her. She suffers a brain haemorrhage; at the hospital he desperately tries to express his feelings before she dies.

April

Heavens Above! (Charter, 118 mins)
prod: Roy Boulting; dir: John Boulting;
scr: Malcolm Muggeridge

Rev. John Smallwood	Peter Sellers
Archdeacon Aspinall	Cecil Parker
Lady Despard	Isabel Jeans
Harry Smith	Eric Sykes
Simpson	Bernard Miles
Matthew	Peter Brock
The Other Smallwood	Ian Carmichael
Rene Smith	Irene Handl
Winnie Smith	Miriam Karlin
Mrs Smith-Gould	Joan Miller
Bank Manager	Eric Barker
Rockerby	Miles Malleson
Maj. Fowler	**William Hartnell**
Fred Smith	Roy Kinnear
Rev. Owen Thomas	Kenneth Griffith
Housewife	Joan Hickson
Shop Steward	Harry Locke
Director General	Nicholas Phipps
Tranquilax Executive	Thorley Walters
Bishop	George Woodbridge
Prison Governor	Basil Dignam

Prime Minister	Colin George
Housewife	Joan Heal
Cleric	Malcolm Muggeridge
PRO	Conrad Phillips
Tramp	Cardew Robinson
Sir Geoffrey Despard	Mark Eden
Fellowes	Billy Milton
Astronaut	Howard Pays
Butcher	John Comer
TV Commentators	Franklyn Engelmann, Tim Brinton, Ludovic Kennedy
Council Official	Geoffrey Hibbert
Women	Olive Sloane, Marjorie Lawrence
Deaf Man	Henry Longhurst
Lady on Council	Elsie Wagstaff
Salvation Army Major	Ian Wilson
Doris Smith	Josephine Woodford
Doris's Boyfriend	Drewe Henley

Smallwood, a prison chaplin, is appointed by mistake to a local church. He has too much compassion and shocks everyone by choosing a black churchwarden, invites gypsies to live with him in the manse, and exhorts the local peeress to give away her fortune. This causes a drop in the share price of the biggest local employers and he is finally hounded out. Reassigned to a missile base on an island, he ties up the astronaut and blasts off into space himself.

July **To Have and to Hold** (Anglo Amalgamated, 71 mins)
prod: Jack Greenwood; dir: Herbert Wise; scr: John Sansom, from story by Edgar Wallace

Sgt Henry Fraser	Ray Barrett
Claudia Matthews	Katherine Beake
George Matthews	Nigel Stock
Insp. Roberts	**William Hartnell**
Lucy	Patricia Bredin

Blake	Noel Trevarthen
Charles Wagner	Richard Clarke

A variation on *Double Indemnity*. Police Sergeant Blake falls in love with Claudia who involves him in a plot to murder her husband for the insurance money. Another not very good Edgar Wallace story.

June   **The World Ten Times Over** (Associated British, 93 mins)
prod: Michael Luke; dir/scr: Wolf Rilla

Billa	Sylvia Syms
Ginnie	June Ritchie
Elizabeth	Sarah Lawson
Compere	Davy Kaye
Bolton	Jack Gwillim
Freddy	Alan White
Bob Shelbourne	Edward Judd
Dad	**William Hartnell**
Shelbourne	Francis de Wolff
Penny	Linda Marlowe
Brian	Kevin Brennan

Billa and Ginnie are nightclub hostesses sharing an apartment. Ginnie is extrovert and attracted to lots of men; Billa exudes cynicism to protect herself. Ginnie becomes involved with wealthy separated Shelbourne who gets her a job in the family firm. WH plays a simple country schoolteacher whom Billa tries to shock when he visits; relations are so strained that he leaves. Shelbourne leaves his wife for good and begs Ginnie to go with him, but she decides to stay with her friend who has discovered she is pregnant.
US title: *Pussycat Alley*

William Hartnell probably also appeared in a version of **Kidnapped**, although I have been unable to verify this.

Appendix Two
PLAY LIST

THIS IS A LIST of the plays in which Bill appeared. There were many more, but I have traced neither programmes nor reviews with which to be able to date them. Productions were often mounted only for one week which makes the process even more difficult.

1926   Sir Frank Benson's Company
King's Theatre, Hammersmith
The Merchant of Venice, Shakespeare
Special matinee 2.30 p.m. Friday 30th April
With Sir Frank Benson as Shylock and Lilian Braithwaite as Portia
William Hartnell and Robert Donat as Venetians and Masquers

1926   Sir Frank Benson's Company (tour)
She Stoops to Conquer, Goldsmith; ***Julius Caesar***, Shakespeare; ***As You Like It***, Shakespeare; ***Hamlet***, Shakespeare; ***The Tempest***, Shakespeare; ***The School for Scandal***, R. B. Sheridan; ***The Merchant of Venice***, Shakespeare; ***Macbeth***, Shakespeare
ASM, walk-on and prompt, billed as 'Henry Hartnell'
Company included: Robert Donat
Dates included: Princes Theatre, Manchester, 7th June

1927   ***Good Morning, Bill***, P. G. Woodhouse
Duke of York's Theatre, West End then tour
Understudied Ernest Truex (lead), then played lead on tour

1928   Sir Frank Benson's Company (tour)
Monsieur Beaucaire, Newton Booth Tarkington & Evelyn
Greenleaf Sutherland; *Hamlet*, Shakespeare; *The School for
Scandal*, R. B. Sheridan; *The Merchant of Venice*, Shakespeare

Mon, Wed, Sat	*Monsieur Beaucaire*
Tues, Thurs matinee, Fri	*Hamlet*
Thurs	*The School for Scandal*
Sat matinee	*The Merchant of Venice*

Company included: Sir Frank Benson and Robert Donat
ASM and walk-on, billed as 'William Henry'
Dates included: King's Theatre, 13th Feb; Wimbledon Theatre,
20th Feb.

1928?   *The Man Responsible* (tour)
Played the lead

1928?   *The Lad*
Played Jimmy

1928?   *Good Morning, Bill*, P. G. Wodehouse
Robert Courtneidge presents, 6th Aug for 6 nights
King's Theatre, Hammersmith
Played the lead, Bill Paradene

1928   *Miss Elizabeth's Prisoner*, Robert Neilson Stevens & E. Lyall Swete
Gordon McLeod Productions, 10th Sep – 21st Nov
Tour of Canada
Played Sergeant Carrington
With Heather McIntyre as Molly Edwards, the Maid

1928/9 *A Bill of Divorcement*, Clemence Dane
Gordon McLeod Productions, 22nd Nov 1928 – 7th Feb 1929
Tour of Canada
Played Kit Pumfrey
With Heather McIntyre playing the lead, Sydney Fairfield

1929   *77 Park Lane* (tour, July for several months)
Venues included: Whitby
Played Philip Baynton
With Heather McIntyre

1930 *The Ugly Duchess*, adapted by Vera Beringer from
Lion Feuchtwanger's novel
prod: W. G. Fay
The Arts Theatre Club, 15th – 25th May
Played Duke Meinhard

1931 *The Man Who Changed His Name*, Edgar Wallace (tour)
prod: Barry O'Brien
Dates included: Brixton Theatre, 6th Apr for 1 week
Grand Theatre, Wolverhampton, 9th Mar
Played Frank O'Ryan, billed as William Hartnell

1931 *The Young Idea*, Noël Coward
Barry O'Brien presents
King's Theatre, Hammersmith, 23rd Nov for 6 nights
8 p.m.
Played Sholto
Preceded by 'Mr Dawson Reed in Selections from his Repertoire'

1932 *The Man I Killed*, Maurice Rostand
prod: Albert de Courville
Apollo Theatre, Shaftesbury Avenue, 2nd Mar
8.30 p.m. + 2 matinees
Starring Emlyn Williams and Celia Johnson
Played Erik, billed as William Hartnell

1932 *Too True to be Good*, George Bernard Shaw
Barry Jackson presents, direct from the New Theatre (tour)
Dates included: Grand Theatre, Leeds, 24th Oct (6 nights);
Lyceum Theatre, Sheffield, 31st Oct; Opera House, Blackpool,
7th Nov; Lyceum Theatre, Edinburgh, 21st Nov; Theatre Royal,
Newcastle, 28th Nov
Starring Donald Wolfit and Greer Garson
Played Private Meek, billed as William Hartnell

1933? *Just Married* (tour)

1934 Arthur Rees presents his Richmond Players
Richmond Theatre
Twice nightly 6.30 & 8.40 p.m.

Billed as 'Billy Hartnell throughout

While Parents Sleep, Anthony Kimmins
17th Sep for 6 nights
Played the lead, Neville Hammond

Behold We Live, John van Druten
24th Sep for 6 nights
Played the lead, Tony Casenove

Good Morning, Bill, P. G. Wodehouse
1st Oct for 6 nights
Played the lead, Bill Paradene

The Brontës, Alfred Sangster
8th Oct for 6 nights
Played Branwell
With Heather McIntyre as Anne

Eliza Comes to Stay, H. V. Esmond
15th Oct for 6 nights
Played the lead, The Hon. Sandy Verall

Counsellor at Law, Elmer Rice
22nd Oct for 6 nights
Played Herbert Weinberg
With Heather McIntyre as Regina Gordon

Apron Strings, Dorrance Davis
29th Oct for 6 nights
Played the lead, Daniel Curtis
With Heather McIntyre as Barbara Oldwood

The Pursuit of Happiness, Lawrence Langer & Armina Marshall
5th Nov for 6 nights
Played the Servant

Nothing but the Truth
12th Nov for 6 nights
Played the lead, Rob Bennett
With Heather McIntyre

Indoor Fireworks
3rd Dec for 6 nights
Played the lead, Pat Swanson
With Heather McIntyre

1935 **Lord Richard in the Pantry**, Sidney Blow & Douglas Hoare
7th Jan for 6 nights
Played the lead, Lord Richard
With Heather McIntyre as Evelyn Lovejoy

Mr Faintheart
21st Jan for 6 nights
Played the lead, Mr Faintheart
With Heather McIntyre

The Maitlands, Ronald MacKenzie
28th Jan for 6 nights
Played the lead
With Heather McIntyre and Basil Langton

It Pays to Advertise, Walter Hackett & R. Cooper Magrue
4th Feb for 6 nights
Played the lead
With Heather McIntyre and Basil Langton

The Ghost Train, Arnold Ridley
11th Feb for 6 nights
Played Teddy Deakin

Charley's Aunt, Brandon Thomas
22nd Apr for 6 nights
Played the lead, Lord Fancourt Babberley
With Heather McIntyre as Kitty and Basil Langton as Jack

White Cargo, Leon Gordon
23rd Sep for 6 nights
Played the lead, Langford
With Heather McIntyre as Tondeleyo

A Little Bit of Fluff, Walter W. Evans
4th Nov for 6 nights

Played the lead, Tully
With Heather McIntyre as Mrs Ayers

1936   *The Ghost Train*, Arnold Ridley
Martin Sabine for the London Repertory Company
Victoria Palace Theatre, Sat 18th Apr for 6 nights
Twice nightly 6.30 & 8.45 p.m.
Played Teddy Deakin
With Basil Langton as Richard Winthrop

1937   *Someone at the Door*, D. & C. Christie
Circle Theatre Presents
Richmond Theatre, 6th Apr for 5 nights
6.30 & 8.40 p.m.
Played the lead, Ronnie Martin

1937   *Paganini*, Paul Knepler, Bela Jenbach, music by Franz Lehar,
lyrics by A. P. Herbert
An operetta in three Acts
Staged by Tyrone Guthrie
Presented by Charles B. Cochran
Lyceum Theatre, from 4th June
Starring Evelyn Laye and Richard Tauber
Played Ricardo and Foletto

1937   *Take it Easy*, book, music & lyrics by Herman & Sammy Timberg
& Barbara Blair
A musical comedy
Staged by Frank Collins
Presented by Barbara Blair Productions
Palace Theatre, from Sep
8.30 p.m. + Wed & Sat matinees 2.30 p.m.
Starring Barbara Blair and Herman Timberg
Played Willie

1938   *Power and Glory*
Savoy Theatre, Apr
Played 1st Journalist, billed as Billy Hartnell

1938   *Happy Returns*, C. B. Cochran

A show with music and dancing
Adelphi Theatre, 12th May onwards
Starring Beatrice Lillie, Bud Flanagan, Chesney Allen
Ensemble and understudied Bud Flanagan

1938/9? *The Second Man*
Sheffield Repertory Theatre
With Heather McIntyre

1939 *Faithfully Yours*, Brandon Fleming & Eric L'Epine Smith
prod: Maxwell Wray
Adele Raymond presents (tour)
Dates included:
Kings Theatre, Southsea, 27th Nov; Devonshire Park Theatre,
Eastbourne, 4th Dec; Swansea Empire, 11th Dec
Starring Cathleen Nesbit
Played Mr Lewis
With Heather McIntyre as Lucille

1940 *Nap Hand*, a farce by Vernon Sylvaine & Guy Bolton
prod: Austin Melford
Frith Shepherd presents
Aldwych Theatre, Mar
Starring Ralph Lynn, Charles Heslop and also Francis de Wolff
Played A Customer, understudied Ralph Lynn and went on for
him

1940? *What Anne Brought Home*, Larry E. Johnson
White Rose Players
Grand Opera House, Harrogate, Jan
Played Douglas Purdie
With Heather McIntyre as Ann

1943 *Brighton Rock*, adapted by Frank Harvey from Graham Greene
Presented by Linnit & Dunfee (tour then West End)

Cubitt	Norman Pierce
Spicer	Beckett Bould
Dallow	Bill Hartnell
Judy	Virginia Winter

Pinkie	Richard Attenborough
Molly Pink	Sheila Keith
Delia	Anna Burden
Fred Hale	Charles Lamb
Ida Arnold	Hermione Baddeley
A Fisherman	Tom Leybourne
A Police Detective	Rupert Siddons
Brewer	Sam Lyons
Rose Wilson	Dulcie Gray
A Waiter	Tom Leybourne
Phil Corkery	Ernest Borrow
Colleoni	Lyn Davies
Manageress	Daphne Newton
Prewitt	Harcourt Williams
A Priest	Rupert Siddon

Tour dates prior to West End included:
Grand Theatre, Blackpool, week beginning 1st Feb
7.00 p.m. + Wed, Thurs, Sat matinees 2.15 p.m.

1950 ***What Anne Brought Home***, Larry E. Johnson
dir: Weyman Mackay
Royal County Theatre, Bedford
Starred as Douglas Purdie
With Rosemary Harris as Ann

1950 ***Seagulls over Sorrento***, Hugh Hastings
dir: Wallace Douglas
George & Alfred Black & H. M. Tennant Ltd (tour then West End)
Apollo Theatre, Shaftesbury Avenue

Able Seaman McIntosh	John Gregson
Able Seaman Sims	Nigel Stock
Able Seaman Turner	Bernard Lee
Able Seaman Badger	Ronald Shiner
Petty Officer Herbert	William Hartnell
Lt-Cmdr Redmond	Peter Gray
Sub-Lieut Granger	Robert Desmond
Able Seaman Hudson	Gerald Anderson
A Telegraphist	David Langton

Tour dates prior to West End included:
Theatre Royal, Brighton, 10th Apr 1950 for 1 week

1954 Tour dates included:
Golders Green Hippodrome, 15th Mar for 2 weeks; Coliseum
Theatre, Harrow, 12th Apr; Wimbledon Theatre, 19th Apr
Cast for tour included Gordon Jackson and Basil Lord

1955 *Treble Trouble*, Heather McIntyre
prod: Tom Wyatt
Alan Miles & Frederick Piffard (for Richmond Rep Co)
Richmond Theatre, 7th Mar
7.45 p.m.
Played the lead, George
With Heather McIntyre as Mrs Jarvis and June Ellis as Elsie
Knowles
Also known as *Home and Away*
Went into the West End in Aug (with different cast)

1956 *Ring for Catty*, Patrick Cargill & Jack Seale
prod: Michael Codron (tour then West End)
dir: Henry Kendal
Lyric Theatre, Shaftesbury Avenue
Co-starred as John Rhodes
With Patrick McGoohan as Leonard White, Mary MacKenzie as
Nurse Catty and Terence Alexander as Donald Gray
Also at:
Coliseum Theatre, Harrow, 6th Feb for 1 week; Golders Green
Hippodrome, 23rd Apr for 1 week

1961 *The Cupboard*
New Arts Theatre, Nov
Played Alf Thompson

1967 *Puss in Boots*
'Dr Who' – William Hartnell in the magnificent Christmas Panto
Odeon Theatre, Cheltenham, 9th Jan for 1 week
Played Buskin the Cobbler
Other dates included: Ipswich; Southend; Taunton

1968 | ***Brother and Sister***, Robert Bolt
dir: Val May
Theatre Royal, Bristol, 29th May for 4 weeks
Played the co-lead, William Brazier
With Sonia Dresdel as Winifred Brazier, Basil Henson as Newton
Reeves

Play which I have been unable to date:

Too True to be Good, George Bernard Shaw
prod: Godfrey Baxter
'Q' Theatre, Kew, 2nd – 7th Mar
With George Wray and Iris Baker

Bibliography

Denis Gifford, *The British Film Catalogue,* David & Charles

Jay Robert Nash and Stanley Ralph Ross, *The Motion Picture Guide 1927-83*, Cinebooks Inc.

David Quinlan, *British Sound Films: The Studio Years 1928-59,* B. T. Batsford

Rachael Low, *Film Making in 1930s Britain*, George Allen & Unwin

Freda Gayle (Ed.), *Who's Who in the Theatre*, Pitman (14th edition)

Leslie Halliwell, *Halliwell's Filmgoer's Companion*, Paladin

Peter Ustinov, *Dear Me,* Heinemann

Hermione Baddeley, *The Unsinkable Hermione Baddeley*, Collins

J. C. Trewin, *Robert Donat*, Heinemann

Peter Noble (Ed.), *British Film Year Book 1947-48*, Skelton Robinson

Peter Haining, *Doctor Who – A Celebration*, W. H. Allen/ Virgin publishing

Howe, Stammers, Walker, *Doctor Who – The Handbook: The First Doctor*, Virgin Publishing

Howe, Stammers, Walker, *Doctor Who – The Sixties*, Virgin Publishing

Jeremy Bentham, *Doctor Who – The Early Years*, W. H. Allen/ Virgin Publishing

John Stather, *Hugh Oswald Blaker* unpublished MA dissertation, University College Wales

Hugh Blaker, *Points of Posterity*, Frank Palmer

Robert Mayrick, Exhibition Catalogue, University College Wales

I have also referred to countless reviews in newspaper, magazines and the *Radio Times.*

Index